nom nom paleo
LET'S GO!

MICHELLE TAM + HENRY FONG

Andrews McMeel
PUBLISHING®

FOR OUR GRANDPARENTS.

HELLO AGAIN!

Long time no see, Nomsters! It's been four long years since we last met in the pages of a cookbook, but I'm back with my family to once again inspire you to get cooking.

For those of you who don't know me, I'm Michelle Tam, the gleefully food-obsessed umami evangelist behind Nom Nom Paleo. I was born in the San Francisco Bay Area to immigrants from Hong Kong who instilled in me and my sister a lifelong passion for all things gustatory. I've said it before: my mom, dad, sister, and I can all be described in Cantonese as *wai sek* (為食)—we live to eat. (An alternative translation of *wai sek* is "gluttonous," which is also an accurate way to describe my family.)

As far back as I can remember, my waking thoughts have always been preoccupied with food: researching it, finding it, savoring it. I read cookbooks like other people read novels. And every time I finish a meal, I start dreaming about my next one.

But in adulthood, while my talented sister became a restaurant chef, I settled into a nightshift job as a hospital pharmacist, relegating my interest in food to a pastime. It's not like I took this hobby frivolously, though; my husband, Henry, and I saved up to travel around the world just to eat, and I never ceased my culinary explorations. Still, it wasn't until 2010 that I started a recipe blog, and a niche one at that.

Our health had vastly improved after Henry and I switched to a paleo eating template—one that prioritized whole, unprocessed ingredients. Naturally, I scoured the internet for recipes that fit this ancestral approach to food. But at the time, most "caveman diet" sites were focused on eating for weight loss or high-intensity exercise; few approached paleo from a flavor-first mindset. So I tried to fill the gap with Nom Nom Paleo, sharing how to prepare deliciously nourishing recipes from scratch. To put kitchen novices at ease, we meticulously documented each step of the cooking process with photos (and a generous sprinkle of snarky humor).

Since then, we've created an award-winning cooking app, written bestselling cookbooks, launched new food products like our Magic Mushroom Powder, and steadily cranked out recipes for our readers. I became a full-time recipe developer in 2014, when I finally quit my gig as a hospital pharmacist. And while Henry loves his day job doing lawyer stuff, he continues to devote his nights and weekends to photographing, illustrating, and designing everything you see on our site and in our cookbooks. With Nom Nom Paleo, we're truly a mom-and-pop operation.

That said, our most important collaboration is raising our two boys, Owen and Ollie. You may remember them as chubby-cheeked tykes, but they're both teenagers now. (We've always intended our books to inspire kids to cook, and the investment has finally paid off: our boys are now old enough to get dinner on the table!) Parenting a pair of teens isn't exactly a walk in the park, but it's been rewarding to juggle my roles as a stay-at-home mom and recipe creator—even during a global crisis.

Every cookbook is a time capsule—a snapshot of the moment. But when we hunkered down to create the dishes in these pages, the moment was unprecedented: a worldwide pandemic that kept most of us sheltered at home for over a year. Like many of you, we were separated from loved ones, lost family members to COVID-19, agonized over the racial reckoning across America, and did our best to adjust to a world that was abruptly shut down by the coronavirus.

There's no escaping the fact that these crises influenced the book you're holding in your hands. For starters, the events of 2020 forced us to think differently about the social, historical, and cultural importance of food, both as a bridge between communities and as a source of comfort in difficult times. No longer able to travel or even dine out at our favorite restaurants, I found myself pining away for all the foods

I used to eat—especially the dishes from my childhood. I considered the importance of cultural representation in areas of everyday life, including the meals we choose to honor, cook, and eat. And even as we were kept apart, I reflected on the power of food to bring and keep people together.

I grew up at the intersection of many immigrant communities in California, which meant I was steeped in an amalgam of diverse cuisines. Night after night, my mom prepared home-style Cantonese dishes for our family, but when I ventured outside the house, I also sought out Indian *chaat*, street tacos, Mission-style burritos, and Vietnamese *bánh mì* sandwiches—not to mention juicy cheeseburgers and french fries. Having been raised on a polyglot diet that fused Asian and Latin flavors with American ingredients, my pandemic cravings leaned toward this familiar mixing and matching of cuisines. So in this book, you'll find comfort food recipes that reflect not only my family's Cantonese heritage but also dishes inspired by the blend of immigrant cultures in the San Francisco Bay Area that helped to shape my palate.

The pandemic also made me focus on protecting and nourishing my family. I came of age in the 1980s and '90s, during the heyday of the California cuisine movement, so seasonal, sustainable ingredients have always been my jam—but making healthy choices during a time of tragedy and stress is easier said than done. A year spent in quarantine taxed us all both physically and mentally, so with that in mind, I worked to create fast, easy, and comforting recipes to combat kitchen fatigue and uplift our spirits. I also included fancier, more complicated fare for those occasions when we just want to lose ourselves in the cooking process. To perk up our palates, I sprinkled in some indispensable flavor boosters like Nom Nom Chili Crisp (page 38) and Umami Stir-Fry Powder (page 43). And to scratch the itch for pandemic baking, I added lots of paleo-friendly desserts to this book. Let's face it, people: stress baking is real.

As I write this in the spring of 2021, we're emerging at last from a year of home confinement, but these recipes feel more relevant than ever. This cookbook is a collection of dishes that—when life put our backs to the wall—I made with love for my family. These recipes truly give me joy, and I'll be returning to them again and again.

I hope this book inspires you to get cooking, whether you're trying to eat for better health or just looking to satisfy your palate with ridiculously tasty noms.

So without further ado, LET'S GO!

OWEN   MICHELLE   HENRY   OLLIE

WHAT'S PALEO?

Paleo is a way of eating that prioritizes whole, unprocessed, nutrient-rich foods (like vegetables, sustainably sourced animal protein, healthy fats, fruit, nuts, and seeds) and avoids ingredients that are likely to be more harmful than healthful (like grains, dairy, soy, refined sugar, and processed seed and vegetable oils). Contrary to popular belief, paleo isn't about mindlessly replicating the diets of prehistoric humans. It's about enjoying wholesome, nourishing foods and avoiding those that trigger inflammation, cause digestive problems, and derail our natural metabolic processes.

All the recipes in this cookbook are paleo-friendly and designed with healthfulness, practicality, and deliciousness in mind. If you're curious to learn more about paleo, check out my other cookbooks or go visit my website, nomnompaleo.com.

HOW WE EAT NOW

As we were dreaming up titles for this book, we briefly flirted with calling it "Nom Nom Paleo-ish" to reflect our more relaxed approach to this way of eating. This is a far cry from when our family first went paleo, scrupulously adhering to all the rules of the so-called "caveman diet." I still clearly remember the day I purged our house of all grains, dairy, beans, and sugar; when the final box of mac and cheese disappeared from the pantry, there was much gnashing of teeth and rending of garments in our house. (I'm exaggerating—but only slightly.)

Going fully paleo—and then adding back some non-paleo foods one at a time—gradually pulled back the curtains on how different ingredients affect us. We learned that rice spikes my blood sugar to diabetic levels, Ollie and I can't tolerate gluten at all, and too much dairy bloats our guts (and makes our butts a bit too musical).

But on the flip side, we also identified the non-paleo foods each of us could tolerate and enjoy—and we gradually reincorporated them into our lives to pleasurable effect. So over time, our family adopted a less rigid approach to the way we eat. These days, Ollie can run to his favorite neighborhood ice cream stand and order a scoop. Owen discovered long ago that gluten doesn't bother him, so when he's out and about, he'll sometimes treat himself to a morning pastry or a burrito. Henry can't pass up a good slice of pizza. And me? I love me some beans.

That said, the food I prepare in my home kitchen has remained mostly paleo for over a decade. Sure, some members of our household insist on eating my dishes with a side of rice (Ollie) or adding fine shavings of Parmesan cheese (Ollie again), but there are simple reasons why I continue to crank out recipes that are steadfastly paleo at the core: they're nutrient-dense and make us feel better.

You may be on different points of the paleo spectrum—or not on it at all. Some of you are strict paleo eaters or follow a similarly health-focused eating program like keto, Whole30®, or AIP. Others of you may be using my recipes in the same way our family does now, mixing and matching paleo and non-paleo dishes. While the recipes in this book are all completely paleo-friendly, I'm happy for you to use them in whatever manner you see fit. Make my food because you want to feel healthier, or because you have food allergies, or because you're looking for something wholesome and delicious to serve alongside rice or noodles, or because you just love California-inspired, umami-forward flavors.

All that matters to me is that you get in the kitchen and cook. After all, the healthiest meal is the one you prepare yourself!

EQUIPMENT

I'm not going to spend much time going over the equipment you'll need to get cooking. Assuming you have the usual assortment of kitchen tools (sharp knives, pots and pans, etc.), you'll have no trouble prepping most of the recipes in this book. That said, here are some items that I find especially helpful in the kitchen:

KITCHEN SCALE

I know you love your measuring cups and spoons, but I'm pleading with you: especially when you're baking, use a kitchen scale. There's a good reason why some recipes call for weight measurements instead of (or in addition to) volume measurements; weight is a much more precise way to specify amounts. And precision counts—especially when you're baking with more expensive alternative flours.

INSTANT-READ THERMOMETER

If you're an inexperienced cook who's anxious about overcooking some pricey cuts of meat, get yourself a reliable instant-read thermometer. Checking the temperature is the best way to truly be sure that your food is perfectly cooked.

KITCHEN SHEARS

Yes, knives can deliver more precise cuts, but kitchen shears offer speed and power. I use shears for everything from snipping fresh herbs to removing the backbone from a chicken. Buy a pair of well-balanced, high-carbon stainless steel shears with micro-serrations on the blades to help firmly grip the slippery foods (like raw poultry) you'll be cutting. And for easy cleaning, make sure the blades can be fully separated.

RASP GRATER

Microplane makes rasp graters with tiny, sharp teeth that slice food into feathery-light ribbons, which in turn add subtle flavors and essences to your dishes without any annoying fiber or grittiness. I'll reach for my rasp grater to finely zest citrus without digging into the bitter white pith, shave frozen ginger to create flavorful snow that melts into hot dishes, and tame raw garlic so that none of my dinner guests are surprised by a big chunk of unpleasant spiciness.

SPIRALIZER + MANDOLINE

Who wants to spend valuable hours hand-cutting stuff? Not me. Henry hates it when I clutter up the kitchen with extra gadgets, but a good vegetable spiralizer and mandoline slicer have proved incredibly useful. A spiralizer creates veggie noodles with the greatest of ease, and nothing slices faster and more consistently than a mandoline. Get yourself a pair of mandoline-safe cut-resistant gloves, too.

RIMMED BAKING SHEET + OVEN-SAFE WIRE RACK

Rimmed baking sheets aren't just for baking cookies. I use them to roast meats and vegetables and to whip up a variety of sheet pan suppers. I recommend getting a few sheets that are no smaller than 13 by 18 inches—otherwise known as half sheets.

I often pair baking sheets with oven-safe wire racks to keep my food elevated while cooking in the oven and to prevent crunchy stuff from going limp and soggy. Wire racks also come in handy for cooling, resting, and draining food. Stainless steel dishwasher-safe wire racks are my favorite—they're practically indestructible!

STAND MIXER

Over the past couple of years, I've done a lot more baking, and while a stand mixer isn't mandatory, it's an incredibly handy (and beautiful!) countertop appliance. I created and tested many of the dessert recipes in this book using my trusty KitchenAid mixer, and it never once let me down.

BLENDER + FOOD PROCESSOR

With an immersion blender (a.k.a. hand blender), whipping up sauces, condiments, and puréed soups is a cinch. A hand blender is relatively inexpensive, too. Got a bit more money to spend? Invest in a high-powered (1,000+ watt) countertop blender. It'll yield faster and more consistent results. Besides, if you're frequently blitzing a lot of sauces, soups, and smoothies, you certainly won't regret the purchase.

Similarly, if you often find yourself buried under an avalanche of ingredients to chop into tiny pieces, a food processor may be well worth the price, too.

INSTANT POT

As a longtime Instant Pot evangelist, I couldn't help but include a bunch of Instant Pot recipes in this book—especially given how much cooking I do in this handy appliance. Through the magic of pressure cooking, this gadget speeds up my meal prep and keeps our food warm until we're ready to eat. That said, I know not everyone has or wants one, so every Instant Pot recipe in this book is accompanied by instructions for how to make the dish on the stovetop and/or in a slow cooker. You're welcome!

PANTRY NOTES

To transform everyday ingredients into truly nomtastic feasts, you'll need an abundant collection of spices, sauces, and other flavor-enhancers. A well-stocked kitchen opens up a universe of flavors and textures—especially for us paleo eaters who can't rely on lab-concocted additives to do the heavy lifting. Thankfully, sourcing whole, healthful pantry items isn't hard, provided you know what to get.

I prioritize components that naturally amplify umami—the elusive, flavor-enhancing fifth taste—so my pantry is filled with wholesome, intrinsically umami-packed foods. Some of these I prepare myself, like my Umami Stir-Fry Powder (page 43). Others are store-bought, like marinara sauce or Thai curry paste. I rarely make bone broth or paleo-friendly mayonnaise now that they're readily available at the grocery store.

In fact, the vast majority of ingredients used in this book are straightforward and easy to find at U.S. supermarkets, though some components may be less familiar to you. For those ingredients, you may need to visit your local Asian or Latin market or shop online. Here are a few pantry staples that merit special mention:

KOSHER SALT

On grocery shelves, you can find over a dozen types of salt: table salt, kosher salt, sea salt, flake salt, *fleur de sel*, Hawaiian salt, Himalayan salt, *kala namak*—you name it. In this book, I generally call for kosher salt, and more specifically, Diamond Crystal kosher salt. Sold in red-and-white boxes, Diamond Crystal kosher salt is very different from its primary competitor, Morton kosher salt (which is packaged in dark blue boxes). The key distinction is that Morton's salt crystals are smaller and more densely packed than Diamond Crystal's light, hollow, and easily dissolvable flakes.

Personally, I prefer the larger, coarser grains of Diamond Crystal kosher salt because they're easier to pinch between my fingers to sprinkle on food and because they're less salty by volume and therefore more forgiving. I developed the recipes in this cookbook using Diamond Crystal kosher salt, but if you prefer to use other salts, here's the approximate conversion:

NOT ALL KOSHER SALTS ARE THE SAME! ONE'S MORE DELICATE, AND THE OTHER'S DENSER AND SALTIER. THE AMOUNT OF SALT YOU USE WILL DEPEND ON WHICH ONE YOU CHOOSE.

1 teaspoon Diamond Crystal kosher salt

=

1 teaspoon Maldon sea salt

=

¾ teaspoon Morton kosher salt

=

¾ teaspoon *fleur de sel*

=

½ teaspoon table salt

COOKING FATS

I try to steer clear of vegetable and seed oils, which are usually marketed as "heart-healthy" but are actually highly processed with chemical solvents and packed with omega-6 polyunsaturated fatty acids. They're so unstable that even when kept at room temperature, they oxidize and turn rancid to some degree. Heat and light accelerate this oxidation, and promote the formation of free radicals that assault the healthy cells in your body. That's why my go-to cooking fats are more natural, less processed oils like ghee, avocado oil, extra-virgin olive oil, and coconut oil.

Ghee, a classic Indian preparation of clarified butter, isn't hard to make at home, but I typically buy it from the store or online these days. (Still want to make it from scratch? I have instructions on nomnompaleo.com and in my other cookbooks.)

Avocado oil is more neutral tasting than olive oil or coconut oil and remains stable when subjected to high heat, so it's perfect for Asian dishes. Unfortunately, some brands are rancid or mixed with other oils, so take special care (as you would with extra-virgin olive oil) to buy avocado oil from reputable brands like Chosen Foods and Marianne's Harvest Brands. Look for a recent harvest date on the label, and pay attention to its smell and taste. (Rancid avocado oil can smell like Play-Doh.)

BONE BROTH

Bone broth is the foundation for my soups and a critical flavoring agent in many of my dishes. I used to make my own broth, incorporating both meat and bones to deliver a full, robust mouthfeel and deep flavor. (My bone broth recipe can be found—you guessed it—at nomnompaleo.com or in my previous cookbooks.) But with plenty of high-quality bone broths now available at the supermarket, I just look for it in the freezer or refrigerator aisles. Two of my favorite brands are Bonafide Provisions and Butcher's by Roli Roti. I prefer bone broth with low or no added salt and lots of jiggle when refrigerated—evidence of its high gelatin content.

By the way, the terms "bone broth" and "stock" are often used interchangeably because, well, they're pretty similar: "stock" is made from bones and cartilage, whereas "broth" is made with both bones and meat. In a pinch, you can substitute store-bought stock for bone broth, but remember: the dish will only be as tasty as the base, so always use the best-quality stock you can find.

FISH SAUCE

Made with salted, fermented anchovies, fish sauce is funky, pungent, powerful magic. It's a potent source of umami and has been a key flavoring agent in the cuisines of Thailand, Vietnam, Myanmar, and the Philippines for centuries. It's a big part of why Southeast Asian cooking has such a distinct flavor profile and why I incorporate fish sauce in so many of my Asian (and non-Asian) dishes.

Before purchasing fish sauce, examine the ingredients carefully. Paleo-friendly fish sauce (like the kind made by my favorite brand, Red Boat) should be made of just anchovies and salt. If it's watered down or adulterated with sugar or chemical additives, leave it on the shelf. Remember also that fish sauce is strong stuff: just a few drops of this golden magic will greatly amplify the umami in savory dishes.

For those who are vegan or allergic to fish, this book includes my recipe for No-Fish Sauce (page 28). But unless you absolutely can't eat fish, try to use the real deal; as much as I love and swear by my No-Fish Sauce, it's not quite the same.

COCONUT AMINOS

Produced from the fermented sap of coconut palm trees, this dark, salty-sweet condiment tastes a lot like soy sauce, but without any soy and gluten. Note that coconut aminos is not the same as Bragg's aminos, which is soy-derived and saltier. I like to mix coconut aminos with fish sauce to make it an even more umami-rich (and paleo-compatible) substitute for soy sauce. My favorite brands include Big Tree Farms, Thrive Market, and Coconut Secret.

FISH SAUCE ISN'T JUST FOR ASIAN RECIPES. IN FACT, ANCIENT ROMANS USED A VERSION OF FISH SAUCE CALLED GARUM. ITS MODERN EQUIVALENT, COLATURA DI ALICI, IS THE ITALIAN EQUIVALENT OF SOUTHEAST ASIAN FISH SAUCE AND IS JUST AS UMAMI-PACKED.

NUTRITIONAL YEAST SEASONING

Affectionately known as "nooch," nutritional yeast seasoning is the inactive form of a yeast similar to the one bakers use to leaven bread—only it's been dried into bright yellow flakes that resemble fish food. It's high in glutamic acid, a compound that imparts lots of umami. Vegans have long used nutritional yeast as a means of adding a savory cheesiness to dairy-free dishes, and I've followed their example, using nutritional yeast as a replacement for Parmesan cheese and as a foundational component of my Cashew Cheese Sauce (page 34).

SHIITAKE MUSHROOMS

A good number of my recipes call for shiitake mushrooms (much to the consternation of Ollie, who hates mushrooms with the intensity of a thousand suns). Cultivated in East Asia for centuries, these forest mushrooms add a wonderfully meaty texture and a rich umami dimension to savory dishes. That said, not all shiitake mushrooms are the same. There are a dozen sub-varieties, ranging from those with thick, deeply cracked caps to wide, smooth-capped mushrooms.

According to experts, the best shiitake mushrooms are from the Ōita Prefecture on the Japanese island of Kyushu. There are many grades of shiitake mushrooms in Japan, but the two main types to keep in mind are *koshin* and *donko.*

Lower-grade, flatter *koshin* mushrooms are picked after the caps bloom into flat, wide umbrellas; by contrast, higher-grade *donko* mushrooms are picked earlier, while the thick, firm caps are still in bud form. *Koshin* shiitake mushrooms are often sliced up and used in stir-fries, soups, and sauces, while *donko* mushrooms are enjoyed whole or in larger pieces because they're prized for their chewy meatiness. Most supermarkets offer only lower-grade *koshin* mushrooms, so you may want to visit an Asian market to seek out more shiitake varieties.

Pro tip: stocking up on dried shiitake mushrooms is a great way to keep umami boosters on hand at all times. On those occasions when I forget to rehydrate dried shiitakes, I'll shave them with a Microplane rasp grater or reach for some dried shiitake mushroom powder instead. Dried shiitake mushroom powder is exactly what it sounds like: shiitakes that have been dehydrated and ground into a powder that's fantastically meaty and bold. You can pulverize your own in a high-powered blender or food processor or buy some at your local Asian market.

ALTERNATIVE FLOURS

I use different grain-free flours for distinct purposes. Arrowroot powder is effective for thickening sauces and gravies, and potato starch adds crispness when coating fried foods. When it comes to preparing baked goods, sweet treats, and skillet flatbreads, I turn to almond flour, cassava flour, and tapioca flour.

A note about cassava flour: I recommend using Otto's Naturals brand cassava flour, which I used to test the recipes in this book. I've found some other brands to be processed inconsistently, resulting in unpleasantly sour or musty flavor notes.

SWEETENERS

When adding sweetness, I reach for natural ingredients like raw organic honey, maple syrup, maple sugar, coconut sugar, dates, fruit juices, and fruit jams. To substitute for powdered sugar in dessert recipes, I'll sometimes use a bit of Swerve Confectioners' Sweetener, a zero-calorie alternative made with erythritol, a sugar alcohol that doesn't affect blood glucose.

USING THIS BOOK

My recipes have never followed the traditional format of *ingredients + directions + photo of the finished dish.* Both Henry and I are visual learners, so ever since we started Nom Nom Paleo back in 2010, we've always presented our recipes in the way we best absorb information, with detailed photographs showing each step of the transformation from raw ingredients to completed dish. That's why we crammed almost 2,000 step-by-step photos and illustrations into this book. If a picture's worth a thousand words, this book contains close to 2 million words. (Kids, please be sure to tell that to your parents and teachers when they nag you to read more.)

If you're feeling overwhelmed or confused about how to navigate my recipes, just treat this cookbook like a comic book. I've even numbered each step-by-step photo, so you can't go wrong (unless you don't know how to count)!

SERVING SIZES + COOKING TIMES

I've included suggested serving sizes and cooking times for the dishes in this book, but note that your mileage may vary depending on your appetite (e.g., you may need more food if you're serving insatiable teenagers), skill level (e.g., it'll take longer if you just learned how to hold a knife today), and equipment (e.g., if your ancient oven takes forever to heat, you'll have to be a bit more patient). You're the best judge of your own appetite and culinary prowess, so cook accordingly.

DIETARY DISTINCTIONS

In this cookbook, I don't bother labeling the recipes as "paleo" because they're all paleo-friendly. (It's in the name of the book, people!) I recognize that not everyone's definition of paleo is the same, so to be clear, every single dish in this book is free of gluten, grains, dairy (except for ghee, which has no lactose or problematic milk proteins), soy, refined sugar, legumes, and processed seed and vegetable oils.

That said, I know that many of you have health-related eating needs beyond paleo, so each recipe in this book is accompanied by labels indicating whether it's also Whole30-compatible, keto-friendly (which to us means it has 10 or fewer net grams of carbohydrates per serving), egg-free, nut-free, nightshade-free, vegetarian, or vegan. (Some of my desserts are technically under the 10-net-grams-of-carbs rule that we set for keto-friendliness, but we didn't label any sweets as keto-friendly.)

NUTRITION INFORMATION

For the first time, I'm also including estimates of the calories, carbohydrates, protein, fat, and fiber in each recipe. Don't take these numbers as immutable truth, though, as they'll fluctuate depending on the brands you use or the natural variations found in fresh ingredients. If down-to-the-decimal-point accuracy is critical to you, input your actual ingredients and amounts into your own preferred nutrition calculator.

THIS IS A COOKBOOK FOR LITTLE CHEFS, TOO!

I absolutely love seeing kids reading and cooking from our books. I don't know if it's the cartoons, the step-by-step photos, or the butt jokes that keep children coming back to our cookbooks, but I get a lot of joy from knowing that little kitchen helpers are taking inspiration from Nom Nom Paleo. If you're raising a budding junior chef, please use this book to encourage them to keep cooking. I believe the children are our future (Whitney Houston said so!) and I can't think of a better use for this book than passing on healthy home cooking habits to the next generation.

BUILDING BLOCKS

NO-FISH SAUCE

MAKES 1½ CUPS
● **1 HOUR**
(30 MINUTES HANDS-ON)

WHOLE30®	KETO-FRIENDLY
NUT-FREE	EGG-FREE
NIGHTSHADE-FREE	VEGAN

2   large dried shiitake mushrooms (about ½ ounce total)

¼   cup packed dried dulse seaweed

¼   cup Diamond Crystal kosher salt

2   tablespoons coconut aminos

3   cups water

USE THIS FOR:

- All-Purpose Stir-Fry Sauce (page 29)
- Hot Dog Fried "Rice" (page 108)
- Chicken Chow Mein (page 126)
- Chinese Velvet and Spinach Soup (page 178)
- Tom Kha Gai (page 180)
- Sheet Pan "Peanut" Sauce Chicken and Broccolini (page 204)
- Sheet Pan Pineapple Chicken (page 206)
- Instant Pot Ground Beef Chili (page 246)
- Moo Shu Pork (page 280)
- Lemongrass Pork Chops (page 286)
- Char Siu (page 290)

FISH SAUCE IS MAGICAL. IT'S ONE OF THE MIGHTIEST UMAMI AMPLIFIERS IN MY COOKING ARSENAL, AND AS MANY OF YOU KNOW, IT'S A KEY INGREDIENT IN MANY OF MY RECIPES. THAT SAID, SOME FOLKS ARE ALLERGIC TO FISH, SO I'VE CREATED A CLOSE FACSIMILE FOR THOSE WHO CAN'T HAVE THE REAL THING. BOTH SHIITAKE MUSHROOMS AND DULSE SEAWEED ARE HIGH IN GLUTAMIC ACID, MAKING THIS SAUCE A POWERFUL FLAVOR BOOSTER.

① BREAK THE DRIED MUSHROOMS (INCLUDING THE STEMS) INTO SMALL PIECES AND TOSS THEM IN A MEDIUM SAUCEPAN.

② DUMP ALL THE OTHER INGREDIENTS INTO THE SAUCEPAN, TOO. BRING EVERYTHING TO A BOIL OVER HIGH HEAT.

③ DECREASE THE HEAT ENOUGH TO MAINTAIN A SIMMER FOR **20** MINUTES, STIRRING OCCASIONALLY, UNTIL REDUCED BY HALF.

④ STRAIN AND COOL TO ROOM TEMPERATURE. THIS SAUCE WILL KEEP IN A SEALED CONTAINER FOR UP TO 1 MONTH IN THE FRIDGE. SHAKE WELL BEFORE USING!

Per 1 tablespoon: 4 calories • 1 g carbohydrates • 1 g protein • 1 g fat • 1 g fiber

ALL-PURPOSE STIR-FRY SAUCE

MAKES 2 CUPS
⏱ **5 MINUTES**

WHOLE30®	KETO-FRIENDLY
NUT-FREE	EGG-FREE
NIGHTSHADE-FREE	VEGAN (IF MODIFIED)

1 cup coconut aminos

½ cup orange or pineapple juice

¼ cup paleo-friendly fish sauce or No-Fish Sauce (page 28)

2 tablespoons rice vinegar

2 teaspoons garlic powder

2 teaspoons ground ginger

1 teaspoon toasted sesame oil

USE THIS FOR:

- Smashed Cucumber and Carrot Salad (page 66)
- Holy Shiitake Mushrooms (page 72)
- Ramen Eggs (page 88)
- Hot Dog Fried "Rice" (page 108)
- Shoyu Ramen (page 134)
- Ahi Avocado Poke (page 142)
- Sheet Pan Teriyaki Salmon (page 148)
- Tsukune (page 184)
- Chicken Karaage (page 190)
- Cantonese Pipa Duck (page 224)
- Kalbi (page 256)
- Shaking Beef (page 262)
- Moo Shu Pork (page 280)
- Instant Pot Buta no Kakuni (page 284)

1 COMBINE ALL OF THE INGREDIENTS IN A MEASURING CUP OR JAR.

2 MIX IT ALL TOGETHER. DONE AND DONE!

DESPITE ITS NAME, MY ALL-PURPOSE STIR-FRY SAUCE ISN'T JUST FOR STIR-FRIES: IT'S A FUNDAMENTAL COMPONENT IN RECIPES OF ALL KINDS. THIS ULTRA-VERSATILE SAUCE KEEPS IN THE REFRIGERATOR FOR UP TO 2 WEEKS. SHAKE WELL AGAIN BEFORE USING IT!

Per 2 tablespoons: 25 calories • 4 g carbohydrates • 1 g protein • 1 g fat • 1 g fiber

DUMPLING DIPPING SAUCE

MAKES 1 CUP
⏱ **5 MINUTES**

WHOLE30®	KETO-FRIENDLY
NUT-FREE	EGG-FREE
NIGHTSHADE-FREE (IF MODIFIED)	
VEGAN (IF MODIFIED)	

½ cup rice vinegar

¼ cup coconut aminos

2 teaspoons paleo-friendly sriracha or ½ teaspoon crushed red pepper flakes (optional)

1 teaspoon toasted sesame oil

USE THIS FOR:

- Scallion Pancakes (page 80)
- Pot Stickers (page 272)
- Wonton Meatballs (page 278)

I THOUGHT YOU SAID DIPPIN' DOTS!

1 DUMPLINGS AND MEATBALLS TASTE GREAT PLAIN, BUT I LIKE 'EM EVEN BETTER WHEN DIPPED IN A TASTY SAUCE. IN A MEASURING CUP, MIX TOGETHER THE RICE VINEGAR...

2 ...COCONUT AMINOS...

3 ...PALEO-FRIENDLY SRIRACHA OR RED PEPPER FLAKES (IF USING)...

4 ...AND TOASTED SESAME OIL.

5 STIR IT ALL TOGETHER, AND YOU'VE GOT YOURSELF A QUICK AND ZINGY DIPPING SAUCE. IT KEEPS FOR UP TO A WEEK IN THE FRIDGE.

Per 2 tablespoons: 15 calories • 2 g carbohydrates • 1 g protein • 1 g fat • 0 g fiber

SPICY, VINEGARY, AND DIVINELY DELICIOUS, THIS SAUCE CAN BE USED FOR MORE THAN JUST DIPPING DUMPLINGS. DRIZZLE IT ON EASY SALADS, MEATY MAINS, OR WHATEVER ELSE NEEDS A SAVORY, TANGY KICK. BUT PERSONALLY, I STILL LIKE IT BEST WITH POT STICKERS (PAGE **272**)!

SUNBUTTER HOISIN SAUCE

MAKES ¾ CUP
⏱ 15 MINUTES

WHOLE30®	NUT-FREE
EGG-FREE	NIGHTSHADE-FREE
VEGAN	

- **4** large dried Medjool dates, pitted
- **¼** cup sunflower seed butter
- **¼** cup coconut aminos
- **¼** cup water
- **2** tablespoons rice vinegar
- **1** tablespoon aged balsamic vinegar
- **½** teaspoon Chinese five-spice powder
- **½** teaspoon toasted sesame oil
- **¼** teaspoon Diamond Crystal kosher salt

USE THIS FOR:

- Scallion Pancake Tacos (page 84)
- Sheet Pan "Peanut" Sauce Chicken and Broccolini (page 204)
- Cantonese Pipa Duck (page 224)
- Moo Shu Pork (page 280)

SUNBUTTER HOISIN SAUCE GOES GREAT WITH GRILLED MEATS AND VEGETABLES!

1 USING A KNIFE, MINCE AND MASH UP THE DATES UNTIL THEY'RE THE CONSISTENCY OF A THICK, STICKY PASTE.

2 IN A SMALL SAUCEPAN OVER MEDIUM HEAT, COMBINE ALL THE INGREDIENTS.

3 COOK, STIRRING, FOR 5 TO 7 MINUTES OR UNTIL THE SAUCE THICKENS AND DARKENS.

4 FOR A SMOOTHER SAUCE, REMOVE THE PAN FROM THE HEAT AND USE AN IMMERSION BLENDER TO BLITZ AWAY ANY LUMPS.

5 COOL AND SERVE. THIS CONDIMENT CAN BE KEPT IN THE FRIDGE FOR UP TO 1 WEEK. (IF IT'S TOO FIRM, JUST STIR IN A TABLESPOON OR TWO OF WATER WHEN YOU'RE REHEATING IT.)

CANTONESE HOISIN SAUCE CAN BE USED AS A TANGY-SWEET GLAZE OR CONDIMENT. USE THIS DATE-SWEETENED PALEO-FRIENDLY VERSION TO LEVEL UP ALL YOUR ASIAN DISHES!

Per 1 tablespoon: 62 calories • 9 g carbohydrates • 1 g protein • 3 g fat • 1 g fiber

GINGER SCALLION SAUCE

MAKES 1 CUP
🌓 **45 MINUTES**
(15 MINUTES HANDS-ON)

WHOLE30®	KETO-FRIENDLY
NUT-FREE	EGG-FREE
NIGHTSHADE-FREE	VEGAN

1 cup finely minced scallions

3 tablespoons finely minced fresh ginger

2 teaspoons Diamond Crystal kosher salt

¼ teaspoon ground white pepper

½ cup avocado oil

USE THIS FOR:

- Scallion Pancake Tacos (page 84)
- Asparagus and Ham Frittata (page 92)
- Ginger Scallion Fish Fillets (page 156)
- Poached Chicken with Ginger Scallion Sauce (page 210)

THIS SALTY, HERBACEOUS CONDIMENT IS EXPONENTIALLY GREATER THAN THE SUM OF ITS PARTS. IT'S TRADITIONALLY SERVED WITH WHOLE POACHED CHICKEN, BUT GROWING UP, I WOULD PUT IT ON EVERYTHING!

1 TOSS THE SCALLIONS, GINGER, SALT, AND WHITE PEPPER IN A LARGE HEAT-PROOF BOWL OR 2-CUP MEASURING CUP.

2 STIR IT ALL TOGETHER.

3 IN A SMALL SAUCEPAN OVER HIGH HEAT, WARM THE OIL UNTIL IT'S SHIMMERING BUT NOT QUITE SMOKING.

4 ADD A TINY PIECE OF SCALLION TO TEST IF THE OIL'S HOT ENOUGH. IF YOU SEE LOTS OF LITTLE BUBBLES, THE OIL'S READY. (OR JUST CHECK THAT THE OIL REACHES 375°F ON AN INSTANT-READ THERMOMETER.)

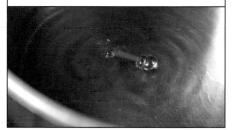

5 POUR THE HOT OIL INTO THE SCALLION AND GINGER MIXTURE A LITTLE AT A TIME. IT'LL SIZZLE AND BOIL, SO BE CAREFUL!

6 STIR WELL AND LET THE SAUCE COOL TO ROOM TEMPERATURE. THE SAUCE CAN BE REFRIGERATED IN A SEALED JAR FOR UP TO 2 WEEKS OR FROZEN IN AN ICE CUBE TRAY FOR UP TO 3 MONTHS.

THIS SIMPLE SAUCE IS TRANSFORMATIVE, LENDING MASSIVE FLAVOR TO ANY SAVORY DISH!

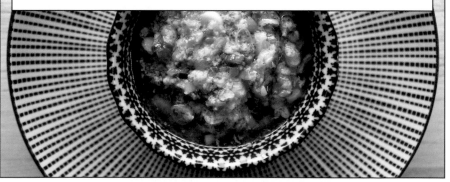

Per 1 tablespoon: 63 calories • 1 g carbohydrates • 1 g protein • 7 g fat • 1 g fiber

CASHEW CHEESE SAUCE

MAKES 1¼ CUPS
◑ **30 MINUTES**

WHOLE30®	KETO-FRIENDLY
EGG-FREE	VEGAN

1 cup raw cashews

4 tablespoons extra-virgin olive oil, divided

½ small onion, diced (about ½ cup)

1 teaspoon Diamond Crystal kosher salt

1 garlic clove, minced

2 teaspoons tomato paste

½ teaspoon ground turmeric

¼ cup nutritional yeast seasoning

½ cup hot water

1 teaspoon lemon juice

USE THIS FOR:

- Crispy Smashed Potatoes (page 86)
- Cheesy Chicken and Kale Casserole (page 212)
- Chicken and Broccoli Hand Pies (page 216)
- Old-School Tacos (page 244)
- Paleo Patty Melts (page 250)
- Bacon Cheeseburger Casserole (page 252)

1 SOAK THE RAW CASHEWS FOR 15 MINUTES IN 2 CUPS OF BOILING WATER. DRAIN THE CASHEWS AND SET THEM ASIDE.

2 WHILE THE CASHEWS ARE SOAKING, HEAT A SMALL PAN OVER MEDIUM HEAT. ONCE IT'S HOT, ADD 2 TABLESPOONS OF OIL.

3 TOSS IN THE ONIONS AND SALT AND SAUTÉ FOR 5 MINUTES OR UNTIL SOFT.

4 ADD THE GARLIC, TOMATO PASTE, AND TURMERIC.

5 COOK, STIRRING, FOR ANOTHER MINUTE OR UNTIL THE INGREDIENTS ARE WELL-MIXED AND FRAGRANT.

6 TRANSFER THE COOKED MIXTURE TO A HIGH-SPEED BLENDER.

7 TOSS IN THE DRAINED CASHEWS AND NUTRITIONAL YEAST.

8 ADD ½ CUP HOT WATER, 2 TABLESPOONS OLIVE OIL, AND THE LEMON JUICE.

Per 2½ tablespoons: 159 calories • 7 g carbohydrates • 4 g protein • 14 g fat • 1 g fiber

9 BLEND ON HIGH SPEED, SCRAPING DOWN THE SIDES . . .

10 . . . UNTIL SMOOTH AND CREAMY. (ADD A TEASPOON OR TWO OF WATER IF NEEDED.)

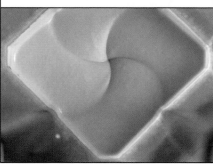

11 TRANSFER TO A BOWL TO SERVE OR COVER AND REFRIGERATE FOR UP TO 4 DAYS.

THIS EASY, CREAMY, DAIRY-FREE CASHEW CHEESE SAUCE IS PACKED WITH UMAMI. IT'LL SATISFY YOUR DEEPEST CRAVINGS FOR A CHEESY SPREAD!

PIPIÁN VERDE (GREEN MOLE SAUCE)

MAKES 6 CUPS
🕐 **45 MINUTES**

WHOLE30®	KETO-FRIENDLY
NUT-FREE	EGG-FREE

1 cup raw pepitas

1 pound tomatillos, husked

3 jalapeño chiles, roughly chopped

1 small onion, roughly chopped

3 garlic cloves

2 cups bone broth or chicken broth, divided

4 cups lightly packed baby spinach

3 large romaine lettuce leaves, roughly chopped (about 2 cups)

1 cup packed coarsely chopped fresh cilantro

1 tablespoon Diamond Crystal kosher salt

2 tablespoons avocado oil

> I LOVE PIPIÁN VERDE WITH CHICKEN OR FISH, BUT IT'S ALSO FANTASTIC ON FLANK STEAK!

USE THIS FOR:

- Shrimp Simmered in Green Mole (page 160)
- Instant Pot Pipián Pork (page 266)

INSPIRED BY A OAXACAN CLASSIC, THIS SPICY, NUTTY-TASTING, AND RICHLY REWARDING MOLE IS THE PERFECT WEEKNIGHT LIFESAVER. IT CAN BE USED TO SIMMER SEAFOOD OR BRAISE MEATS OR AS A FINISHING SAUCE FOR ANYTHING HOT OFF YOUR BACKYARD GRILL.

1 HEAT A LARGE SKILLET OVER MEDIUM HEAT. WHEN IT'S HOT, ADD THE PEPITAS IN A SINGLE LAYER.

2 TOAST THE SEEDS, STIRRING OCCASIONALLY, FOR 3 TO 5 MINUTES OR UNTIL THE PEPITAS ARE FRAGRANT AND YOU CAN HEAR THEM POPPING.

Per ½ cup serving: 89 calories • 6 g carbohydrates • 3 g protein • 7 g fat • 2 g fiber

3 Transfer the toasted pepitas to a plate to cool.

4 In a high-speed blender, combine the pepitas, tomatillos, jalapeños, onion, garlic, and ½ cup broth.

5 Blend until smooth.

6 Add the spinach, lettuce, cilantro, and salt. (If your blender's not big enough, add the greens in batches.)

7 Blitz until liquefied.

8 Heat a large pot over medium heat. Once it's hot, add the avocado oil.

9 Pour in the purée. (It'll probably splatter, so have a lid or towel ready!) Bring the sauce to a simmer.

10 Decrease the heat to maintain a simmer. Cook, stirring occasionally, for 8 to 10 minutes or until the sauce thickens. (Keep the saucepan partially covered to reduce splattering.)

11 Add in the remaining 1½ cups of broth. Increase the heat to bring the sauce back to a simmer for 5 more minutes.

12 The mole should have the texture of a creamy soup. (If it's too chunky for your liking, just blend it some more.)

13 Taste and add more salt if needed.

14 In a sealed container, this mole can be kept for up to 4 days in the fridge or up to 4 months in the freezer.

NOM NOM CHILI CRISP

MAKES 1 CUP
◐ 1½ HOURS

WHOLE30®	KETO-FRIENDLY
NUT-FREE	EGG-FREE
VEGAN	

- 1½ cups dried Chinese red chili peppers, *chiles Japones*, or *chiles de árbol*
- 1½ tablespoons dehydrated minced garlic
- 1½ tablespoons dehydrated minced onion
- 2 teaspoons Sichuan peppercorns, crushed with a mortar and pestle or meat pounder
- 2 tablespoons toasted sesame seeds
- 1 tablespoon dried shiitake mushroom powder
- 2 teaspoons Diamond Crystal kosher salt
- 1¼ cups avocado oil
- 2 medium shallots, thinly sliced (about ½ cup)
- 4 large garlic cloves, peeled and smashed
- 1 (2-inch) piece fresh ginger, cut into ¼-inch-thick coins and smashed
- 4 star anise pods
- 1 (3-inch) cinnamon stick
- 2 dried bay leaves

USE THIS FOR:

- Scallion Pancake Tacos (page 84)
- Seared Scallops with Chili Crisp (page 158)

1. FIRST, SOME NOTES ABOUT THE INGREDIENTS. FOR THE BEST CHILI CRISP, USE WHOLE, HIGH-QUALITY, DARK RED CHILIES. (TRY TO AVOID PALE OR STALE PEPPERS.)

2. WANNA KNOW THE SECRET SHORTCUT TO ACHIEVING A GREAT CRUNCH WITH LESS FUSS? USE DEHYDRATED MINCED GARLIC AND ONIONS! YOU CAN FIND THEM IN THE SPICE AISLE AT YOUR LOCAL SUPERMARKET.

3. SICHUAN (OR SZECHUAN) PEPPERCORNS ADD A PLEASURABLY TINGLY, MOUTH-NUMBING EFFECT TO THE CHILI CRISP. GET 'EM AT YOUR LOCAL ASIAN MARKET OR ONLINE.

4. LET'S GET STARTED. WITH GLOVED HANDS, REMOVE AND DISCARD THE STEMS FROM THE CHILI PEPPERS. (I MEAN IT: PUT ON GLOVES OR YOU'LL BE SORRY YOU DIDN'T!)

5. OPEN UP THE CHILIES, AND DISCARD THE SEEDS, TOO.

6. TOSS THE DE-SEEDED CHILIES INTO A MINI-FOOD PROCESSOR OR SPICE GRINDER AND PULSE TO CHOP THEM . . .

7. . . . UNTIL THE PIECES ARE ROUGHLY TWICE THE SIZE OF REGULAR CRUSHED RED PEPPER FLAKES. YOU SHOULD END UP WITH ABOUT ½ CUP OF CHOPPED CHILIES.

8. DUMP THE CHOPPED CHILIES INTO A LARGE HEAT-PROOF MEASURING CUP OR JAR . . .

Per 1 tablespoon: 124 calories • 2 g carbohydrates • 1 g protein • 13 g fat • 1 g fiber

9 ...WITH THE DEHYDRATED MINCED GARLIC AND ONION, SICHUAN PEPPERCORNS, SESAME SEEDS, SHIITAKE POWDER, AND SALT.

10 MIX WELL AND SET ASIDE. (LATER, YOU'RE GOING TO STRAIN SOME HOT OIL INTO THIS CHILI MIXTURE, SO BE SURE TO HAVE A FINE-MESH SIEVE ON HAND, TOO.)

11 IN A MEDIUM SAUCEPAN, COMBINE THE OIL, SHALLOTS, GARLIC CLOVES, GINGER ...

12 ...STAR ANISE, CINNAMON, AND BAY LEAVES.

13 COOK FOR 5 MINUTES OVER MEDIUM HEAT OR UNTIL THE TEMPERATURE OF THE OIL REACHES 225° TO 250°F. YOU SHOULD SEE SMALL BUBBLES POPPING ON THE SURFACE.

14 SIMMER TO INFUSE THE OIL, DECREASING THE HEAT AS NEEDED TO MAINTAIN THE OIL AT THIS TEMPERATURE FOR 30 MINUTES. (IF THE AROMATICS START TO BURN, YOU CAN FISH THEM OUT EARLY.)

15 USE A SLOTTED SPOON OR STRAINER TO REMOVE AND DISCARD THE AROMATICS FROM THE OIL.

16 IF THERE ARE ANY LINGERING BITS IN THE OIL, USE A SPOON TO REMOVE THEM. YOU DON'T WANT THEM TO BURN DURING THE NEXT STEP.

17 INCREASE THE HEAT TO HIGH AND COOK THE OIL FOR ABOUT 3 TO 5 MINUTES. AS SOON AS THE OIL REACHES 375°F ...

18 ...CAREFULLY POUR THE HOT OIL THROUGH A FINE-MESH SIEVE OVER THE MIXTURE OF CHILIES AND SEASONINGS. (YOU MAY NEED A HELPER TO HOLD THE SIEVE.) AND AVERT YOUR EYES FROM THE BUBBLING FUMES!

19 STIR TO COMBINE AND COOL TO ROOM TEMPERATURE. THEN, STRAIN OUT ABOUT ½ CUP OF THE OIL. (FLIP THE PAGE TO SEE WHAT YOU CAN DO WITH THE INFUSED OIL.)

20 REFRIGERATE THE CHILI CRISP IN AN AIRTIGHT CONTAINER FOR UP TO 3 MONTHS. GIVE IT A GOOD STIR BEFORE SERVING.

An insanely popular, cult-favorite spicy condiment that originated from Guizhou province in southwest China, chili crisp adds a crunchy, lip-tingling bite to any dish that needs a hit of flavor, heat, and texture. My paleo-fied version is just as maddeningly delicious as the original, so go spoon it on some boring leftovers, bland old meat and vegetables, seafood, scrambled eggs, paleo dumplings, and anything else you feel like cramming into your chili-crunch-lovin' mouth!

SWITCH IT UP:
NOM NOM CHILI OIL

Remember the infused oil you strained off? Keep it in an airtight bottle or jar in the refrigerator for up to 3 months. (I like to use a squeeze bottle.) Then, bring this fiery condiment to room temperature to use as a seasoning for stir-fries, a dipping sauce for dumplings, or drizzled over just about anything and everything.

BASIL PESTO

MAKES ¾ CUP
🕐 10 MINUTES

WHOLE30®	KETO-FRIENDLY
EGG-FREE	NIGHTSHADE-FREE
VEGAN	

1 large garlic clove, peeled

2 cups packed fresh basil leaves

¼ cup pine nuts

2 tablespoons nutritional yeast seasoning

½ teaspoon Diamond Crystal kosher salt

⅓ cup extra-virgin olive oil

USE THIS FOR:

- Roasted Winter Vegetables (page 78)
- Pesto Garden Scramble (page 98)
- Pesto Potato Meatza (page 268)

REFRIGERATE THIS PESTO IN A JAR TOPPED WITH A THIN LAYER OF OLIVE OIL FOR UP TO A WEEK, OR FREEZE IT IN AN ICE CUBE TRAY FOR UP TO 4 MONTHS.

1 DUNK THE GARLIC IN 1 CUP OF BOILING WATER FOR 30 SECONDS TO MELLOW OUT THE SPICY SHARPNESS OF THE GARLIC.

2 FISH THE GARLIC OUT WITH A SLOTTED SPOON AND TOSS IT INTO THE BOWL OF A FOOD PROCESSOR.

3 ADD THE BASIL, PINE NUTS, NUTRITIONAL YEAST, SALT, AND OLIVE OIL.

4 BLITZ UNTIL IT'S MOSTLY SMOOTH, SCRAPING DOWN THE SIDES AS NEEDED. TASTE FOR SEASONING AND ADJUST WITH MORE SALT OR NUTRITIONAL YEAST AS NEEDED.

NUTRITIONAL YEAST SEASONING GIVES THIS DAIRY-FREE PESTO A PARMESAN-LIKE PUNCH OF UMAMI THAT'S OFTEN MISSING FROM OTHER VEGAN PESTOS.

Per 1 tablespoon: 117 calories • 2 g carbohydrates • 2 g protein • 12 g fat • 1 g fiber

UMAMI STIR-FRY POWDER

MAKES ⅔ CUP
⏱ 10 MINUTES

WHOLE30®	KETO-FRIENDLY
NUT-FREE	EGG-FREE
NIGHTSHADE-FREE	VEGAN

⅔ cup dehydrated chopped green onions

6½ tablespoons Diamond Crystal kosher salt

¼ cup dried shiitake mushroom powder

1 tablespoon garlic powder

1 tablespoon onion powder

1 tablespoon ground ginger

½ teaspoon ground white pepper

USE THIS FOR:

- Garlic Mushroom Noodles (page 122)
- Hash Brown Fish (page 150)
- Shrimp and Sugar Snap Peas (page 162)
- Umami Fried Shrimp (page 164)
- Baby Bok Choy with Crab Meat Sauce (page 166)
- 2-Ingredient Crispy Chicken (page 188)

TRY IT ON SCRAMBLED EGGS!

1 TOSS ALL OF THE INGREDIENTS INTO A MINI FOOD PROCESSOR OR SPICE GRINDER.

2 BLEND TO MAKE A FINE POWDER . . .

3 . . . SCRAPING DOWN THE SIDES OCCASIONALLY TO MAKE SURE THE DEHYDRATED GREEN ONIONS ARE TOTALLY POWDERIZED.

4 THIS SEASONING SALT BLEND WILL KEEP IN AN AIRTIGHT CONTAINER STORED IN A COOL, DRY PLACE FOR UP TO 6 MONTHS.

INSPIRED BY THE FLAVORS OF THE CHINESE HOME COOKING OF MY CHILDHOOD, THIS ALL-PURPOSE SEASONING SALT IS ANOTHER SECRET SHORTCUT TO DELICIOUSNESS. IN PLACE OF SALT, BREAK OUT THIS HEAVENLY BLEND OF DRIED SHIITAKE MUSHROOMS, GARLIC, GINGER, AND GREEN ONION WHENEVER YOU'RE PREPARING DISHES WITH AN ASIAN FLAIR.

Per ¼ teaspoon: 0 calories • 0 g carbohydrates • 0 g protein • 0 g fat • 0 g fiber

NOMTASTIC GRILLING POWDER

MAKES ⅔ CUP
⏱ 10 MINUTES

WHOLE30®	KETO-FRIENDLY
NUT-FREE	EGG-FREE
NIGHTSHADE-FREE	VEGAN

½ cup Diamond Crystal kosher salt

1½ tablespoons dried parsley

2 teaspoons freshly ground black pepper

2 teaspoons onion powder

2 teaspoons ground yellow mustard

1½ teaspoons garlic powder

1¼ teaspoons ground coriander

1 teaspoon ground cumin

½ teaspoon ground allspice

USE THIS FOR:

- Roasted Winter Vegetables (page 78)
- 2-Ingredient Crispy Chicken (page 188)

DON'T BE FOOLED BY ITS NAME; THIS POWDER ISN'T JUST FOR GRILLING. YOU CAN USE IT IN PLACE OF SALT ON JUST ABOUT ANYTHING!

1 PUT ALL OF THE INGREDIENTS INTO A MINI FOOD PROCESSOR OR SPICE GRINDER.

2 GRIND THE INGREDIENTS INTO A POWDER, AND STORE IT IN AN AIRTIGHT CONTAINER FOR UP TO 6 MONTHS.

AS A RULE OF THUMB, SEASON EACH POUND OF MEAT OR VEGETABLES WITH 1 TEASPOON OF NOMTASTIC GRILLING POWDER BEFORE YOU TOSS YOUR FOOD ON THE GRILL (THOUGH SKIN-ON, BONE-IN MEATS MAY NEED MORE).

Per ¼ teaspoon: 0 calories • 0 g carbohydrates • 0 g protein • 0 g fat • 0 g fiber

MAGIC MUSHROOM POWDER

MAKES 1¼ CUPS
⏱ 10 MINUTES

WHOLE30®	KETO-FRIENDLY
NUT-FREE	EGG-FREE
VEGAN	

- **1** cup (1 ounce) dried porcini mushrooms
- **⅔** cup Diamond Crystal kosher salt
- **1** tablespoon crushed red pepper flakes
- **2** teaspoons dried thyme
- **1** teaspoon freshly ground black pepper

USE THIS FOR:

- Warm Autumn Slaw (page 64)
- Roasted Winter Vegetables (page 78)
- Crispy Smashed Potatoes (page 86)
- Sunday Night Lasagna (page 114)
- Instant Pot Zucchini Bolognese (page 118)
- Instant Pot Meat Sauce (page 120)
- Sheet Pan Italian Chicken (page 202)
- Cheesy Chicken and Kale Casserole (page 212)
- Bacon Cheeseburger Casserole (page 252)
- Instant Pot Balsamic Beef Stew (page 258)

1. DUMP THE DRIED MUSHROOMS IN A FOOD PROCESSOR OR SPICE GRINDER. PULSE A FEW TIMES TO ROUGHLY CHOP THEM UP.

2. NEXT, TURN THE FOOD PROCESSOR ON FOR 2 MINUTES OR UNTIL THE 'SHROOMS BREAK DOWN INTO A FINE POWDER. COVER THE TOP WITH A TOWEL TO KEEP THE POWDER FROM ESCAPING.

3. WAIT A FEW MINUTES FOR THE MUSHROOM POWDER TO SETTLE. THEN, ADD THE SALT, RED PEPPER FLAKES, DRIED THYME, AND BLACK PEPPER TO THE FOOD PROCESSOR.

4. PULSE TO MIX THOROUGHLY. WAIT A FEW MORE MINUTES, AND THEN TRANSFER TO AN AIRTIGHT CONTAINER. THIS MAGICAL SALT BLEND WILL LAST UP TO 6 MONTHS.

MAGIC MUSHROOM POWDER IS THE ULTIMATE NOT-SO-SECRET WEAPON IN MY KITCHEN. I USE IT IN PLACE OF SALT TO ADD A BURST OF UMAMI TO VIRTUALLY ANY SAVORY DISH. (OH, AND IF YOU DON'T FEEL LIKE MAKING YOUR OWN, YOU CAN ALWAYS JUST BUY SOME!)

Per ¼ teaspoon: 0 calories • 0 g carbohydrates • 0 g protein • 0 g fat • 0 g fiber

PALEO SANDWICH BREAD

MAKES 1 LOAF (16 SLICES)
●● 2 HOURS
(20 MINUTES HANDS-ON)

NIGHTSHADE-FREE	VEGETARIAN

1   teaspoon ghee or avocado oil

6   large eggs

½   cup (128 grams) raw unsweetened cashew butter

½   cup unsweetened almond milk or cashew milk

¼   cup avocado oil

1   tablespoon apple cider vinegar

1¼ cups (160 grams) cassava flour

¼   cup (26 grams) golden flaxseed meal

2   tablespoons (20 grams) psyllium husk powder

1½ teaspoons Diamond Crystal kosher salt

1½ teaspoons baking soda

NO CASHEW BUTTER ON HAND? ALMOND BUTTER WORKS, TOO!

USE THIS FOR:

- Michelle's Breakfast Toast (page 90)
- Paleo Patty Melts (page 250)

"PALEO SANDWICH BREAD" MIGHT SOUND LIKE AN OXYMORON, BUT WHO CARES? IT'S SIMPLE TO MAKE, DELICIOUS TO A FAULT, AND A WELCOME ALTERNATIVE WHEN YOU'RE WEARY OF LETTUCE WRAPS. BESIDES, I KNOW YOU'VE BEEN CRAVING GRAIN-FREE TOAST AND SAMMIES!

Per slice: 136 calories • 14 g carbohydrates • 4 g protein • 7 g fat • 2 g fiber

1 HEAT THE OVEN TO 350°F AND LIGHTLY GREASE A 8½ X 4½-INCH LOAF PAN WITH GHEE OR OIL. LINE THE PAN WITH A STRIP OF PARCHMENT PAPER THAT COVERS THE BOTTOM AND HANGS OVER THE SIDES.

2 POUR THE EGGS INTO THE BOWL OF A STAND MIXER.

3 ADD THE CASHEW BUTTER, ALMOND MILK, AVOCADO OIL, AND APPLE CIDER VINEGAR.

4 MIX ON LOW UNTIL WELL COMBINED.

5 ADD THE CASSAVA FLOUR, FLAXSEED MEAL, PSYLLIUM HUSK POWDER, SALT, AND BAKING SODA TO THE MIXTURE IN THE BOWL.

6 MIX ON MEDIUM-HIGH FOR APPROXIMATELY A MINUTE OR UNTIL A UNIFORM BATTER DEVELOPS, SCRAPING DOWN THE SIDES AS NEEDED. THE BAKING SODA AND VINEGAR WILL START REACTING, SO DON'T DAWDLE!

7 IMMEDIATELY TRANSFER THE BATTER INTO THE PREPARED LOAF PAN. USE A SPATULA TO SMOOTH THE TOP.

8 BAKE FOR 20 MINUTES. AFTERWARD, USE A SHARP PARING KNIFE TO SCORE THE LOAF ABOUT ¼ INCH DEEP LENGTHWISE DOWN THE MIDDLE. ROTATE THE LOAF PAN 180°.

9 BAKE THE BREAD FOR 20 TO 30 MINUTES MORE OR UNTIL THE CENTER REACHES BETWEEN 180°F AND 190°F (OR AN INSERTED TOOTHPICK COMES OUT CLEAN).

10 USING THE PARCHMENT FLAPS, LIFT THE LOAF OUT OF THE PAN AND SET IT ON A WIRE RACK TO COOL.

11 COOL COMPLETELY, AT LEAST 1 HOUR.

12 CUT THE LOAF INTO ½-INCH SLICES. KEPT IN AN AIRTIGHT CONTAINER, THESE SLICES CAN BE REFRIGERATED FOR UP TO 1 WEEK OR FROZEN FOR UP TO 3 MONTHS.

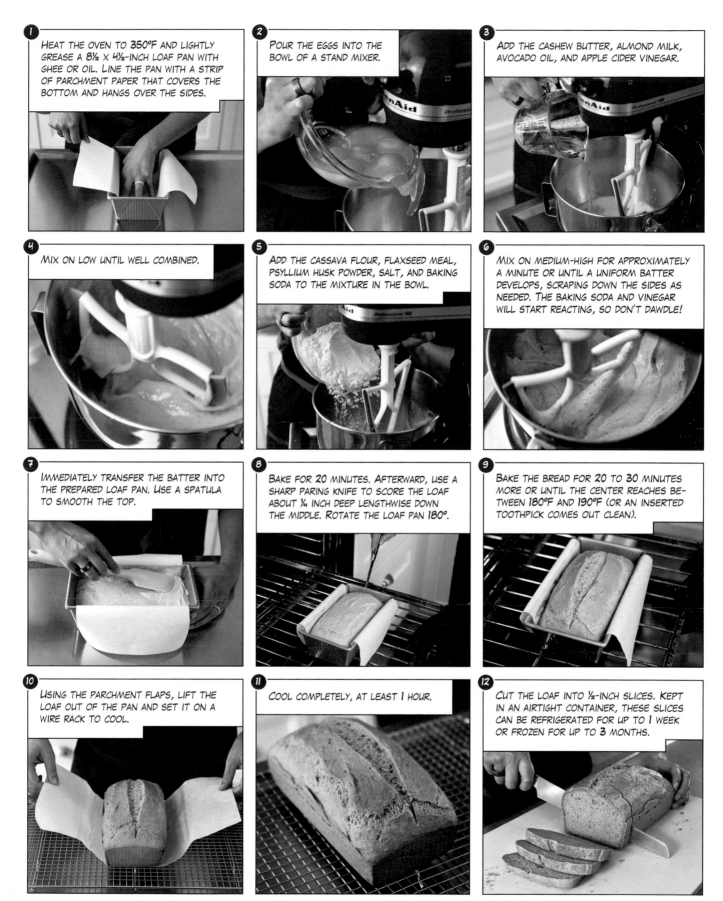

GRAIN-FREE TORTILLAS

MAKES 12 TORTILLAS
30 MINUTES

NUT-FREE	EGG-FREE
NIGHTSHADE-FREE	VEGAN (IF MODIFIED)

- **2** cups (270 grams) cassava flour
- **¾** cup (96 grams) arrowroot powder
- **1** teaspoon Diamond Crystal kosher salt
- **¼** cup softened ghee or avocado oil
- **1¼** cups hot water

USE THIS FOR:

- Instant Pot Duck Carnitas (page 220)
- Old-School Tacos (page 244)
- Moo Shu Pork (page 280)

I HAVE A GREAT DAD JOKE ABOUT GRAIN-FREE TORTILLAS, BUT DON'T WORRY: IT'S NOT CORNY AT ALL!

1 ADD THE CASSAVA FLOUR, ARROWROOT POWDER, SALT, AND FAT TO A LARGE BOWL.

2 WORK IN THE FAT WITH YOUR FINGERS UNTIL IT'S INCORPORATED. ADD WATER AND KNEAD UNTIL A BALL OF DOUGH IS FORMED.

3 DIVIDE THE DOUGH EQUALLY INTO A DOZEN PIECES. ROLL EACH INTO A BALL. COVER THE BOWL SO YOUR BALLS DON'T DRY OUT. ALWAYS KEEP YOUR BALLS MOIST, PEOPLE!

4 ONE BY ONE, FLATTEN EACH DOUGH BALL BETWEEN PARCHMENT PAPER OR PLASTIC WRAP USING A TORTILLA PRESS, A ROLLING PIN, OR A COUPLE OF SUPER HEAVY BOOKS.

5 HEAT A DRY SKILLET OR GRIDDLE OVER MEDIUM-HIGH HEAT. TRANSFER A FLATTENED TORTILLA TO THE HOT SKILLET...

6 ...AND COOK FOR 1 MINUTE OR UNTIL AIR BUBBLES FORM ON THE SURFACE. FLIP THE TORTILLA, AND COOK FOR 1 MINUTE MORE, OR UNTIL EACH SIDE IS LIGHTLY BROWNED.

7 TRANSFER EACH TORTILLA TO A PLATE AS IT FINISHES COOKING, AND COVER WITH A CLEAN TOWEL UNTIL YOU'RE READY TO EAT.

Per tortilla: 131 calories • 23 g carbohydrates • 1 g protein • 4 g fat • 1 g fiber

I DON'T OFTEN MAKE MY OWN GRAIN-FREE TORTILLAS NOW THAT I CAN BUY THEM AT THE SUPERMARKET. BUT SOMETIMES, YOU JUST CAN'T BEAT A HOT-OFF-THE-GRIDDLE HOMEMADE TORTILLA!

IF YOU MAKE EXTRA TORTILLAS, KEEP 'EM IN THE REFRIGERATOR FOR UP TO 4 DAYS OR IN THE FREEZER FOR UP TO 2 MONTHS. REHEAT THEM IN A HOT PAN UNTIL SOFT AND PLIABLE, AND EAT.

49

PLANTS + EGGS

INSTANT POT GREEN SOUP WITH TANGY CASHEW CREAM

MAKES 5 SERVINGS
◐ **45 MINUTES**
(25 MINUTES HANDS-ON)

WHOLE30®	EGG-FREE
NIGHTSHADE-FREE	VEGAN (IF MODIFIED)

• CASHEW CREAM •

1 cup raw cashews, soaked in 1 cup boiling water for 15 minutes

½ cup water

2 tablespoons extra-virgin olive oil

2 tablespoons lemon juice

2 small garlic cloves, peeled

1 teaspoon Diamond Crystal kosher salt

• SOUP •

2 tablespoons extra-virgin olive oil

1 large onion, chopped

Diamond Crystal kosher salt

3 garlic cloves, roughly chopped

1 tablespoon chopped fresh ginger

1 medium head broccoli, roughly chopped

2 small zucchini, roughly chopped

4 scallions, trimmed and roughly chopped

½ cup peeled and diced apple

4 cups bone broth, chicken broth, or vegetable broth

5 cups lightly packed baby spinach

Freshly ground black pepper

1. LET'S MAKE THE CASHEW CREAM FIRST. DRAIN THE SOAKED CASHEWS ...

2. ...AND TOSS THEM IN A BLENDER WITH ½ CUP WATER, OLIVE OIL, LEMON JUICE, GARLIC, AND SALT.

3. BLITZ THE CONTENTS UNTIL SMOOTH.

4. TASTE AND ADJUST THE SEASONING WITH MORE SALT OR LEMON JUICE IF NEEDED. SET ASIDE THE CASHEW SAUCE.

5. NOW, LET'S MAKE THE SOUP. SWITCH ON THE SAUTÉ FUNCTION ON THE INSTANT POT. ONCE IT'S HOT, SWIRL IN THE OIL.

6. TOSS IN THE ONION AND ½ TEASPOON OF KOSHER SALT.

7. COOK FOR **2** TO **3** MINUTES, STIRRING THE ONION FREQUENTLY, UNTIL SLIGHTLY SOFTENED. TURN OFF THE SAUTÉ FUNCTION.

8. STIR IN THE GARLIC AND GINGER AND COOK FOR ABOUT **30** SECONDS UNTIL FRAGRANT.

Per serving: 220 calories • 18 g carbohydrates • 7 g protein • 15 g fat • 4 g fiber

9 DUMP THE BROCCOLI...

10 ...ZUCCHINI, SCALLIONS, AND APPLE INTO THE INSTANT POT. MIX WELL.

11 POUR IN THE BROTH...

12 ...AND ADD ANOTHER ½ TEASPOON SALT.

13 COVER THE INSTANT POT AND COOK FOR 1 MINUTE UNDER HIGH PRESSURE.

14 THEN, TURN OFF THE INSTANT POT AND RELEASE THE PRESSURE MANUALLY.

15 OPEN UP THE INSTANT POT AND ADD THE BABY SPINACH.

16 STIR UNTIL THE SPINACH IS WILTED.

17 BLEND THE SOUP IN BATCHES USING A HIGH-SPEED BLENDER.

18 MAKE SURE TO FILL THE BLENDER NO MORE THAN ⅔ FULL, REMOVE THE CENTER OF THE LID, AND COVER THE TOP WITH A TOWEL. (ALTERNATIVELY, YOU CAN BLEND THE SOUP WITH AN IMMERSION BLENDER.)

19 TASTE FOR SEASONING AND ADJUST WITH SALT AND PEPPER TO TASTE.

20 POUR THE SOUP INTO BOWLS. TOP EACH WITH SOME CASHEW CREAM AND SERVE.

Overindulging with too many treats? Get back on track by cooking up a big batch of this emerald-green soup packed with healthy vegetables.

SWITCH IT UP:
STOVETOP GREEN SOUP

No Instant Pot? Make this recipe on the stovetop instead. In Step 5, add the olive oil to a large saucepan over medium heat. Add the onion and ½ teaspoon kosher salt, and sauté for 8 to 10 minutes until softened and translucent. Add the garlic and ginger and cook until fragrant, about 30 seconds. Throw in the broccoli, zucchini, scallions, apple, broth, and ½ teaspoon kosher salt. Bring everything to a boil over high heat, and then decrease the heat to maintain a simmer for 4 to 8 minutes or until the vegetables are fork-tender. Then, finish the recipe from Step 15 by adding the spinach and continuing through Step 20.

PRO TIP: THIS SOUP WILL TASTE ONLY AS GOOD AS YOUR BROTH BASE, SO USE THE RICHEST, HIGHEST-QUALITY CHICKEN OR VEGETABLE BROTH YOU CAN FIND. AFTER ALL, YOU DON'T WANT YOUR HEARTY SOUP TO TASTE LIKE HOT GREEN JUICE, RIGHT?

SWIRL IN A DOLLOP OF SMOOTH, LEMONY CASHEW CREAM TO MAKE THIS SOUP IRRESISTIBLE TO EVEN THE FUSSIEST EATERS. SAVE THE EXTRA CASHEW CREAM IN THE REFRIGERATOR FOR UP TO 1 WEEK. YOU CAN USE IT TO DRESS SIMPLE SALADS OR DRIZZLE IT ON SOME ROASTED VEGGIES!

ZUCCHINI CARPACCIO SALAD

MAKES 4 SERVINGS
🕐 **45 MINUTES**
(15 MINUTES HANDS-ON)

WHOLE30®	KETO-FRIENDLY
EGG-FREE	NIGHTSHADE-FREE
VEGAN	

3   medium zucchini, ends trimmed

     Diamond Crystal kosher salt

2   tablespoons lemon juice

¼   cup extra-virgin olive oil

2   tablespoons minced fresh mint

2   tablespoons minced fresh basil

2   tablespoons roasted and salted pistachios, shelled and roughly chopped

¼   teaspoon freshly ground black pepper

2   tablespoons nutritional yeast seasoning (optional)

> THIS TASTES AS AMAZING AS IT LOOKS!

1   USING A VEGETABLE PEELER OR MANDOLIN SLICER, CAREFULLY SLICE THE ZUCCHINI INTO THIN STRIPS.

2   DUMP THE ZUCCHINI STRIPS IN A COLANDER AND TOSS THEM WITH ½ TEASPOON SALT.

3   SET 'EM ASIDE FOR 30 MINUTES TO ALLOW THE EXCESS LIQUID TO DRAIN.

4   BLOT THE ZUCCHINI STRIPS DRY WITH PAPER TOWELS . . .

5   . . . AND ARRANGE THEM ON A PLATTER. (NOT READY TO EAT YET? YOU CAN REFRIGERATE THE ZUCCHINI FOR UP TO 2 DAYS.)

6   DRIZZLE ON THE LEMON JUICE AND OLIVE OIL.

7   GARNISH WITH A SHOWER OF FRESH MINT, BASIL, PISTACHIOS, AND PEPPER. TASTE AND ADJUST THE SEASONING WITH MORE SALT OR LEMON JUICE IF NEEDED.

8   SPRINKLE ON THE NUTRITIONAL YEAST IF DESIRED. (IT'S OPTIONAL, BUT I ALWAYS DO IT TO ADD SOME EXTRA UMAMI.)

Per serving: 178 calories • 7 g carbohydrates • 4 g protein • 16 g fat • 3 g fiber

GOT A BOATLOAD OF ZUCCHINI? ASSEMBLE THIS NO-COOK, SUMMERTIME SALAD. THE BALANCE OF ACIDITY, CRUNCH, AND UMAMI PAIRS BEAUTIFULLY WITH WHATEVER YOU DECIDE TO TOSS ON YOUR BACKYARD GRILL!

JAPANESE POTATO SALAD

MAKES 8 SERVINGS
◖ 45 MINUTES
(35 MINUTES HANDS-ON)

WHOLE30®	NUT-FREE
VEGETARIAN (IF MODIFIED)	

1½   pounds russet potatoes, peeled and cut into 1½-inch cubes

     Diamond Crystal kosher salt

2   Japanese or Persian cucumbers, thinly sliced into half moons

⅓   cup paleo-friendly mayonnaise

2   teaspoons rice wine vinegar

1   teaspoon Dijon-style mustard

1   small carrot, thinly sliced into half moons

¼   cup thinly sliced shallot or red onion, soaked for 10 minutes in ice water and drained

2   hard-boiled eggs, roughly chopped

½   cup diced ham (optional)

2   scallions, thinly sliced

     Freshly ground black pepper

I'M A HUGE FAN OF YOSHOKU, OR WESTERN-INFLUENCED JAPANESE COOKING, AND THIS DISH IS A PARTICULARLY TASTY EXAMPLE OF EAST-WEST FUSION CUISINE. COMBINING ROUGHLY MASHED POTATOES AND CRUNCHY VEGETABLES AND FLAVORED WITH MAYO, RICE VINEGAR, AND MUSTARD, JAPANESE POTATO SALAD IS ONE OF OWEN'S ALL-TIME FAVORITE SIDES FOR GOOD REASON.

I LOVE THAT IT'S LIKE MASHED POTATOES MADE INTO SALAD!

Per serving: 181 calories • 17 g carbohydrates • 6 g protein • 11 g fat • 2 g fiber

1 PLOP THE POTATOES INTO A LARGE POT. ADD ENOUGH COLD WATER TO SUBMERGE THE POTATOES SO THAT THEY'RE AT LEAST AN INCH BELOW THE WATER'S SURFACE.

2 TOSS IN A GENEROUS PINCH OF SALT AND BRING THE CONTENTS OF THE POT TO A BOIL OVER HIGH HEAT.

3 LOWER THE HEAT TO MAINTAIN A STEADY SIMMER. COOK FOR 10 MINUTES OR UNTIL THE POTATOES ARE TENDER AND CAN BE EASILY PIERCED WITH A FORK.

4 WHILE THE POTATOES ARE COOKING, TOSS THE CUCUMBER SLICES AND ½ TEASPOON OF KOSHER SALT IN A SMALL BOWL. SET ASIDE FOR AT LEAST 10 MINUTES.

5 DRAIN THE COOKED POTATOES AND COOL TO ROOM TEMPERATURE. (POP THEM IN THE FRIDGE TO CHILL THEM FASTER.)

6 PLACE THE SALTED CUCUMBER SLICES IN A CLEAN KITCHEN TOWEL.

7 SQUEEZE OUT AND DISCARD THE RELEASED LIQUID. SET ASIDE THE CUCUMBER SLICES.

8 IN A LARGE BOWL, STIR TOGETHER THE PALEO MAYONNAISE, RICE WINE VINEGAR, AND MUSTARD.

9 ADD THE COOLED POTATOES TO THE BOWL.

10 MASH WELL WITH A FORK TO INCORPORATE THE POTATOES WITH THE MAYONNAISE MIXTURE. THE RESULTING TEXTURE SHOULD RESEMBLE CHUNKY MASHED POTATOES.

11 STIR IN THE CUCUMBERS, CARROTS, SHALLOTS, EGGS, HAM, AND SCALLIONS. TASTE FOR SEASONING AND ADJUST WITH SALT AND PEPPER TO TASTE.

12 SERVE OR KEEP IN THE REFRIGERATOR FOR UP TO FOUR DAYS.

INSALATA TRICOLORE WITH PERSIMMONS

MAKES 4 SERVINGS
◑ **30 MINUTES**

WHOLE30®	KETO-FRIENDLY
EGG-FREE	NIGHTSHADE-FREE
VEGAN	

• LEMON VINAIGRETTE •

1 tablespoon finely minced shallot

1 tablespoon lemon zest

2 tablespoons lemon juice

Diamond Crystal kosher salt

Freshly ground black pepper

6 tablespoons extra-virgin olive oil

• SALAD •

2 medium endive heads, cut crosswise into ½-inch slices

1 medium radicchio head, cut lengthwise into ½-inch slices

4 cups baby arugula

2 Fuyu persimmons or 1 apple, peeled and thinly sliced

2 tablespoons roughly chopped toasted hazelnuts

HELLO, MY SWEETS!

1 MAKE THE LEMON VINAIGRETTE. COMBINE THE MINCED SHALLOT, LEMON ZEST, AND LEMON JUICE IN A LIQUID MEASURING CUP. LET THE SHALLOT SOAK FOR 5 MINUTES.

2 ADD ½ TEASPOON SALT AND ¼ TEASPOON FRESHLY GROUND BLACK PEPPER TO THE CONTENTS IN THE MEASURING CUP.

3 POUR IN THE OLIVE OIL AND WHISK WELL. TASTE AND ADJUST FOR SEASONING.

4 PUT THE ENDIVE, RADICCHIO, AND ARUGULA IN A BOWL. ADD A SPRINKLE OF SALT.

5 POUR IN HALF OF THE LEMON VINAIGRETTE AND TOSS WELL. TASTE AND ADD MORE DRESSING IF NEEDED.

6 TRANSFER THE SALAD TO A LARGE SERVING PLATTER AND ADD THE PERSIMMON SLICES.

7 SPRINKLE THE TOASTED HAZELNUTS ON THE SALAD AND ADD MORE BLACK PEPPER.

8 SERVE!

Per serving: 267 calories • 11 g carbohydrates • 3 g protein • 25 g fat • 3 g fiber

THIS SALAD IS A MASH-UP OF TWO OF HENRY'S FAVORITE THINGS: FUYU PERSIMMONS AND THE INSALATA TRICO-LORE SALAD FROM SAN FRANCISCO'S PIZZERIA DELFINA. (SERIOUSLY: GET YOURSELF SOMEONE WHO LOOKS AT YOU LIKE HENRY LOOKS AT A BOWL OF WINTER PERSIMMONS.) PERSIMMON SEASON IS SHORT, THOUGH, SO IF YOU CAN'T FIND THEM, USE FUJI OR HONEYCRISP APPLES INSTEAD.

WARM AUTUMN SLAW

MAKES 6 SERVINGS
● **1 HOUR**
(45 MINUTES HANDS-ON)

WHOLE30®	NUT-FREE
EGG-FREE	VEGAN

1 pound brussels sprouts, ends trimmed

1 small delicata squash, seeded and cut into thin half moons

4 tablespoons extra-virgin olive oil, divided

1½ teaspoons Magic Mushroom Powder (page 45) or Diamond Crystal kosher salt

2 tablespoons raw pepitas

1 large Fuji or Honeycrisp apple, cored and thinly sliced

¼ cup pomegranate arils

¼ teaspoon freshly ground black pepper

2 tablespoons aged balsamic vinegar

2 tablespoons minced chives

WAIT, AUTUMN IS A SEASON? I THOUGHT IT WAS CALLED *PUMPKIN SEASON!*

WHEN THE LEAVES CHANGE COLOR AND THE AIR OUTSIDE TURNS BRISK AND CHILLY, I CAN'T WAIT TO TOSS TOGETHER A TOASTY, COMFORTING SALAD WITH AUTUMNAL INGREDIENTS. THIS SLAW COMBINES ROASTED FALL VEGETABLES, CRISP FRUIT, AND NUTTY PEPITAS FOR A HEARTY SIDE DISH THAT MIGHT EVEN OVERSHADOW YOUR MAIN COURSE.

AS PRESENTED HERE, THIS DISH IS NUT-FREE, BUT IF YOU'RE NOT ALLERGIC, I RECOMMEND A GARNISH OF CRUSHED, TOASTED HAZELNUTS TO ADD EVEN MORE CRUNCH TO THIS SLAW.

Per serving: 183 calories • 20 g carbohydrates • 5 g protein • 11 g fat • 5 g fiber

1 HEAT THE OVEN TO 450°F WITH THE RACK IN THE MIDDLE POSITION.

2 USING A KNIFE OR FOOD PROCESSOR, CUT THE BRUSSELS SPROUTS INTO ⅛-INCH-THICK SLICES.

3 IN A LARGE BOWL, TOSS THE SQUASH AND BRUSSELS SPROUTS WITH 2 TABLESPOONS OF OLIVE OIL AND THE MAGIC MUSHROOM POWDER (OR KOSHER SALT).

4 SPREAD THE VEGETABLES IN A SINGLE LAYER ON A RIMMED BAKING SHEET, MAKING SURE THE SQUASH SLICES ARE FLUSH AGAINST THE BOTTOM.

5 ROAST IN THE OVEN FOR 15 TO 20 MINUTES, TURNING THE TRAY AROUND AT THE HALFWAY POINT.

6 MEANWHILE, TOAST THE PEPITAS. HEAT A SMALL PAN OVER MEDIUM HEAT. ONCE IT'S HOT, ADD THE PEPITAS IN A SINGLE LAYER.

7 COOK, STIRRING, FOR 3 TO 5 MINUTES OR UNTIL THE PEPITAS ARE FRAGRANT AND YOU CAN HEAR THEM POPPING. TRANSFER THE PEPITAS TO A PLATE TO COOL.

8 WHEN THE DELICATA SQUASH AND BRUSSELS SPROUTS ARE DONE ROASTING, TAKE THE TRAY OUT OF THE OVEN AND COOL FOR ABOUT 15 MINUTES.

9 ADD THE SLICED APPLES, POMEGRANATE ARILS, AND PEPITAS. SEASON WITH PEPPER.

10 DRIZZLE ON THE AGED BALSAMIC VINEGAR AND 2 TABLESPOONS OLIVE OIL. SPRINKLE FRESH CHIVES ON THE SLAW.

11 TRANSFER TO A LARGE SERVING BOWL.

12 TASTE FOR SEASONING AND SERVE.

SMASHED CUCUMBER AND CARROT SALAD

MAKES 4 SERVINGS
⏱ **15 MINUTES**

WHOLE30®	KETO-FRIENDLY
NUT-FREE	EGG-FREE
VEGAN (IF MODIFIED)	

- **¼** cup All-Purpose Stir-Fry Sauce (page 29) (to make vegan, use No-Fish Sauce variation)

- **1** pound Japanese or Persian cucumbers

- **1** teaspoon Diamond Crystal kosher salt

- **1** garlic clove, minced

- **½** teaspoon toasted sesame oil

- **¼** teaspoon crushed red pepper flakes

- **2** medium carrots, sliced into thin ribbons with a vegetable peeler

- **2** scallions, thinly sliced

- **2** teaspoons toasted sesame seeds

LET'S SMASH SOME CUKES!

1 YOU'LL NEED ALL-PURPOSE STIR-FRY SAUCE, SO MAKE SOME IF YOU DON'T ALREADY HAVE A BOTTLE IN YOUR FRIDGE.

2 ON A CUTTING BOARD, GENTLY SMASH THE CUCUMBERS WITH A MEAT POUNDER OR SMALL CAST-IRON SKILLET UNTIL THEY SPLIT OPEN.

3 TRIM OFF THE ENDS AND CUT THE BASHED CUCUMBERS INTO BITE-SIZE PIECES.

4 PUT A FINE-MESH STRAINER OR COLANDER IN A MEDIUM BOWL, AND DUMP THE CUCUMBER PIECES INTO THE STRAINER.

5 TOSS THE CUCUMBERS WITH SALT. THEN, PUT THE STRAINER AND BOWL WITH THE SALTED CUCUMBER IN THE FRIDGE WHILE YOU MAKE THE DRESSING.

6 IN A SMALL MEASURING CUP OR BOWL, STIR TOGETHER THE ALL-PURPOSE STIR-FRY SAUCE, GARLIC, SESAME OIL, AND CRUSHED RED PEPPER FLAKES.

7 PLOP THE DRAINED CUCUMBERS INTO A BOWL WITH THE CARROT NOODLES AND MOST OF THE SCALLIONS.

8 ADD THE DRESSING AND TOSS WELL.

Per serving: 60 calories • 11 g carbohydrates • 2 g protein • 1 g fat • 2 g fiber

9 Transfer to a serving bowl and top with the rest of the scallions and sesame seeds.

This is my paleo version of a classic Sichuanese chilled cucumber salad seasoned with nutty sesame oil, spicy garlic, and tangy vinegar. Why smash the cucumbers, you ask? Gently crushing them with something heavy helps expel some of the extra liquid during the initial salting process; plus, the umami-rich dressing clings better to the jagged bits of bashed cucumber.

A NICE GREEN SALAD

MAKES 4 SERVINGS
◑ **30 MINUTES**
(15 MINUTES HANDS-ON)

WHOLE30® (IF MODIFIED)	
NUT-FREE (IF MODIFIED)	
EGG-FREE	NIGHTSHADE-FREE
VEGAN (IF MODIFIED)	

• SALAD •

2 cups sugar snap peas

Diamond Crystal kosher salt

6 cups mixed greens or lettuce

1 medium Chioggia beet, sliced paper-thin with a mandolin slicer

2 medium carrots, sliced into thin ribbons with a vegetable peeler

2 Japanese or Persian cucumbers, thinly sliced

1 medium Hass avocado, pitted, peeled, and cubed

1 cup broccoli sprouts

Freshly ground black pepper

¼ cup toasted almond slivers, sunflower seeds, or pepitas

• JORY'S DRESSING •

3 tablespoons sherry vinegar

1 teaspoon Dijon-style mustard

1 teaspoon honey (optional, not Whole30)

½ teaspoon Diamond Crystal kosher salt

¼ teaspoon freshly ground black pepper

⅓ cup extra-virgin olive oil

I'M OFTEN ASKED "WHAT SHOULD I SERVE WITH THIS MAIN DISH?" AND MY ANSWER'S ALWAYS THE SAME: "A NICE GREEN SALAD." SALADS DON'T HAVE TO BE COMPLICATED TO BE TASTY; THIS SIMPLE COMBINATION OF GREENS AND VEGETABLES CAN BE HASTILY TOSSED TOGETHER AND SERVED ALONGSIDE ANY WEEKNIGHT SUPPER. AS FOR THE SALAD DRESSING, I'M PARTIAL TO THIS EASY SHAKE-IT-UP-YOURSELF VINAIGRETTE PERFECTED BY MY SUPERFRIEND JORY!

DON'T FEEL LIMITED BY THE LISTED INGREDIENTS. USE WHATEVER GREENS ARE IN SEASON OR IN YOUR FRIDGE!

Per serving: 273 calories • 19 g carbohydrates • 6 g protein • 21 g fat • 7 g fiber

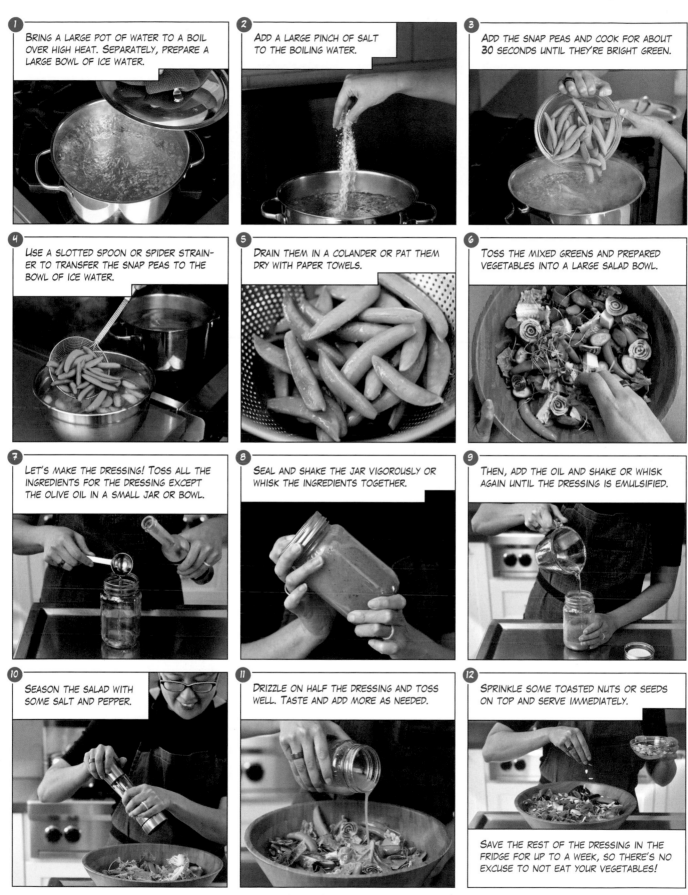

1. BRING A LARGE POT OF WATER TO A BOIL OVER HIGH HEAT. SEPARATELY, PREPARE A LARGE BOWL OF ICE WATER.

2. ADD A LARGE PINCH OF SALT TO THE BOILING WATER.

3. ADD THE SNAP PEAS AND COOK FOR ABOUT 30 SECONDS UNTIL THEY'RE BRIGHT GREEN.

4. USE A SLOTTED SPOON OR SPIDER STRAINER TO TRANSFER THE SNAP PEAS TO THE BOWL OF ICE WATER.

5. DRAIN THEM IN A COLANDER OR PAT THEM DRY WITH PAPER TOWELS.

6. TOSS THE MIXED GREENS AND PREPARED VEGETABLES INTO A LARGE SALAD BOWL.

7. LET'S MAKE THE DRESSING! TOSS ALL THE INGREDIENTS FOR THE DRESSING EXCEPT THE OLIVE OIL IN A SMALL JAR OR BOWL.

8. SEAL AND SHAKE THE JAR VIGOROUSLY OR WHISK THE INGREDIENTS TOGETHER.

9. THEN, ADD THE OIL AND SHAKE OR WHISK AGAIN UNTIL THE DRESSING IS EMULSIFIED.

10. SEASON THE SALAD WITH SOME SALT AND PEPPER.

11. DRIZZLE ON HALF THE DRESSING AND TOSS WELL. TASTE AND ADD MORE AS NEEDED.

12. SPRINKLE SOME TOASTED NUTS OR SEEDS ON TOP AND SERVE IMMEDIATELY.

SAVE THE REST OF THE DRESSING IN THE FRIDGE FOR UP TO A WEEK, SO THERE'S NO EXCUSE TO NOT EAT YOUR VEGETABLES!

AVOCADO SASHIMI

MAKES 4 SERVINGS
⏱ 10 MINUTES

WHOLE30®	KETO-FRIENDLY
NUT-FREE	EGG-FREE
VEGAN	

- **2** large Hass avocados
- **2** tablespoons coconut aminos
- **2** teaspoons paleo-friendly furikake
- **¼** teaspoon shichimi togarashi (Japanese seven-spice blend)
- **1** teaspoon flake sea salt
- **2** scallions, thinly sliced

> THIS FAST AND EASY NO-COOK SIDE IS EQUAL PARTS BEAUTIFUL AND CRAZY DELICIOUS.

> THAT SAID, THIS ISN'T A CLASSIC JAPANESE DISH. DESPITE THE POPULARITY OF CRAB-AND-AVOCADO ROLLS IN THE WEST, AVOCADOS WEREN'T EVEN INTRODUCED TO JAPAN UNTIL THE 1970S.

1 CUT THE AVOCADOS IN HALF LENGTHWISE.

2 REMOVE THE PITS . . .

3 . . . AND CAREFULLY PEEL OFF THE SKIN.

4 THINLY SLICE THE AVOCADO HALVES . . .

5 . . . AND GENTLY FAN 'EM OUT ON A PLATE. (DON'T BE A SLOB. MAKE IT LOOK PRETTY!)

6 DRIZZLE THE COCONUT AMINOS ON TOP.

7 SPRINKLE ON THE FURIKAKE, SHICHIMI, AND FLAKE SEA SALT.

8 ADORN WITH SCALLIONS AND SERVE.

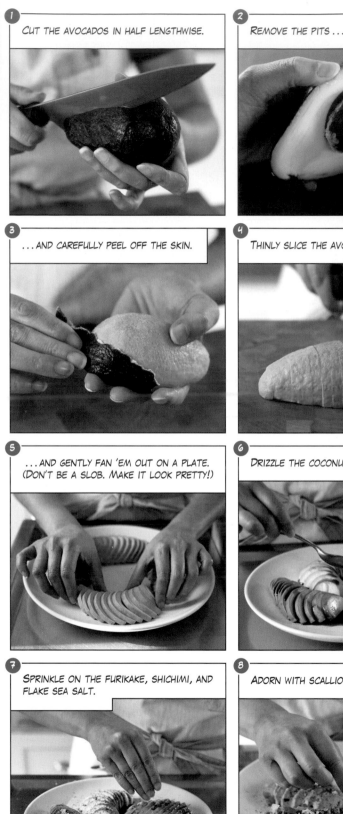

Per serving: 185 calories • 14 g carbohydrates • 2 g protein • 15 g fat • 10 g fiber

WITH JUST A COUPLE OF AVOCADOS AND SOME PANTRY STAPLES, YOU CAN APPROXIMATE THE FLAVORS AND TEXTURES OF CREAMY, DELICATE SLICES OF SASHIMI ANYTIME, EVEN WHEN YOU HAVE NO FRESH FISH ON HAND. WITH A SALTY-SWEET SAUCE AND A DASH OF SPICY SHICHIMI TOGARASHI, THIS PALEO AND VEGAN SASHIMI IS DELICIOUS ENOUGH FOR EATERS OF ALL STRIPES.

HOLY SHIITAKE MUSHROOMS

MAKES 6 SERVINGS
⚠ 7 HOURS
(40 MINUTES HANDS-ON)

WHOLE30®	NUT-FREE
EGG-FREE	NIGHTSHADE-FREE
VEGAN (IF MODIFIED)	

3 cups (3.5 ounces) dried shiitake mushrooms

4 cups water

½ cup All-Purpose Stir-Fry Sauce (page 29) (to make vegan, use No-Fish Sauce variation)

USE THIS FOR:

- Michelle's Breakfast Toast (page 90)

- Shoyu Ramen (page 134)

"HOLY SHIITAKE" IS ONE OF MY TOP THREE FAKE PROFANITIES, ALONG WITH "MOTHERFATHER" AND "SON OF A BUSINESSMAN"!

SHIITAKE MUSHROOMS ARE FREQUENTLY SHOWCASED AT CELEBRATORY CANTONESE FEASTS, ESPECIALLY DURING THE LUNAR NEW YEAR. THIS SAVORY SIMMERED DISH IS A RIFF ON ONE OF MY FAMILY'S FAVORITES, MADE EVEN EASIER WITH MY ALL-PURPOSE STIR-FRY SAUCE. TO DO THIS RECIPE JUSTICE, MAKE AN EFFORT TO SOURCE PLUMP, HIGH-QUALITY SHIITAKE MUSHROOMS; AFTER ALL, THEY'RE THE STAR OF THIS SHOW.

BECAUSE THEY'RE HARVESTED WHILE STILL BUDDING, DONKO OR DONGGU (A.K.A. "WINTER MUSHROOM") SHIITAKES FEATURE THICKER, MEATIER MUSHROOM CAPS THAN THOSE OF THE FLATTER, WIDER KOSHIN VARIETY. AS A RESULT, WHOLE DONKO SHIITAKES ARE IDEAL FOR THIS RECIPE, YIELDING A PLEASANTLY CHEWY TEXTURE AND A RICH, UMAMI-FORWARD FLAVOR.

Per serving: 66 calories • 15 g carbohydrates • 2 g protein • 1 g fat • 3 g fiber

1 IN A LARGE BOWL, SOAK THE SHIITAKE MUSHROOMS IN 4 CUPS OF WATER.

2 COVER THE BOWL AND POP IT IN THE FRIDGE. LET THE MUSHROOMS REHYDRATE FOR AT LEAST 6 HOURS OR UNTIL SOFT.

3 IF YOU DON'T HAVE ALL-PURPOSE STIR-FRY SAUCE AT THE READY, MAKE SOME BEFORE THE MUSHROOMS ARE DONE SOAKING.

4 TRIM AND DISCARD THE STEMS FROM THE HYDRATED MUSHROOMS.

5 TOSS THE MUSHROOM CAPS INTO A MEDIUM SAUCEPAN. THEN, STRAIN THE SOAKING LIQUID THROUGH A FINE-MESH SIEVE.

6 MEASURE OUT 2 CUPS OF THE STRAINED LIQUID AND POUR IT INTO THE SAUCEPAN.

7 POUR IN THE ALL-PURPOSE STIR-FRY SAUCE AND STIR TO COMBINE.

8 BRING THE CONTENTS TO A BOIL OVER HIGH HEAT.

9 ONCE THE LIQUID STARTS BOILING, SKIM OFF ANY SCUM THAT FLOATS TO THE TOP.

10 TURN THE HEAT DOWN TO MAINTAIN A SIMMER AND PLACE A LID ON TOP, LEAVING IT SLIGHTLY ASKEW TO ALLOW STEAM TO ESCAPE. COOK FOR 15 MINUTES.

11 REMOVE THE LID AND CONTINUE SIMMERING FOR 10 TO 15 MINUTES, STIRRING OCCASIONALLY, UNTIL SOME OF THE LIQUID COOKS OFF AND THE SAUCE THICKENS.

12 SLICE 'EM UP OR EAT AS-IS! LADLE THE SAUCE OVER THE MUSHROOMS AND SERVE. THEY'LL KEEP FOR UP TO A WEEK IN AN AIRTIGHT CONTAINER IN THE FRIDGE.

BROCCOLINI WITH TAHINI SAUCE

MAKES 4 SERVINGS
⏱ 20 MINUTES
(10 MINUTES HANDS-ON)

WHOLE30®	KETO-FRIENDLY
NUT-FREE	EGG-FREE
VEGAN	

Diamond Crystal kosher salt

1   pound broccolini, ends trimmed

¼   cup tahini

3   tablespoons extra-virgin olive oil

     Zest from 1 lemon

2   tablespoons lemon juice

¼   teaspoon ground cumin

1   garlic clove, minced

¼   cup ice water

2   teaspoons toasted black sesame seeds

½   teaspoon crushed red pepper flakes

FEEL FREE TO ALSO DRIZZLE THIS CREAMY, TANGY TAHINI SAUCE ON GRILLED MEATS AND ROASTED VEGETABLES, OR USE IT AS A SALAD DRESSING!

1   BRING A LARGE POT OF WATER TO A ROLLING BOIL OVER HIGH HEAT, COVERED. THEN, ADD A BIG PINCH OF SALT.

2   CAREFULLY DROP THE BROCCOLINI INTO THE BOILING WATER. COOK THE BROCCOLINI FOR 1 MINUTE OR UNTIL IT TURNS BRIGHT GREEN AND TENDER-CRISP.

3   TRANSFER THE BROCCOLINI TO A COLANDER TO DRAIN. THEN, ARRANGE THE BROCCOLINI ON A SERVING PLATE. SET IT ASIDE.

4   IN A MEDIUM BOWL, WHISK TOGETHER THE TAHINI, OLIVE OIL, LEMON ZEST, LEMON JUICE, ¾ TEASPOON KOSHER SALT, CUMIN, AND GARLIC. (DON'T WORRY IF IT LOOKS CLUMPY OR CURDLED AT THIS STAGE.)

5   SLOWLY WHISK IN 1 TABLESPOON OF ICE WATER AT A TIME . . .

6   . . . UNTIL THE CHUNKY TAHINI PASTE MAGICALLY TURNS INTO A CREAMY SAUCE. (I'VE FOUND IT USUALLY TAKES ABOUT 4 TABLESPOONS OF ICE WATER, GIVE OR TAKE.)

7   TASTE THE SAUCE AND ADJUST WITH MORE SALT OR LEMON JUICE IF NEEDED. SPOON THE TAHINI SAUCE ON THE BROCCOLINI.

8   TOP WITH TOASTED SESAME SEEDS AND CRUSHED RED PEPPER FLAKES. SERVE!

Per serving: 238 calories • 12 g carbohydrates • 7 g protein • 19 g fat • 2 g fiber

A HYBRID OF BROCCOLI AND CHINESE BROCCOLI (A.K.A. GAI LAN), BROCCOLINI OFFERS A PLEASANT CRUNCH AND A MILD SWEETNESS MISSING FROM STANDARD-ISSUE BROCCOLI.

DELICIOUSLY UNFUSSY, THIS QUICK SIDE ADDS BRIGHTNESS AND FLAIR TO ANY SIT-DOWN SUPPER. YOU CAN EVEN MAKE THE BROCCOLINI AHEAD OF TIME AND SERVE IT CHILLED.

GARLICKY COLLARDS AND BACON

MAKES 4 SERVINGS
◑ 30 MINUTES

WHOLE30®	KETO-FRIENDLY
NUT-FREE	EGG-FREE
NIGHTSHADE-FREE	

- **1½** pounds collard greens, thick stems removed

- **4** slices bacon, cut crosswise into ¼-inch pieces

- **6** garlic cloves, minced

- **1** tablespoon red wine vinegar or lemon juice

- **¾** teaspoon Diamond Crystal kosher salt

- **¼** teaspoon freshly ground black pepper

Is there anything that doesn't taste better with bacon?

THIS BRIGHT, TASTY SIDE IS INSPIRED BY *COUVE À MINEIRA*, A BRAZILIAN DISH OF COLLARD GREENS QUICKLY COOKED IN GARLIC AND OLIVE OIL. THESE GARLICKY COLLARDS ARE EASY TO PREPARE AND A WELCOME ADDITION TO ANY DINNER TABLE. FINISHED WITH A GENEROUS SPRINKLE OF CRUNCHY BACON, I BET YOU'LL FIND THIS DISH AS SWOONWORTHY AS WE DO.

Per serving: 153 calories • 11 g carbohydrates • 8 g protein • 10 g fat • 7 g fiber

1. WASH THE STEMMED COLLARDS AND DRAIN THEM IN A COLANDER. DON'T SPIN OFF ALL THE WATER WITH A SALAD SPINNER.

2. LAYER THE COLLARD LEAVES INTO STACKS.

3. ROLL EACH STACK INTO A CIGAR SHAPE.

4. CUT INTO FINE STRIPS AND REPEAT WITH THE REST OF THE GREENS. SET 'EM ASIDE.

5. TOSS THE BACON STRIPS INTO A LARGE SKILLET WITH THE HEAT OFF. THEN, TURN THE HEAT TO MEDIUM.

6. COOK FOR 8 TO 10 MINUTES, STIRRING THE BACON BITS UNTIL THEY'RE CRISPY AND ALL THE FAT IS RENDERED.

7. USE A SLOTTED SPOON TO TRANSFER THE BACON TO A PAPER TOWEL-LINED PLATE.

8. STIR THE GARLIC INTO THE BACON DRIPPINGS IN THE PAN. COOK FOR 30 SECONDS OR UNTIL FRAGRANT. DON'T LET IT BURN!

9. QUICKLY ADD IN THE COLLARD GREENS.

10. TOSS THE COLLARD GREENS WELL WITH TONGS FOR 2 TO 3 MINUTES OR UNTIL VIVIDLY GREEN AND SLIGHTLY WILTED.

11. STIR IN THE VINEGAR, SALT, AND PEPPER. TASTE AND ADD MORE IF NEEDED.

12. TRANSFER THE GREENS TO A PLATTER AND TOP WITH CRISPY BACON BEFORE SERVING.

ROASTED WINTER VEGETABLES

MAKES 6 SERVINGS

🕐 **45 MINUTES**
(10 MINUTES HANDS-ON)

WHOLE30®	EGG-FREE
VEGAN	

2 teaspoons Magic Mushroom Powder (page 45) or Nomtastic Grilling Powder (page 44)

1 pound brussels sprouts, cut in half (or quartered if large)

1 medium delicata squash, seeded and cut into ½-inch-thick half moons

½ pound king trumpet mushrooms, cut into 1-inch pieces

1 small red onion, cut into ½-inch wedges

2 tablespoons avocado oil or extra-virgin olive oil

2 tablespoons aged balsamic vinegar, lemon juice, or Basil Pesto (page 42)

¼ cup minced fresh chives, parsley, and/or basil

I LOVE WINTERTIME BECAUSE THESE VEGETABLES ROAST UP SWEET AND CRUNCHY ON THE OUTSIDE!

BUT MOSTLY, I LOVE WINTER 'CAUSE I GET CHRISTMAS PRESENTS.

1 GRAB SOME MAGIC MUSHROOM POWDER OR NOMTASTIC GRILLING POWDER. YOU'LL NEED IT FOR THIS RECIPE.

2 HEAT THE OVEN TO 400°F ON CONVECTION MODE OR 425°F ON REGULAR MODE WITH THE RACK SET IN THE MIDDLE POSITION.

3 TOSS TOGETHER THE VEGETABLES, OIL, AND MAGIC MUSHROOM POWDER OR NOMTASTIC GRILLING POWDER ON A RIMMED BAKING SHEET.

4 SPREAD OUT THE VEGETABLES IN A SINGLE LAYER ON THE SHEET PAN.

5 COOK THE VEGETABLES IN THE OVEN FOR 30 TO 40 MINUTES, ROTATING THE TRAY MIDWAY THROUGH THE ROASTING TIME.

6 THE ROASTED VEGGIES ARE READY WHEN THEY'RE TENDER AND BROWNED IN PLACES.

7 DRIZZLE WITH YOUR CHOICE OF BALSAMIC VINEGAR, LEMON JUICE, OR PESTO.

8 GARNISH WITH FRESH HERBS AND SERVE.

Per serving: 120 calories • 17 g carbohydrates • 5 g protein • 5 g fat • 5 g fiber

When you've got an abundance of winter vegetables, hack them up, toss 'em with oil, and pop them into a hot oven until they're roast-y, tender, and concentrated in flavors. You'll cut down on food waste and have tasty leftovers that you can quickly add to frittatas and scrambles.

SCALLION PANCAKES

MAKES 8 PANCAKES
● ◖ **1½ HOURS**

NUT-FREE	EGG-FREE
NIGHTSHADE-FREE	VEGAN

2 cups (256 grams) cassava flour

½ cup (64 grams) arrowroot powder

Diamond Crystal kosher salt

1½ cups boiling water

2 tablespoons toasted sesame oil

2 cups thinly sliced scallions

Avocado oil (for frying)

½ cup Dumpling Dipping Sauce (page 30) or Sunbutter Hoisin Sauce (page 32) (optional)

CHINESE SCALLION PANCAKES ARE FLATBREADS THAT ARE IRRESISTIBLY CRISPY ON THE OUTSIDE AND CHEWY ON THE INSIDE.

IN CHINA, THEY'RE TYPICALLY ENJOYED AS A BREAKFAST STREET FOOD, BUT THESE PANCAKES CAN BE ENJOYED ANYWHERE AND ANYTIME!

1 IN A LARGE BOWL, WHISK TOGETHER THE CASSAVA FLOUR, ARROWROOT POWDER, AND 1 TEASPOON OF KOSHER SALT.

2 ADD ABOUT 1 CUP OF THE BOILING WATER AND MIX WELL WITH A SPOON (OR WITH YOUR HANDS IF YOUR NERVE ENDINGS ARE GONE LIKE MINE).

3 SLOWLY ADD THE REST OF THE HOT WATER AND KNEAD WELL TO FORM A DOUGH.

4 THE RESULTING DOUGH SHOULD BE SPRINGY AND NOT STICKY. IF IT SEEMS TOO DRY, ADD JUST A TOUCH MORE WATER, BUT YOU DON'T WANT THE DOUGH TO BE WET OR MUSHY. IF IT'S TOO MOIST, KNEAD IN A BIT MORE CASSAVA FLOUR.

5 DIVIDE THE DOUGH INTO 8 EQUAL-SIZED PORTIONS. ROLL 'EM INTO BALLS WITH YOUR HANDS.

6 GRAB A DOUGH BALL, MAKING SURE TO KEEP THE REST OF THEM COVERED WITH A DAMP KITCHEN TOWEL. SMUSH DOWN THE BALL WITH YOUR FINGERS, AND THEN FLATTEN IT BETWEEN 2 PIECES OF PARCHMENT.

7 USE A ROLLING PIN OR DOWEL TO FLATTEN THE PIECE OF DOUGH BETWEEN THE PARCHMENT UNTIL IT'S ABOUT ⅛ INCH THICK.

8 USING A BRUSH, APPLY A THIN LAYER OF TOASTED SESAME OIL ONTO THE PANCAKE.

Per pancake: 222 calories • 33 g carbohydrates • 1 g protein • 9 g fat • 2 g fiber

9 Add ¼ cup of the sliced scallions in a single layer to the flattened dough. Sprinkle on some kosher salt, too.

10 Carefully roll up the circle of dough into a cigar shape.

11 Then, take one end and tuck it in.

12 Coil the cigar around until you end up with something that looks like a pinwheel or a little cinnamon bun.

13 Place the "cinnamon bun" between 2 pieces of parchment paper, and either flatten it into a thin circular pancake with a tortilla press (which helps give your pancake a nice circular shape)...

14 ...or roll it out with a dowel. (I like to do both: I smush mine with a tortilla press and then roll it out even thinner with a dowel 'cause I like my pancakes extra thin and crispy.)

15 Repeat steps 6 to 14 with the rest of the balls, flattening as many scallion pancakes as you feel like making. Keep them between parchment until you're ready to cook so they don't dry out.

16 Heat a large skillet over medium heat. Once the pan is hot, add enough oil so it covers the bottom of the skillet. Carefully transfer a pancake (without the parchment) to the pan.

17 Cook the pancake for 5 minutes on one side or until it's nicely browned. Brush some hot oil onto the not-yet-fried side, then flip the pancake over.

18 Fry the other side for about 3 minutes or until it's crispy and browned.

19 Transfer the scallion pancake to a wire rack to cool a bit while you fry up the rest of the scallion pancakes.

20 Cut and serve while warm. If desired, pair with Dumpling Dipping Sauce or Sunbutter Hoisin Sauce.

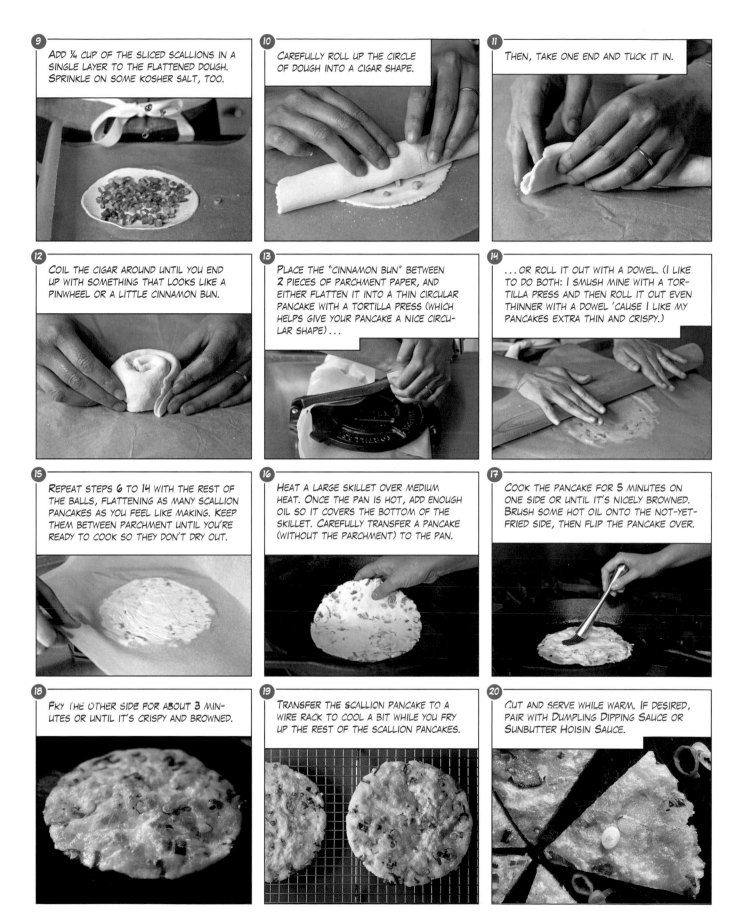

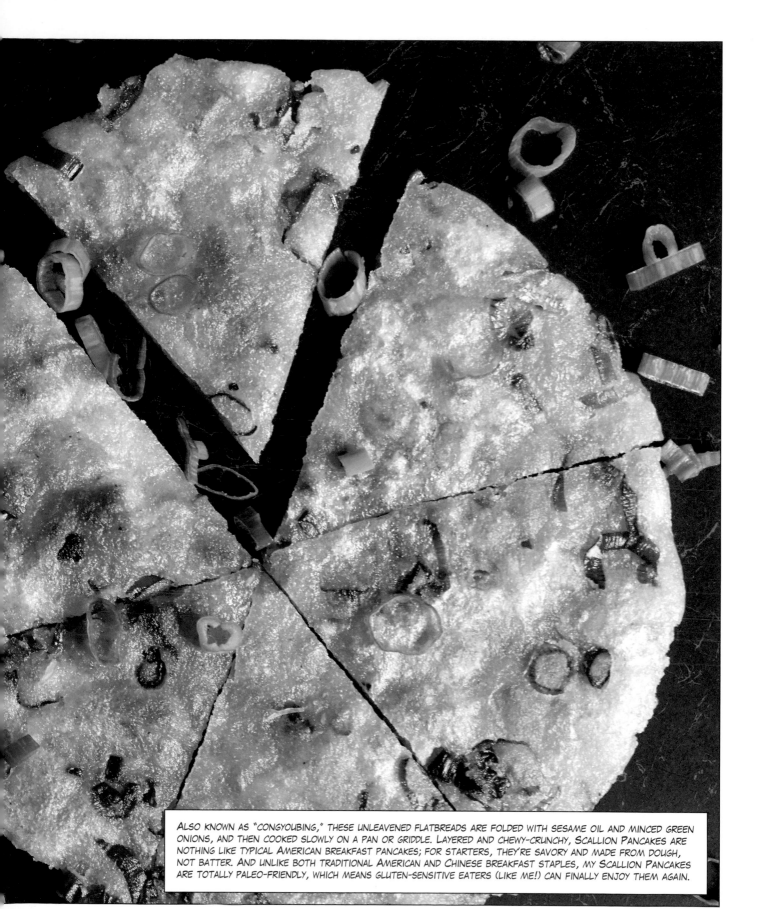

ALSO KNOWN AS "CONGYOUBING," THESE UNLEAVENED FLATBREADS ARE FOLDED WITH SESAME OIL AND MINCED GREEN ONIONS, AND THEN COOKED SLOWLY ON A PAN OR GRIDDLE. LAYERED AND CHEWY-CRUNCHY, SCALLION PANCAKES ARE NOTHING LIKE TYPICAL AMERICAN BREAKFAST PANCAKES; FOR STARTERS, THEY'RE SAVORY AND MADE FROM DOUGH, NOT BATTER. AND UNLIKE BOTH TRADITIONAL AMERICAN AND CHINESE BREAKFAST STAPLES, MY SCALLION PANCAKES ARE TOTALLY PALEO-FRIENDLY, WHICH MEANS GLUTEN-SENSITIVE EATERS (LIKE ME!) CAN FINALLY ENJOY THEM AGAIN.

As I've said before, my upbringing in the San Francisco Bay Area exposed me to a mash-up of all sorts of food cultures, and I especially love the fusion of Asian and Mexican cuisines. Hence, Scallion Pancake Tacos. As soon as you make Scallion Pancakes (and before they firm up), tuck them into a V-shaped stainless steel taco holder. Then, stuff them with your favorite Asian (or non-Asian) fillings.

THE POSSIBILITIES ARE ENDLESS, BUT SHOWN HERE ARE 3 SCALLION PANCAKE TACO VARIETIES YOU NEED TO TRY.

ONE'S FILLED WITH POACHED CHICKEN WITH GINGER SCALLION SAUCE (PAGE 210), ANOTHER ONE'S STUFFED WITH SCRAMBLED EGGS TOPPED WITH NOM NOM CHILI CRISP (PAGE 38), AND THE LAST ONE'S PACKED WITH CHAR SIU (PAGE 290), CUCUMBER SLICES, AND SUNBUTTER HOISIN SAUCE (PAGE 32).

CRISPY SMASHED POTATOES

MAKES 8 SERVINGS
● **1 HOUR**
(15 MINUTES HANDS-ON)

WHOLE30®	NUT-FREE
EGG-FREE	VEGAN

1½ pounds small Yukon Gold potatoes (1½ to 2 inches long)

1½ teaspoons Magic Mushroom Powder (page 45) or Diamond Crystal kosher salt

¼ cup avocado oil, divided

½ cup Cashew Cheese Sauce (page 34), room temperature (optional, not nut-free)

> NO INSTANT POT? BOIL THE SPUDS IN A LARGE POT OF SALTED WATER FOR 20 TO 30 MINUTES OR UNTIL FORK-TENDER, AND THEN PICK UP THE RECIPE FROM STEP 4.

1 POUR 1 CUP OF WATER INTO THE INSERT OF AN INSTANT POT. PLACE A STEAMER BASKET ON THE BOTTOM, AND PUT THE POTATOES IN THE BASKET.

2 COVER THE INSTANT POT AND COOK UNDER HIGH PRESSURE FOR 10 MINUTES. THEN, RELEASE THE PRESSURE IMMEDIATELY.

3 WHEN DONE, THE POTATOES SHOULD BE EASILY PIERCED WITH A KNIFE. TAKE THEM OUT OF THE INSTANT POT AND COOL TO ROOM TEMPERATURE.

(IF NOT EATING RIGHT AWAY, REFRIGERATE THESE COOKED SPUDS FOR UP TO 4 DAYS.)

4 HEAT THE OVEN TO 475°F (OR 450°F ON CONVECTION SETTING) WITH THE RACK IN THE MIDDLE POSITION. DRIZZLE HALF THE OIL ON A RIMMED BAKING SHEET, AND ARRANGE THE POTATOES ON IT.

5 USE A MEAT POUNDER OR THE BOTTOM OF A CUP TO SMUSH THE POTATOES UNTIL THEY'RE ABOUT ½ INCH THICK.

6 SPRINKLE THE MAGIC MUSHROOM POWDER ON TOP AND DRIZZLE THE REMAINING AVOCADO OIL ON THE SMASHED POTATOES.

7 COOK THE POTATOES IN THE OVEN FOR 25 TO 30 MINUTES, ROTATING AT THE HALFWAY POINT, UNTIL CRISP AND GOLDEN ON THE EDGES.

8 SERVE THESE CRISPY BITES AS-IS, OR DIP 'EM IN CASHEW CHEESE SAUCE (PAGE 34).

Per serving: 127 calories • 15 g carbohydrates • 2 g protein • 7 g fat • 2 g fiber

THE PROBLEM WITH OVEN-BAKED FRENCH FRIES IS THAT THEY ALMOST ALWAYS DISAPPOINT. THE TIME AND EFFORT IT TAKES TO HAND-CUT PERFECTLY UNIFORM FRIES RARELY PAYS OFF; THE RESULTS ARE OFTEN LIMP AND SOGGY, AND NOTHING LIKE THE SALTY, GOLDEN-CRISP TATER STRINGS WE CRAVE. IN CONTRAST, THESE CRISPY SMASHED POTATOES ARE EASY TO PREPARE AND ALWAYS CRUNCHY AND DELICIOUS. TRY 'EM!

WANT TO GET A HEAD START? COOK THE POTATOES IN THE INSTANT POT (STEPS 1 TO 3) IN ADVANCE, AND KEEP THEM IN THE FRIDGE. THEN, WHENEVER YOU NEED A SIMPLE SIDE DISH, SNACK, OR APPETIZER, SMASH AND ROAST THEM TO ORDER.

RAMEN EGGS

MAKES 6 EGGS

●●●●◐ **4½ HOURS**
(30 MINUTES HANDS-ON)

WHOLE30®	KETO-FRIENDLY
NUT-FREE	NIGHTSHADE-FREE
VEGETARIAN (IF MODIFIED)	

6 large eggs, straight from the fridge

1 cup water

½ cup All-Purpose Stir-Fry Sauce (page 29) (to make vegetarian, use No-Fish Sauce variation)

USE THIS FOR:

- Michelle's Breakfast Toast (page 90)
- Shoyu Ramen (page 134)

SWITCH IT UP: JAMMY EGGS

WANT JAMMY EGGS TO TOP THE SALMON NIÇOISE SALAD ON PAGE 144? FOLLOW STEPS 1 THROUGH 4, SLICE UP THE EGGS, AND PRESTO-CHANGE-O: LUXURIOUSLY SPOONABLE SOFT-BOILED EGGS FEATURING BRIGHT, CREAMY YOLKS AND FIRM WHITES.

1. FILL A LARGE SAUCEPAN MORE THAN HALFWAY WITH WATER, AND BRING IT TO A BOIL. THEN, CAREFULLY AND COMPLETELY SUBMERGE THE EGGS IN THE WATER.

2. BOIL THE EGGS UNCOVERED FOR 7 MINUTES. GENTLY MOVE THE EGGS AROUND OCCASIONALLY. THIS'LL HELP KEEP THE EGG YOLKS CENTERED.

3. ONCE THE 7 MINUTES ARE UP, USE A SLOTTED SPOON TO TRANSFER THE EGGS TO A LARGE BOWL OF ICE WATER.

4. LEAVE THE EGGS IN THE ICE BATH FOR ABOUT 10 MINUTES, AND THEN PEEL THEM.

5. IN A MEASURING CUP, STIR 1 CUP WATER WITH ALL-PURPOSE STIR-FRY SAUCE TO FORM A MARINADE.

6. PLACE THE EGGS IN A BOWL OR MEASURING CUP AND POUR THE MARINADE ON TOP.

7. COVER AND PLACE THE MARINATING EGGS IN THE FRIDGE FOR AT LEAST 4 HOURS OR UP TO 3 DAYS. IF THE EGGS AREN'T FULLY SUBMERGED, MAKE SURE TO ROTATE THEM OCCASIONALLY. THE LONGER THEY SOAK, THE MORE FLAVORFUL THEY'LL BECOME.

8. CAREFULLY CUT THE EGGS IN HALF. EAT 'EM AS-IS, OR USE THEM TO ADORN SALADS, SOUPS, OR A TASTY BOWL OF RAMEN.

Per egg: 86 calories • 2 g carbohydrates • 6 g protein • 5 g fat • 1 g fiber

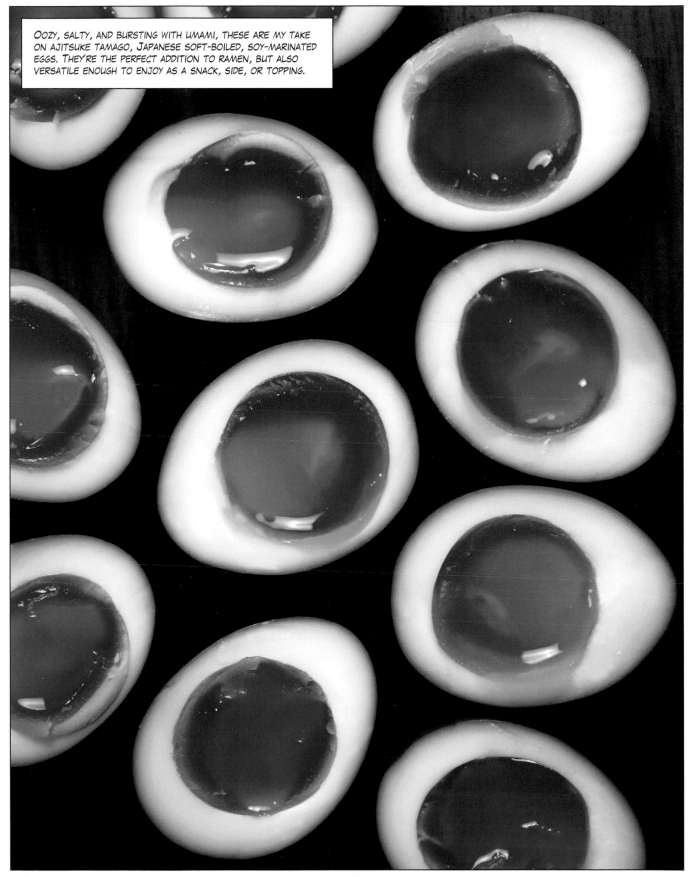

OOZY, SALTY, AND BURSTING WITH UMAMI, THESE ARE MY TAKE ON AJITSUKE TAMAGO, JAPANESE SOFT-BOILED, SOY-MARINATED EGGS. THEY'RE THE PERFECT ADDITION TO RAMEN, BUT ALSO VERSATILE ENOUGH TO ENJOY AS A SNACK, SIDE, OR TOPPING.

MICHELLE'S BREAKFAST TOAST

MAKES 2 SERVINGS
⏱ **10 MINUTES**

- **2** slices Paleo Sandwich Bread (page 46) or other paleo-friendly bread
- **1** medium Haas avocado
- **2** Holy Shiitake Mushrooms (page 72)
- **2** Jammy Eggs (page 88) or Ramen Eggs (page 88)

Shichimi togarashi (Japanese seven-spice blend)

Flake sea salt

I'M NO MILLENNIAL, BUT THIS OLD LADY STILL LOVES HER AVOCADO TOAST.

THIS IS MY ASIAN SPIN ON CLASSIC AVOCADO TOAST, WITH ADDED PROTEIN TO BOOT. IT'S UMAMI ON UMAMI ON UMAMI ON GRAIN-FREE TOAST!

1 TOAST THE BREAD.

2 SLICE THE AVOCADO IN HALF. CAREFULLY REMOVE THE PIT AND PEEL.

3 THINLY SLICE UP THE AVOCADO HALVES . . .

4 . . . AND THE HOLY SHIITAKE MUSHROOMS.

5 CUT THE JAMMY EGGS IN HALF.

6 ON EACH SLICE OF TOAST, FAN OUT THE SLICED AVOCADO HALF. MAKE IT PRETTY!

7 ADD THE SLICED MUSHROOMS AND EGGS.

8 SPRINKLE WITH SHICHIMI TOGARASHI AND FLAKE SEA SALT. NOW, GOBBLE IT ALL UP!

Per serving: 408 calories • 30 g carbohydrates • 13 g protein • 27 g fat • 10 g fiber

I'M OFTEN ASKED WHAT PALEO EATERS
CAN POSSIBLY HAVE FOR BREAKFAST, AND
MY ANSWER IS INVARIABLY "LEFTOVERS."
BUT THAT DOESN'T MEAN YOU CAN'T MAKE
OVER YOUR LEFTOVERS INTO SOMETHING
NEW, DIFFERENT, AND YUMMY. TAKE THIS
BREAKFAST TOAST, FOR EXAMPLE: ADDING
AVOCADO TO JAMMY EGGS (PAGE 88),
HOLY SHIITAKE MUSHROOMS (PAGE 72),
AND PALEO SANDWICH BREAD (PAGE 46)
YIELDS A CRAVEWORTHY DELIGHT THAT YOU
CAN PICK UP AND EAT WITH YOUR HANDS.

ASPARAGUS AND HAM FRITTATA

MAKES 6 SERVINGS
⏱ **45 MINUTES**
(30 MINUTES HANDS-ON)

WHOLE30®	KETO-FRIENDLY
NUT-FREE	NIGHTSHADE-FREE

- **¼** cup Ginger Scallion Sauce (page 33)
- **10** large eggs
- **¼** cup full-fat coconut milk
- **¼** cup finely sliced scallions or chives
- **1½** teaspoons Diamond Crystal kosher salt, divided
- **¼** teaspoon freshly ground black pepper
- **1** tablespoon avocado oil or fat of choice
- **1** medium shallot, minced
- **1** pound asparagus, trimmed and cut crosswise into ½-inch pieces
- **6** ounces ham, diced

HEY! THIS IS ACTUALLY GOOD!

THIS EASY FRITTATA IS SPRINGTIME ON A PLATE: A VIVIDLY SUNNY SLICE FILLED WITH FRESH EGGS, ASPARAGUS COINS, AND DICED HAM. AND WHEN IT GETS COLD OUTSIDE, USE ROASTED WINTER VEGETABLES (PAGE **78**) AS THE FILLING INSTEAD. WHILE IT'S LISTED AS OPTIONAL, THE GINGER SCALLION SAUCE DEFINITELY AMPS UP THE DELICIOUSNESS, SO USE IT, PEOPLE!

Per serving: 300 calories • 6 g carbohydrates • 19 g protein • 22 g fat • 2 g fiber

1 GO GRAB SOME GINGER SCALLION SAUCE FROM THE REFRIGERATOR. HEAT THE OVEN TO 350°F WITH THE RACK IN THE MIDDLE.

2 IN A LARGE BOWL, ADD THE EGGS, COCONUT MILK, SCALLIONS, 1 TEASPOON SALT, AND PEPPER. WHISK TOGETHER UNTIL THOROUGHLY COMBINED.

3 HEAT A 10-INCH CAST-IRON SKILLET OR OVEN-SAFE NON-STICK PAN OVER MEDIUM HEAT AND SWIRL IN THE OIL.

4 ADD THE MINCED SHALLOT AND COOK, STIRRING, FOR 1 MINUTE.

5 TOSS IN THE ASPARAGUS, DICED HAM, AND ½ TEASPOON SALT.

6 COOK, STIRRING, FOR 2 TO 3 MINUTES OR UNTIL THE ASPARAGUS IS BRIGHT GREEN AND TENDER-CRISP.

7 POUR IN THE EGG MIXTURE.

8 COOK, STIRRING OCCASIONALLY TO KEEP THE FILLING FROM SETTLING, FOR 3 TO 5 MINUTES OR UNTIL THE SIDES OF THE FRITTATA BEGIN TO SET.

9 TRANSFER THE SKILLET TO THE OVEN AND COOK FOR 10 TO 15 MINUTES OR UNTIL THE TOP IS SET.

10 CRANK THE HEAT UP TO BROIL AND COOK FOR ANOTHER 2 MINUTES OR UNTIL THE FRITTATA PUFFS UP AND IS COOKED ALL THE WAY THROUGH.

11 PLATE, SLICE, AND SERVE . . .

12 . . . WITH A DOLLOP OF GINGER SCALLION SAUCE. (THIS SAUCE TOTALLY PUTS THIS FRITTATA OVER THE TOP!)

93

SHIRAAZ'S EGG MASALA

MAKES 4 SERVINGS
● **1 HOUR**

WHOLE30®	NUT-FREE
VEGETARIAN	

• SAUCE •

- ¼ cup ghee or avocado oil
- 2 medium onions, finely minced
- 1½ tablespoons minced fresh ginger
- 5 garlic cloves, minced
- 1 jalapeño pepper, finely chopped
- 1 teaspoon ground cumin
- 1 teaspoon turmeric powder
- ¼ teaspoon Indian red chili powder or cayenne pepper
- 1 (14.5-ounce) can diced tomatoes
- 1 teaspoon Diamond Crystal kosher salt
- 1 cup boiling water
- ½ teaspoon garam masala

• EGGS •

- 4 hard-boiled eggs, peeled
- 6 large eggs, uncooked
- 1 teaspoon Diamond Crystal kosher salt
- 1 medium jalapeño pepper, finely chopped
- 3 tablespoons minced fresh cilantro, divided
- 2 tablespoons ghee or avocado oil

1 HEAT A LARGE HEAVY-BOTTOMED SKILLET OVER MEDIUM-HIGH HEAT. WHEN THE PAN IS HOT, SWIRL IN THE GHEE.

2 ADD THE ONIONS.

3 COOK THE ONIONS FOR 10 MINUTES, STIR-RING FREQUENTLY, AND THEN LOWER THE HEAT TO MEDIUM.

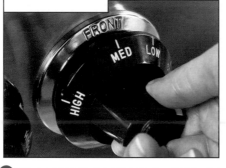

4 COOK FOR ANOTHER 10 MINUTES OR UNTIL THE ONIONS ARE NICELY BROWNED.

5 TOSS IN THE GINGER, GARLIC, AND JALA-PEÑO. COOK FOR 30 SECONDS, STIRRING, UNTIL FRAGRANT.

6 QUICKLY MIX IN THE CUMIN, TURMERIC, AND CHILI POWDER . . .

7 . . . AND POUR IN THE DICED TOMATOES.

8 ADD THE SALT AND THE BOILING WATER. SCRAPE UP ANY BROWNED BITS ON THE BOTTOM OF THE PAN.

Per serving: 354 calories • 14 g carbohydrates • 17 g protein • 24 g fat • 2 g fiber

9 COVER AND SIMMER THE SAUCE ON LOW HEAT FOR 15 TO 20 MINUTES.

10 WHILE THE SAUCE IS SIMMERING, MAKE THE EGGS. TURN ON THE BROILER WITH THE OVEN RACK 6 INCHES FROM THE HEATING ELEMENT.

11 THINLY SLICE THE 4 HARD-BOILED EGGS CROSSWISE. SET 'EM ASIDE.

12 THEN, CRACK THE 6 UNCOOKED EGGS INTO A LARGE BOWL. WHISK TOGETHER THE EGGS AND THE SALT.

13 ADD THE JALAPEÑO PEPPER AND 2 TABLE-SPOONS OF MINCED CILANTRO.

14 WHISK TO INCORPORATE.

15 HEAT A 10-INCH OVEN-SAFE CAST-IRON OR NON-STICK SKILLET OVER MEDIUM-HIGH HEAT. ONCE IT'S HOT, ADD THE GHEE.

16 CAREFULLY POUR THE EGG MIXTURE INTO THE HOT SKILLET.

17 ARRANGE THE SLICED HARD-BOILED EGGS IN A SINGLE LAYER ON TOP OF THE LIQUID EGG MIXTURE.

18 COOK THE EGGS FOR 2 MINUTES OR UNTIL THE BOTTOM AND EDGES ARE SET.

19 PLACE THE SKILLET UNDER THE BROILER.

20 COOK FOR 2 TO 3 MINUTES OR UNTIL THE EGGS ARE COOKED THROUGH.

(RECIPE CONTINUES ON THE NEXT PAGE.)

21 TAKE THE SKILLET OUT OF THE OVEN AND SET IT ASIDE. LET'S CHECK ON THE SAUCE.

22 STIR IN ½ TEASPOON OF GARAM MASALA INTO THE SPICY SAUCE . . .

23 . . . AND ADD A BIT MORE SALT IF NEEDED.

24 SPOON SOME SAUCE ONTO A PLATTER . . .

25 . . . AND THEN TRANSFER THE EGGS ON TOP.

26 DRIZZLE MORE SAUCE ONTO THE EGGS.

27 GARNISH WITH THE REMAINING 1 TABLE-SPOON OF CILANTRO.

28 SLICE AND SERVE.

MY GOOD FRIEND SHIRAAZ WAS KIND ENOUGH TO SHARE THIS RICH AND FIERY EGG MASALA RECIPE WITH ME. INSPIRED BY A DISH SERVED AT A POPULAR MUMBAI STREET FOOD STAND, HER VERSION IS AN OPEN-FACED OMELET FILLED WITH SLICED HARD-BOILED EGGS, DICED HOT PEPPERS, AND CILANTRO, ACCOMPANIED BY A THICK-SIMMERED SAUCE OF SPICE AND HEAT AND TOMATO. BEST OF ALL, SHIRAAZ'S EGG MASALA CAN BE MADE WITH SIMPLE PANTRY ITEMS, MAKING IT THE PERFECT ANYTIME MEAL: YOU CAN ENJOY IT MORNING, NOON, OR NIGHT.

PESTO GARDEN SCRAMBLE

MAKES 2 SERVINGS
🕐 **15 MINUTES**

WHOLE30®	VEGETARIAN

2 tablespoons Basil Pesto (page 42) or store-bought pesto

6 large eggs

¾ teaspoon Diamond Crystal kosher salt, divided

1 tablespoon ghee or avocado oil

2 cups lightly packed baby kale or spinach

½ cup cherry tomatoes, halved

2 garlic cloves, minced

2 tablespoons toasted walnuts, roughly chopped

¼ teaspoon freshly ground black pepper

SCRAMBLES ARE A CLASSIC BREAKFAST DISH, BUT THEY'RE KINDA PERFECT FOR DINNER, TOO!

1 MAKE OR GRAB SOME BASIL PESTO. THEN, HEAT A 10-INCH CAST-IRON OR NON-STICK SKILLET OVER MEDIUM HEAT. CRACK THE EGGS INTO A BOWL.

2 ADD ½ TEASPOON SALT TO THE EGGS AND WHISK WELL. SET IT ASIDE.

3 ONCE THE SKILLET IS HOT, SWIRL IN THE COOKING FAT. THEN, ADD THE KALE TO THE SKILLET ALONG WITH ¼ TEASPOON SALT.

4 SAUTÉ FOR 1 TO 2 MINUTES OR UNTIL THE KALE IS WILTED.

5 ADD THE CHERRY TOMATOES AND MINCED GARLIC AND COOK FOR ABOUT 30 SECONDS OR UNTIL FRAGRANT.

6 POUR THE BEATEN EGGS INTO THE SKILLET.

7 COOK, STIRRING AND SCRAPING THE PAN, UNTIL THE EGGS ARE ALMOST SET, ABOUT 3 TO 5 MINUTES.

8 TAKE THE PAN OFF THE HEAT AND GENTLY STIR IN THE PESTO. TASTE AND ADJUST WITH MORE SALT IF DESIRED.

Per serving: 526 calories • 14 g carbohydrates • 25 g protein • 42 g fat • 2 g fiber

9 PLATE THE SCRAMBLE AND TOP WITH TOASTED WALNUTS AND FRESHLY GROUND BLACK PEPPER.

MY TAKE ON ONE OF OUR SATURDAY MORNING FAVORITES AT PORTLAND'S HARLOW, THIS SUPER-EASY ONE-PAN BREAKFAST IS FAST, VIBRANT, AND HEARTY ENOUGH TO POWER US THROUGH EVEN THE BUSIEST WEEKENDS.

"RICE + NOODLES"

INSTANT POT SPAGHETTI SQUASH

MAKES 2 SERVINGS
◑ 30 MINUTES
(5 MINUTES HANDS-ON)

WHOLE30®	NUT-FREE
EGG-FREE	NIGHTSHADE-FREE
VEGAN	

1 small (2-pound) spaghetti squash

USE THIS FOR:

- Instant Pot Meat Sauce (page 120)
- Singapore Noodles (page 128)

> IF YOU DON'T HAVE AN INSTANT POT, FLIP THE PAGE AND FIND OUT HOW TO COOK YOUR SPAGHETTI SQUASH IN THE OVEN. SURE, IT TAKES A BIT LONGER, BUT IT'S JUST AS TASTY AND EASY!

1 PLACE A STEAMER INSERT OR TRIVET INTO THE INSTANT POT. ADD 1 CUP OF WATER.

2 CUT THE SPAGHETTI SQUASH CROSSWISE IN HALF WITH A SHARP PARING KNIFE.

3 WITH A SPOON, SCOOP THE SEEDS OUT OF THE CENTER OF EACH SQUASH HALF AND DISCARD THE GUNK.

4 PUT THE SQUASH ON THE STEAMER INSERT IN THE INSTANT POT. (IT DOESN'T MATTER WHETHER THE CUT-SIDE IS UP OR DOWN, BUT MAKE SURE BOTH HALVES FIT INSIDE.)

5 COVER THE INSTANT POT AND COOK UNDER HIGH PRESSURE FOR **7** MINUTES.

6 MANUALLY RELEASE THE PRESSURE.

7 OPEN UP THE INSTANT POT AND TIP THE SQUASH HALVES TO POUR OUT ANY COLLECTED LIQUID. THEN, TAKE THE SQUASH OUT OF THE POT ...

8 ...AND SHRED IT UP WITH A FORK. SERVE!

Per serving: 140 calories • 32 g carbohydrates • 3 g protein • 3 g fat • 7 g fiber

IT'S NO SECRET THAT SPAGHETTI SQUASH IS A FABULOUS VEHICLE FOR JUST ABOUT ANY UMAMI-PACKED SAUCE. BUT DID YOU KNOW YOU CAN PRESSURE COOK IT IN JUST MINUTES USING AN INSTANT POT?

OVEN-BAKED SPAGHETTI SQUASH

MAKES 2 SERVINGS
⏱ **45 MINUTES**
(10 MINUTES HANDS-ON)

WHOLE30®	NUT-FREE
EGG-FREE	NIGHTSHADE-FREE
VEGAN	

1 small (2-pound) spaghetti squash

2 teaspoons avocado oil or extra-virgin olive oil

USE THIS FOR:

- Instant Pot Meat Sauce (page 120)
- Singapore Noodles (page 128)

WHAT DO YOU CALL FAKE NOODLES?

IMPASTA!

1. HEAT THE OVEN TO 400°F WITH THE RACK IN THE MIDDLE POSITION.

2. WITH A SHARP PARING KNIFE, CUT THE SPAGHETTI SQUASH CROSSWISE IN HALF.

3. WITH A SPOON, SCOOP THE SEEDS OUT OF THE CENTER OF EACH SQUASH HALF AND DISCARD THE GUNK.

4. LINE A RIMMED BAKING SHEET WITH PARCHMENT PAPER.

5. PUT THE SQUASH HALVES ON THE BAKING SHEET. LIGHTLY COAT THE CUT SURFACE OF EACH HALF WITH THE OIL.

6. ARRANGE THE SQUASH HALVES CUT-SIDE DOWN ON THE BAKING SHEET AND STAB THEM ALL OVER WITH THE TIP OF A SHARP PARING KNIFE.

7. BAKE FOR **30** TO **35** MINUTES OR UNTIL THE SQUASH STRANDS PULL AWAY FROM THE EDGE BUT ARE STILL TOOTHSOME AND NOT MUSHY.

8. SHRED INTO "SPAGHETTI" WITH A FORK AND SERVE.

Per serving: 179 calories • 32 g carbohydrates • 3 g protein • 6 g fat • 7 g fiber

CAULIFLOWER RICE / RICED CAULIFLOWER

MAKES 6 SERVINGS
🕐 **15 MINUTES**

WHOLE30®	KETO-FRIENDLY
NUT-FREE	EGG-FREE
NIGHTSHADE-FREE	VEGAN

1 medium (1-pound) cauliflower head, cut into uniform pieces

2 tablespoons avocado oil

Diamond Crystal kosher salt

USE THIS FOR:

- Hot Dog Fried "Rice" (page 108)
- Kimchi Fried "Rice" (page 110)
- Cheesy Chicken and Kale Casserole (page 212)
- Bacon Cheeseburger Casserole (page 252)
- Kalbi (page 256)

SWITCH IT UP: BROCCOLI RICE / RICED BROCCOLI

GUESS WHAT? THIS RECIPE WORKS WITH BROCCOLI, TOO, SO FEEL FREE TO CHANGE THINGS UP A BIT BY MAKING GREEN RICE.

HEY OLLIE! LEAVE THE DUMB DAD JOKES FOR DAD!

1. IN A FOOD PROCESSOR, PULSE THE CAULIFLOWER PIECES...

2. ...UNTIL THEY'RE CHOPPED UP INTO THE SIZE OF RICE GRAINS. (IF A RECIPE CALLS FOR "RICED CAULIFLOWER" AS AN INGREDIENT, YOU CAN STOP HERE AT THIS STEP.)

3. IN A LARGE SKILLET, HEAT THE OIL OVER MEDIUM HEAT. ADD THE CAULIFLOWER.

4. COOK, STIRRING, FOR 5 TO 10 MINUTES OR UNTIL SOFT. SEASON WITH SALT TO TASTE.

5. SERVE CAULIFLOWER RICE AS AN ACCOMPANIMENT TO A MAIN DISH, OR PACK IT AWAY FOR LATER! IT CAN BE REFRIGERATED FOR UP TO 4 DAYS, OR KEPT FROZEN FOR UP TO 2 MONTHS.

Per serving: 76 calories • 7 g carbohydrates • 3 g protein • 8 g fat • 3 g fiber

HOT DOG FRIED "RICE"

MAKES 4 SERVINGS
◑ 30 MINUTES

WHOLE30®	KETO-FRIENDLY
NUT-FREE	

¼ cup All-Purpose Stir-Fry Sauce (page 29)

3 large eggs

¾ teaspoon paleo-friendly fish sauce or No-Fish Sauce (page 28)

2 tablespoons avocado oil or cooking fat of choice, divided

5 grass-fed all-beef hot dogs (with no added sugar), cut into ½-inch coins

1 large carrot, diced

½ small onion, finely chopped

¼ teaspoon Diamond Crystal kosher salt

1 medium broccoli or cauliflower head, riced (or 16 ounces fresh or frozen riced broccoli or cauliflower) (page 107)

3 garlic cloves, minced

2 scallions, thinly sliced

Paleo-friendly ketchup or sriracha

THIS IS MY VERSION OF ARROZ CHAUFA, A CHINESE-PERUVIAN FRIED RICE FEATURING CUT-UP HOT DOGS.

MY CHILDHOOD BEST FRIEND, EVELYN, IS PERUVIAN, SO THIS RECIPE IS LIKE THE TWO OF US IN A BOWL!

HOT DOGS DON'T HAVE TO BE SERVED ON BUNS, YOU KNOW. IN FACT, HIGH-QUALITY, ALL-BEEF WIENERS ARE THE PERFECT ADDITION TO A QUICK AND EASY FRIED RICE. (AND FOR THOSE OF YOU WHO SNEER AT HOT DOGS, GO AHEAD AND USE SOME NICE, PALEO-FRIENDLY SAUSAGES INSTEAD, YOU SNOBBY SNOB.)

1 FIRST, GRAB OR MAKE SOME ALL-PURPOSE STIR-FRY SAUCE.

2 IN A MEDIUM BOWL, WHISK TOGETHER THE EGGS AND FISH SAUCE.

Per serving: 310 calories • 13 g carbohydrates • 16 g protein • 22 g fat • 3 g fiber

3 HEAT A LARGE SKILLET OVER MEDIUM HEAT. SWIRL IN 2 TEASPOONS OF OIL. THEN, ADD THE EGGS.

4 STIR AND SCRAPE THE PAN CONSTANTLY UNTIL THE EGGS ARE SOFTLY SCRAMBLED. THEN, TRANSFER THE EGGS TO A PLATTER.

5 SWIRL ANOTHER TEASPOON OF OIL INTO THE PAN AND ADD THE HOT DOG PIECES.

6 COOK UNTIL BROWNED ON THE OUTSIDE AND WARMED THROUGH.

7 TRANSFER THE HOT DOGS TO THE PLATTER WITH THE EGGS.

8 POUR A TABLESPOON OF AVOCADO OIL INTO THE EMPTY SKILLET AND TOSS IN THE CARROT AND ONION. SPRINKLE THE SALT ON THE VEGETABLES.

9 COOK, STIRRING, FOR 10 MINUTES OR UNTIL THE ONION IS TRANSLUCENT.

10 STIR IN THE RICED BROCCOLI OR CAULIFLOWER AND MINCED GARLIC.

11 COVER AND COOK FOR 3 TO 5 MINUTES OR UNTIL THE "RICE" IS TENDER-CRISP.

12 ADD THE ALL-PURPOSE STIR-FRY SAUCE AND COOK, STIRRING FREQUENTLY, UNTIL THE LIQUID IS ABSORBED.

13 MIX IN THE RESERVED SCRAMBLED EGGS, HOT DOG PIECES, AND SCALLIONS. TASTE FOR SEASONING AND ADJUST WITH MORE SALT IF NEEDED.

14 SERVE WITH A SQUIRT OF KETCHUP OR SRIRACHA.

KIMCHI FRIED "RICE"

MAKES 4 SERVINGS
🌗 30 MINUTES

WHOLE30®	KETO-FRIENDLY
NUT-FREE	

3 tablespoons avocado oil or melted ghee, divided

3 large eggs

Diamond Crystal kosher salt

½ small onion, finely chopped

2 garlic cloves, minced

1 cup roughly chopped kimchi

2 cups cubed cooked chicken or leftover cooked meat

1 medium cauliflower head, riced (or 16 ounces fresh or frozen riced cauliflower) (page 107)

2 tablespoons kimchi juice (the brining liquid in the kimchi jar)

2 tablespoons coconut aminos

1 teaspoon toasted sesame oil

2 scallions, finely sliced

1 toasted seaweed sheet, cut into strips

1 tablespoon toasted sesame seeds

IT TAKES A LITTLE LONGER, BUT A CLASSIC ALTERNATIVE TO ADDING STRIPS OF COOKED EGG IS TO TOP EACH BOWL OF KIMCHI FRIED RICE WITH A CRISPY FRIED EGG!

1 HEAT A LARGE SKILLET OVER MEDIUM HEAT, AND ADD 1 TABLESPOON OF OIL.

2 WHISK THE EGGS IN A LARGE BOWL WITH ½ TEASPOON SALT.

3 ONCE THE OIL IN THE PAN IS SHIMMERING, POUR IN THE WHISKED EGGS AND GENTLY TILT THE PAN SO THE EGG FORMS A FLAT, EVEN LAYER.

4 COOK FOR 1 TO 2 MINUTES OR UNTIL THE EGG FIRMS UP. FLIP THE EGG OVER TO COOK IT THROUGH ON THE OTHER SIDE.

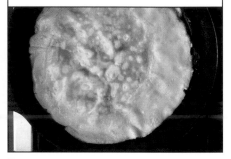

5 TRANSFER THE EGG TO A CUTTING BOARD. SLICE IT INTO THIN STRIPS AND SET ASIDE.

6 HEAT THE REMAINING 2 TABLESPOONS OF OIL IN THE NOW-EMPTY PAN, AND ADD THE ONION AND A SPRINKLE OF SALT.

7 COOK THE ONIONS FOR 2 TO 3 MINUTES OR UNTIL SOFTENED.

8 ADD THE MINCED GARLIC AND SAUTÉ FOR 30 SECONDS OR UNTIL FRAGRANT.

Per serving: 347 calories • 13 g carbohydrates • 30 g protein • 19 g fat • 3 g fiber

9 TOSS IN THE KIMCHI AND INCREASE THE HEAT TO MEDIUM-HIGH.

10 COOK, STIRRING, FOR 5 MINUTES OR UNTIL THE KIMCHI STARTS TO BROWN IN PARTS.

11 ADD THE CUBED CHICKEN.

12 STIR FOR 1 MINUTE TO WARM THROUGH.

13 TOSS IN THE RICED CAULIFLOWER.

14 MIX WELL TO INCORPORATE.

15 STIR IN THE KIMCHI JUICE AND COCONUT AMINOS.

16 DECREASE THE HEAT TO MEDIUM-LOW. COVER AND COOK FOR 3 TO 5 MINUTES OR UNTIL THE RICED CAULIFLOWER IS TENDER (BUT NOT MUSHY).

17 TASTE THE CAULI RICE FOR SEASONING AND ADJUST WITH SALT IF NEEDED. REMOVE THE PAN FROM THE HEAT AND STIR IN THE SESAME OIL.

18 MIX IN THE EGG STRIPS AND SCALLIONS.

19 SCOOP THE FRIED RICE INTO SERVING BOWLS.

20 GARNISH WITH SEAWEED STRIPS AND SESAME SEEDS AND SERVE. LEFTOVERS CAN BE KEPT REFRIGERATED FOR UP TO 4 DAYS.

KIMCHI FRIED RICE, OR KIMCHI BOKKEUM-BAP, ORIGINATED AS A LEFTOVER MAKEOVER IN KOREA, REPURPOSING OVERRIPE KIMCHI AND SURPLUS COLD RICE. IT'S EASY AND INEXPENSIVE TO MAKE, AND WITH PALEO-FRIENDLY INGREDIENTS, THIS VERSION IS JUST AS FAST AND DELICIOUS AS THE ORIGINAL!

I LOVE KIMCHI IN ALL ITS TANGY, SALTY, SPICY, UMAMI-PACKED GLORY. KIMCHI LENDS INCREDIBLE DEPTH AND A FLAVORFUL FUNK TO THIS ANYTHING-BUT-ORDINARY FRIED RICE RECIPE. MAKE YOUR OWN KIMCHI (I HAVE A RECIPE ON PAGE 62 OF MY *READY OR NOT!* COOKBOOK) OR BUY SUGAR-FREE KIMCHI TO USE IN THIS RECIPE.

SUNDAY NIGHT LASAGNA

MAKES 10 SERVINGS
●● 2 HOURS
(1½ HOURS HANDS-ON)

WHOLE30®	KETO-FRIENDLY
EGG-FREE	

• LASAGNA SHEETS •

5 medium (about 2 pounds) yellow summer squash, ends trimmed

2 tablespoons extra-virgin olive oil, divided

Diamond Crystal kosher salt

• MAC NUT "RICOTTA" •

3 cups raw macadamia nuts

½ cup packed fresh basil, roughly chopped

3 tablespoons nutritional yeast seasoning

1 tablespoon lemon zest

2 tablespoons lemon juice

1½ teaspoons Diamond Crystal kosher salt

¼ teaspoon freshly ground black pepper

⅔ cup water, plus more as needed

• MEAT SAUCE •

1 tablespoon extra-virgin olive oil

1 medium onion, finely chopped

4 medium garlic cloves, minced

1 pound ground beef

1 pound bulk mild Italian sausage

1 teaspoon Magic Mushroom Powder (page 45) or Diamond Crystal kosher salt

¼ teaspoon ground black pepper

1 (28-ounce) jar marinara sauce

① FIRST, MAKE THE SQUASH PASTA! (YOU CAN DO THIS UP TO **3** DAYS IN ADVANCE AND REFRIGERATE IT.) TURN THE BROILER ON HIGH WITH THE RACK IN THE MIDDLE.

② WITH A MANDOLIN SLICER (AS WELL AS A CUT-RESISTANT GLOVE), CUT THE SQUASH LENGTHWISE INTO ¼-INCH-THICK SLICES.

③ BRUSH **2** RIMMED BAKING SHEETS WITH A TABLESPOON OF OIL. LAY THE SQUASH IN A SINGLE LAYER ON EACH OF THE SHEETS.

④ BRUSH ANOTHER TABLESPOON OF OLIVE OIL ON THE SQUASH SLICES AND SPRINKLE LIGHTLY WITH SALT.

⑤ ONE BAKING SHEET AT A TIME, BROIL THE SQUASH SLICES FOR **10** TO **12** MINUTES OR UNTIL SOFTENED AND LIGHTLY BROWNED.

⑥ SET ASIDE THE SQUASH. TURN OFF THE BROILER AND SET THE OVEN TO **400°F**.

⑦ NOW WE CAN MAKE THE CHEESE. START BY ADDING THE MACADAMIA NUTS TO A FOOD PROCESSOR OR BLENDER.

⑧ PROCESS THE MACADAMIA NUTS, SCRAPING DOWN THE SIDES AS NEEDED . . .

Per serving: 678 calories • 13 g carbohydrates • 21 g protein • 61 g fat • 6 g fiber

9 ...UNTIL A COARSE, CORN-MEAL-LIKE TEXTURE FORMS.

10 ADD THE REMAINING RICOTTA INGREDIENTS: BASIL, NUTRITIONAL YEAST, LEMON ZEST, LEMON JUICE, SALT, PEPPER, AND WATER.

11 PURÉE UNTIL SMOOTH. (THIN WITH A BIT OF WATER IF NEEDED.) TASTE AND ADJUST THE SEASONING. SET THE CHEESE ASIDE.

12 NOW, LET'S MAKE THE SAUCE. HEAT A LARGE SKILLET OVER MEDIUM HEAT. ADD THE OLIVE OIL AND TOSS IN THE ONIONS.

13 COOK THE ONIONS FOR **2** TO **3** MINUTES OR UNTIL SOFTENED.

14 ADD THE GARLIC AND COOK UNTIL FRAGRANT, ABOUT **30** SECONDS.

15 DUMP IN THE GROUND BEEF AND SAUSAGE.

16 BREAK UP THE MEAT WITH A SPATULA AND COOK FOR ABOUT **10** MINUTES ...

17 ...UNTIL IT'S NO LONGER PINK.

18 ADD THE MAGIC MUSHROOM POWDER (OR SALT) AND PEPPER. STIR TO COMBINE.

19 POUR IN THE JAR OF MARINARA SAUCE, AND BRING THE CONTENTS TO A BOIL.

20 DECREASE THE HEAT AND MAINTAIN A LOW SIMMER FOR **3** TO **5** MINUTES. THEN, TAKE THE SAUCE OFF THE HEAT AND SET ASIDE.

(RECIPE CONTINUES ON THE NEXT PAGE.)

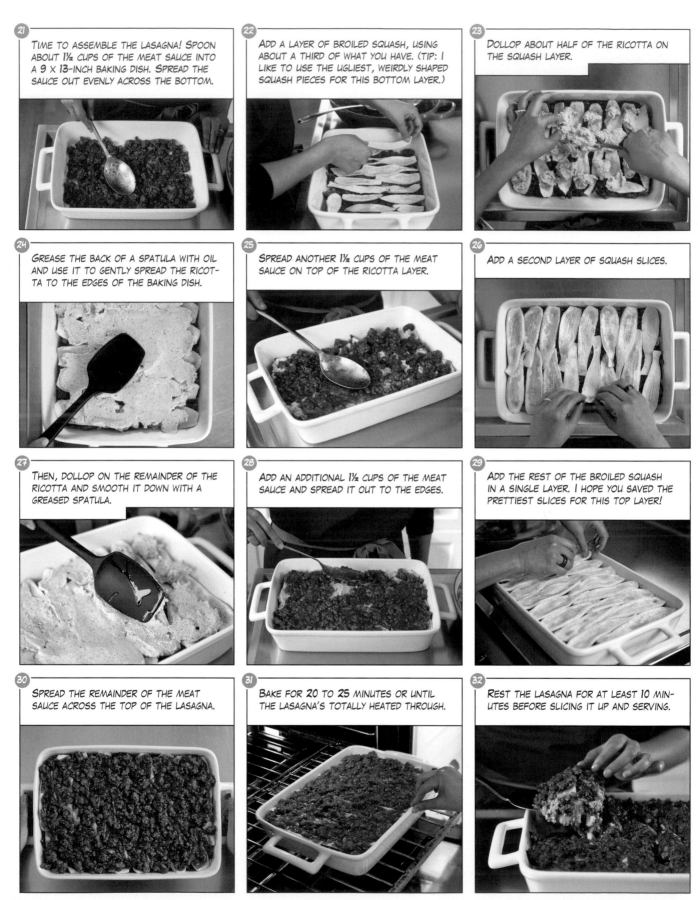

21 Time to assemble the lasagna! Spoon about 1½ cups of the meat sauce into a 9 × 13-inch baking dish. Spread the sauce out evenly across the bottom.

22 Add a layer of broiled squash, using about a third of what you have. (Tip: I like to use the ugliest, weirdly shaped squash pieces for this bottom layer.)

23 Dollop about half of the ricotta on the squash layer.

24 Grease the back of a spatula with oil and use it to gently spread the ricotta to the edges of the baking dish.

25 Spread another 1½ cups of the meat sauce on top of the ricotta layer.

26 Add a second layer of squash slices.

27 Then, dollop on the remainder of the ricotta and smooth it down with a greased spatula.

28 Add an additional 1½ cups of the meat sauce and spread it out to the edges.

29 Add the rest of the broiled squash in a single layer. I hope you saved the prettiest slices for this top layer!

30 Spread the remainder of the meat sauce across the top of the lasagna.

31 Bake for 20 to 25 minutes or until the lasagna's totally heated through.

32 Rest the lasagna for at least 10 minutes before slicing it up and serving.

Is it possible to capture the rich, hearty spirit of a traditional lasagna without the traditional ingredients? Absolutely. With layers of summer squash "noodles," creamy macadamia nut ricotta, and a rib-sticking meat sauce, this irresistibly delicious one-pan meal hits all the right notes. Serve it with A Nice Green Salad (page 68), and your Sunday supper is all set!

INSTANT POT ZUCCHINI BOLOGNESE

MAKES 4 SERVINGS
● **1 HOUR**
(20 MINUTES HANDS-ON)

WHOLE30®	NUT-FREE
EGG-FREE	

• BOLOGNESE SAUCE •

2 tablespoons extra-virgin olive oil or avocado oil

1 large yellow onion, diced

1 pound bulk Italian sausage

4 medium (1½ pounds) zucchini, diced into ½-inch pieces

3 garlic cloves, minced

Magic Mushroom Powder (page 45) or Diamond Crystal kosher salt

Freshly ground black pepper

1½ tablespoons lemon juice

¼ cup minced Italian parsley or basil

• ZUCCHINI NOODLES •

4 medium zucchini, ends trimmed and spiralized

SWITCH IT UP: SLOW COOKER ZUCCHINI BOLOGNESE

IF YOU WANT TO COOK THE BOLOGNESE IN A SLOW COOKER, SAUTÉ THE ONIONS AND SAUSAGE BEFORE ADDING THEM WITH THE REST OF THE INGREDIENTS TO THE SLOW COOKER. COOK ON LOW FOR 6 TO 8 HOURS OR UNTIL THE ZUCCHINI IS SUPER TENDER. FINISH UP BY FOLLOWING STEPS 9 TO 14.

THIS IS MY TAKE ON MEGHAN MARKLE'S FAMOUS PASTA SAUCE MADE WITH ZUCCHINI (OR COURGETTES, FOR YOU PROPER BRITS). ACCORDING TO THE DUCHESS OF SUSSEX, THE TRICK TO A CREAMY, DREAMY SAUCE IS TO COOK EVERYTHING LOW AND SLOW FOR HOURS ON END. BUT WHO WANTS TO BABYSIT A POT OF SAUCE ALL DAY, ESPECIALLY WHEN YOU HAVE AN INSTANT POT ON STANDBY?

1 SWITCH ON THE SAUTÉ FUNCTION ON YOUR INSTANT POT. ONCE THE METAL INSERT IS HOT, POUR IN THE OLIVE OIL.

2 TOSS IN THE DICED ONIONS. COOK, STIRRING FREQUENTLY, FOR 2 TO 3 MINUTES OR UNTIL SLIGHTLY SOFTENED.

Per serving: 533 calories • 16 g carbohydrates • 21 g protein • 44 g fat • 4 g fiber

3 Add the Italian sausage and break it up with a spatula.

4 Cook the sausage until it's no longer pink.

5 Throw in the zucchini, minced garlic, and 1 teaspoon of Magic Mushroom Powder or salt.

6 Stir it all together.

7 Lock the lid and program the Instant Pot to cook for **35** minutes under high pressure. (No need to add any extra liquid! The zucchini will release enough liquid for the contents to reach high pressure.)

8 Once the sauce is done cooking, wait for the pressure to release naturally (or just manually vent it if you're feeling antsy).

9 The cooked zucchini and onions should be fork-tender and easily mashed with a spatula . . .

10 . . . to produce a chunky sauce.

11 Taste the sauce and adjust the seasoning with additional Magic Mushroom Powder (or salt) and black pepper. Stir in the lemon juice.

12 If you haven't already, use a spiralizer to prepare some zucchini noodles.

13 Drop the raw spiralized zucchini straight into the Instant Pot and toss it around until the hot sauce softens the zoodles to your liking.

14 Top with your favorite herbs and dig in. This tasty sauce freezes incredibly well, so make a batch whenever your fridge is overflowing with zucchini!

INSTANT POT MEAT SAUCE

MAKES 8 SERVINGS
◐◐◑ 1½ HOURS
(15 MINUTES HANDS-ON)

WHOLE30®	KETO-FRIENDLY
NUT-FREE	EGG-FREE

1 pound bulk mild Italian sausage

1 small onion, diced

6 garlic cloves, minced

2½ pounds beef chuck roast, cut into 1½-inch cubes

1 teaspoon Magic Mushroom Powder (page 45) or Diamond Crystal kosher salt

1 cup marinara sauce

1 (14.5-ounce) can diced fire-roasted tomatoes, drained

1 small (2-pound) spaghetti squash, cooked and shredded using the instructions on pages 104–106

¼ cup chopped Italian parsley

SWITCH IT UP: STOVETOP MEAT SAUCE

MAKE THIS ON THE STOVETOP INSTEAD BY INCREASING THE AMOUNT OF MARINARA SAUCE TO 3 CUPS. SIMMER PARTLY COVERED FOR 3 HOURS OR UNTIL TENDER.

SWITCH IT UP: SLOW COOKER MEAT SAUCE

USING A SLOW COOKER? INCREASE THE AMOUNT OF MARINARA SAUCE TO 2 CUPS AND COOK IT ALL ON LOW FOR 8 HOURS.

1. SWITCH ON THE SAUTÉ FUNCTION ON YOUR INSTANT POT. ONCE IT'S HOT, ADD IN THE SAUSAGE AND DICED ONIONS.

2. BREAK UP THE SAUSAGE WITH A SPATULA AND COOK UNTIL IT'S NO LONGER PINK AND THE ONIONS ARE SOFTENED. STIR IN THE GARLIC AND CANCEL THE SAUTÉ FUNCTION.

3. ADD THE CUBED CHUCK ROAST AND SPRINKLE ON 1 TEASPOON OF MAGIC MUSHROOM POWDER OR SALT. STIR WELL TO COMBINE.

4. POUR THE MARINARA SAUCE ON TOP AND ADD THE DICED TOMATOES. NO NEED TO STIR AT THIS POINT OR ADD EXTRA LIQUID.

5. LOCK THE LID ON THE INSTANT POT AND PROGRAM IT TO COOK UNDER HIGH PRESSURE FOR 35 MINUTES. WHEN THE MEAT SAUCE IS FINISHED COOKING, LET THE PRESSURE DROP NATURALLY OR RELEASE IT MANUALLY AFTER WAITING 15 MINUTES.

6. STIR THE SAUCE. THEN, TURN ON THE SAUTÉ FUNCTION AND BRING THE SAUCE TO A ROLLING BOIL. COOK, REDUCING THE SAUCE FOR ABOUT 15 MINUTES OR UNTIL YOU COOK OFF ½ LITER OR ABOUT 2 CUPS.

7. WHILE THE SAUCE IS SIMMERING, USE A SILICONE SPATULA OR WOODEN SPOON TO SMUSH AND SHRED THE CHUCK ROAST AGAINST THE SIDE OF THE POT.

8. ONCE THE SAUCE HAS REDUCED AND THICKENED, TASTE IT AND ADJUST THE SEASONING WITH MORE MAGIC MUSHROOM POWDER OR SALT IF NEEDED.

Per serving: 505 calories • 12 g carbohydrates • 37 g protein • 35 g fat • 2 g fiber

9

SERVE OVER COOKED SPAGHETTI SQUASH, AND GARNISH WITH MINCED ITALIAN PARSLEY.

SUNDAY GRAVY ISN'T JUST FOR SUNDAYS. IN FACT, THIS WEEKDAY MEAT SAUCE IS A CINCH TO MAKE IN AN INSTANT POT USING JUST A FEW PANTRY STAPLES. IT'S HEARTY, COMFORTING, AND PERFECT OVER SPAGHETTI SQUASH OR ANY OTHER NOODLE-IZED VEGETABLES.

GARLIC MUSHROOM NOODLES

MAKES 4 SERVINGS
◖ 30 MINUTES

WHOLE30®	KETO-FRIENDLY
NUT-FREE	EGG-FREE
NIGHTSHADE-FREE	VEGAN

2 tablespoons coconut aminos

1 tablespoon nutritional yeast seasoning

1½ teaspoons Umami Stir-Fry Powder (page 43), divided

1–2 large daikon radishes (1½ pounds total), peeled

Diamond Crystal kosher salt

4 tablespoons avocado oil or extra-virgin olive oil, divided

½ pound fresh shiitake mushrooms, stemmed and thinly sliced

1½ tablespoons minced garlic cloves

1 tablespoon water

2 scallions, thinly sliced

> DAIKON NOODLES HAVE A PEPPERY BITE, SO YOU GOTTA BLANCH 'EM TO MELLOW OUT THE FLAVOR!

1 IN A SMALL BOWL, COMBINE THE COCONUT AMINOS, NUTRITIONAL YEAST, AND 1 TEASPOON OF UMAMI STIR-FRY POWDER.

2 STIR IT ALL TOGETHER TO MAKE AN UMAMI-PACKED SAUCE. SET IT ASIDE.

3 FILL A LARGE STOCKPOT WITH WATER AND BRING IT TO A BOIL OVER HIGH HEAT.

4 WHILE THE WATER BOILS, SPIRALIZE THE DAIKON INTO NOODLES. SET THEM ASIDE.

5 ONCE THE WATER IS BOILING, ADD A LARGE PINCH OF SALT.

6 SUBMERGE THE SPIRALIZED DAIKON IN THE BOILING WATER.

7 COOK ABOUT 1 TO 2 MINUTES, STIRRING FREQUENTLY, UNTIL THE NOODLES ARE SLIGHTLY SOFTENED BUT STILL FIRM.

8 DRAIN THE DAIKON NOODLES IN A COLANDER AND RINSE WELL WITH COLD WATER.

Per serving: 190 calories • 14 g carbohydrates • 3 g protein • 14 g fat • 5 g fiber

9 Set aside to drain completely.

10 Heat a 12-inch skillet over medium-high heat. When the skillet is hot, add 2 tablespoons of oil.

11 Toss in the mushrooms and add the remaining ½ teaspoon of Umami Stir-Fry Powder.

12 Sauté the mushrooms for 3 minutes or until browned in bits.

13 Add the remaining 2 tablespoons oil, garlic, and 1 tablespoon of water. (The water will help keep the garlic from burning.)

14 Cook, stirring, until the garlic is fragrant and lightly browned.

15 Toss in the daikon noodles . . .

16 . . . and pour in the sauce from Step 2.

17 Cook for 3 to 5 minutes or until heated through.

18 Taste and season with more salt, coconut aminos, or nutritional yeast if necessary.

19 Transfer to a serving platter . . .

20 . . . garnish with scallions and serve.

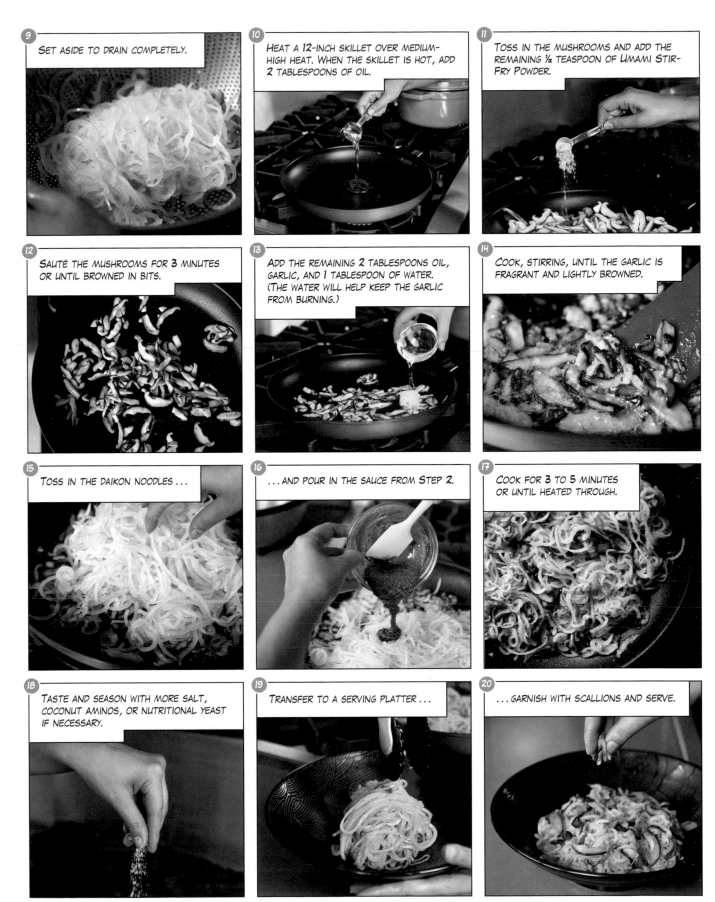

Back when we lived in San Francisco's Outer Sunset, Thanh Long, the city's oldest Vietnamese restaurant, was one of our favorite neighborhood mainstays. It actually started as an Italian deli before the owner, who had recently immigrated to the U.S. after the fall of Saigon, started incorporating her Vietnamese family recipes into the menu. Helene An's attempt at spaghetti ultimately became Thanh Long's famous Garlic Noodles, fusing Asian components like oyster sauce with Western ones like Parmesan.

My homage to this famous dish keeps garlic as its foundation, but I've used paleo-friendly options to stay true to the umami-rich spirit of the original, such as mushrooms, nutritional yeast, and Umami Stir-Fry Powder.

Don't be afraid of nutritional yeast! "Nooch" is just an umami-packed, nutrient-dense flavor booster. Vegans popularized its use as a dairy-free substitute for Parmesan cheese, but it's also paleo and keto-friendly.
Nutritional yeast is grown on molasses and then harvested, washed, and heat-dried to inactivate it.
More importantly, it's crazy delicious. Some even call this superfood "Nature's Cheeto dust"!
And just like with Cheeto dust, you can use nooch to coat all ten of your fingers with lickable deliciousness!
Ollie!

CHICKEN CHOW MEIN

MAKES 4 SERVINGS
🌗 30 MINUTES

WHOLE30®	NUT-FREE
EGG-FREE	

- **1** pound boneless, skinless chicken thighs, cut into bite-sized pieces
- **6** tablespoons avocado oil, divided
- **2** tablespoons coconut aminos, divided
- **1** teaspoon aged balsamic vinegar
- **1** teaspoon paleo-friendly fish sauce or No-Fish Sauce (page 28)
- **½** teaspoon toasted sesame oil
- **2** teaspoons arrowroot powder
- **1** pound white-fleshed Hannah sweet potatoes or 6 medium carrots, peeled
- **1** small yellow onion, halved and thinly sliced

    Diamond Crystal kosher salt
- **¼** pound shiitake mushrooms, stemmed and thinly sliced
- **1** (1-inch) piece fresh ginger, peeled and cut into thin coins
- **2** scallions, cut diagonally into ½-inch segments
- **5** cups baby spinach
- **½** teaspoon crushed red pepper flakes

CHOW MEIN'S A STAPLE OF CHINESE-AMERICAN CUISINE, BUT ITS PREPARATION CAN VARY FROM COAST TO COAST. HERE ON THE WEST COAST, CHOW MEIN NOODLES ARE SOFT AND COOKED TOGETHER WITH MEAT AND VEGGIES, WHILE BACK EAST, THEY'RE FRIED SUPER-CRISPY (A.K.A. HONG KONG STYLE) AND SERVED BENEATH A PILE OF COOKED INGREDIENTS AND A THICK BROWN GRAVY. MY PALEO VERSION IS A MASH-UP OF BOTH STYLES, COMBINING THE SOFTER NOODLES (OR IN THIS CASE, SWEET POTATO NOODLES) OF THE WEST COAST WITH SOME CRISPY BITS MORE REMINISCENT OF EAST COAST CHOW MEIN.

> WEST COAST CHOW MEIN IS CALLED LO MEIN ON THE EAST COAST!

① IN A MEDIUM BOWL, TOSS TOGETHER THE CHICKEN PIECES, 1 TABLESPOON AVOCADO OIL, AND 1 TABLESPOON COCONUT AMINOS.

② ADD THE BALSAMIC VINEGAR, FISH SAUCE, SESAME OIL, AND ARROWROOT POWDER.

Per serving: 441 calories • 33 g carbohydrates • 26 g protein • 23 g fat • 6 g fiber

3 STIR WELL TO COMBINE, AND SET IT ASIDE.

4 TURN THE SWEET POTATO INTO NOODLES USING A SPIRALIZER. THEN, HEAT A LARGE SKILLET OVER MEDIUM HEAT.

5 WHEN IT'S HOT, ADD **2** TABLESPOONS OF AVOCADO OIL TO THE PAN. ONCE THE OIL IS SHIMMERING, ADD THE SWEET POTATO NOODLES IN A SINGLE LAYER.

6 FRY UNDISTURBED FOR **2** TO **3** MINUTES UNTIL SOME OF THE SWEET POTATO NOODLES START TO BROWN AND CRISP.

7 SPRINKLE ON ½ TEASPOON OF SALT AND THEN CAREFULLY FLIP THE SWEET POTATO NOODLES OVER. COOK THEM UNDISTURBED FOR ANOTHER **2** TO **3** MINUTES. TRANSFER THE NOODLES TO A PLATE AND SET ASIDE.

8 NEXT, HEAT THE NOW-EMPTY PAN OVER MEDIUM-HIGH AND ADD **2** TABLESPOONS OF AVOCADO OIL. ONCE THE OIL IS HOT, ADD THE SLICED ONIONS ALONG WITH A LIBERAL SPRINKLE OF SALT.

9 COOK THE ONIONS, STIRRING, FOR **3** TO **5** MINUTES OR UNTIL SOFTENED. TOSS IN THE MUSHROOMS, GINGER, AND ANOTHER SPRINKLE OF SALT.

10 COOK, STIRRING, FOR ABOUT **2** MINUTES OR UNTIL THE MUSHROOMS ARE COOKED THROUGH AND THE GINGER IS FRAGRANT. IF THE PAN'S LOOKING A LITTLE DRY, ADD ANOTHER TABLESPOON OF OIL.

11 ADD THE CHICKEN PIECES AND COOK, STIRRING, UNTIL NO LONGER PINK.

12 STIR IN THE SCALLIONS AND THE SPINACH. SEASON WITH 1 TABLESPOON COCONUT AMINOS AND RED PEPPER FLAKES. TASTE AND ADJUST THE SEASONING AS NEEDED.

13 ONCE THE SPINACH IS WILTED, PLATE THE CHICKEN AND VEGGIES ATOP THE SWEET POTATO NOODLES.

14 SERVE THE CHOW MEIN IMMEDIATELY.

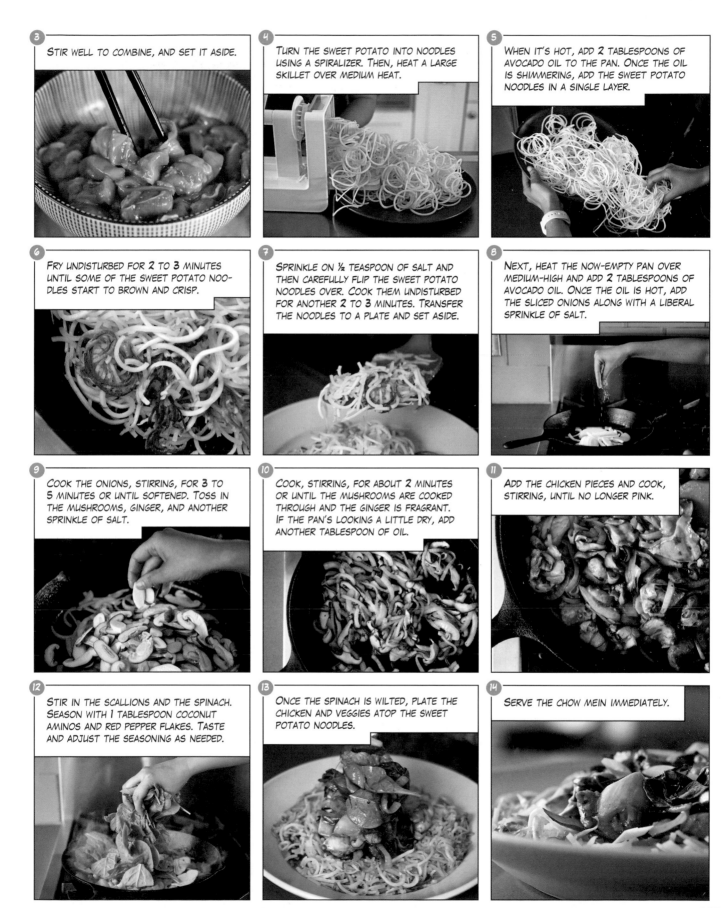

SINGAPORE NOODLES

MAKES 4 SERVINGS
🌓 30 MINUTES

WHOLE30®

1 small (2-pound) spaghetti squash, cooked and shredded (pages 104–106)

½ pound Char Siu (page 290) or ham, cut into matchsticks

½ pound shrimp (16–20 count per pound), shelled and deveined

1 teaspoon arrowroot powder

½ teaspoon Diamond Crystal kosher salt

2 tablespoons coconut aminos

3 teaspoons paleo-friendly fish sauce, divided

4 teaspoons Madras curry powder, divided

4 large eggs

4 tablespoons avocado oil, divided

1 small red bell pepper, cored and thinly sliced

1 medium carrot, cut into matchsticks

½ small onion, peeled and thinly sliced lengthwise

½ teaspoon toasted sesame oil

2 scallions, thinly sliced

> DESPITE THEIR NAME, SINGAPORE NOODLES AREN'T FROM SINGAPORE. THIS IS ACTUALLY A HONG KONG DISH INSPIRED BY SINGAPORE'S INDIAN-CHINESE FUSION CUISINE!

1 COOK UP SOME SPAGHETTI SQUASH AND GRAB SOME CHAR SIU.

2 IN A MEDIUM BOWL, COMBINE THE SHRIMP, ARROWROOT POWDER, AND SALT.

3 MIX WELL AND SET ASIDE.

4 NOW, WE'RE GOING TO MAKE THE SAUCE! IN A SMALL BOWL, COMBINE THE COCONUT AMINOS, 2 TEASPOONS OF FISH SAUCE, AND 2 TEASPOONS OF CURRY POWDER.

5 WHISK IT ALL TOGETHER AND SET THE SAUCE ASIDE.

6 IN A MEASURING CUP OR BOWL, WHISK THE EGGS TOGETHER WITH THE REMAINING TEA-SPOON OF FISH SAUCE.

7 HEAT A LARGE CAST-IRON OR NON-STICK SKILLET OVER MEDIUM HEAT. ONCE IT'S HOT, SWIRL IN 1 TABLESPOON OF THE OIL.

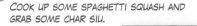

8 POUR THE EGGS INTO THE PAN AND COOK, STIRRING, UNTIL SET.

Per serving: 527 calories • 23 g carbohydrates • 32 g protein • 26 g fat • 5 g fiber

9 BREAK THE EGGS INTO SMALL PIECES AND TRANSFER THEM TO A PLATE. WIPE THE SKILLET CLEAN.

10 INCREASE THE HEAT TO MEDIUM-HIGH. ONCE IT'S HOT, ADD 1 TABLESPOON OF OIL TO THE NOW-EMPTY PAN.

11 TOSS IN THE SHRIMP.

12 COOK, STIRRING FREQUENTLY, FOR ABOUT 30 SECONDS.

13 NEXT, TOSS IN THE BELL PEPPER, CARROT, ONION, CHAR SIU . . .

14 . . . AND ADD THE REMAINING 2 TEASPOONS OF CURRY POWDER.

15 COOK, STIRRING FREQUENTLY, FOR ABOUT 2 TO 3 MINUTES OR UNTIL THE MEAT IS HEATED THROUGH AND THE VEGETABLES ARE TENDER-CRISP.

16 TRANSFER THE CONTENTS OF THE PAN TO A LARGE PLATE.

17 WIPE THE SKILLET CLEAN, AND THEN ADD THE REMAINING 2 TABLESPOONS OF OIL.

18 TOSS IN THE SPAGHETTI SQUASH. SAUTÉ FOR 1 TO 2 MINUTES TO COOK OFF SOME OF THE MOISTURE FROM THE "NOODLES."

19 GIVE THE SAUCE ONE MORE STIR AND POUR IT IN THE PAN.

20 STIR TO DISTRIBUTE THE SAUCE EVENLY.

(RECIPE CONTINUES ON THE NEXT PAGE.)

21 ADD THE VEGETABLES, CHAR SIU, AND RESERVED EGGS.

22 STIR WELL TO COMBINE. TASTE FOR SEASONING AND ADJUST IF NEEDED.

23 STIR IN ½ TEASPOON OF TOASTED SESAME OIL. PLATE THE NOODLES . . .

24 . . . AND GARNISH WITH **2** THINLY-SLICED SCALLIONS BEFORE SERVING.

THE CLASSIC PREPARATION OF SINGAPORE NOODLES INVOLVES QUICKLY STIR-FRYING RICE VERMICELLI TOGETHER WITH JULIENNED VEGETABLES, PORK, SHRIMP, AND SCRAMBLED EGGS, ALL SEASONED WITH CURRY POWDER TO LEND THE DISH A PUNCH OF HEAT AND A DISTINCTIVE YELLOW HUE. MY PALEO-FRIENDLY VERSION MAKES A FEW KEY SUBSTITUTIONS, BUT OTHERWISE HEWS CLOSELY TO THE FORMULA THAT MADE THE ORIGINAL DISH A GLOBAL HIT.

CRISPY SWOODLES WITH BACON

MAKES 4 SERVINGS
● 1 HOUR
(20 MINUTES HANDS-ON)

WHOLE30®	NUT-FREE
EGG-FREE	NIGHTSHADE-FREE

½   pound bacon, cut crosswise into ¼-inch pieces

2   pounds Hannah white-fleshed sweet potatoes, peeled

2   large carrots, peeled

1   small yellow onion, peeled

     Diamond Crystal kosher salt

     Juice from 1 medium lime

     Freshly ground black pepper

2   tablespoons chopped Italian parsley

2   tablespoons minced chives

> WANNA ADD SOME HEAT TO THESE CRISPY SWOODLES? TOP THEM WITH SOME NOM NOM CHILI OIL (PAGE 41)!

1 HEAT THE OVEN TO 400°F ON CONVECTION MODE (OR 425°F ON REGULAR MODE) WITH THE RACK IN THE MIDDLE. MEANWHILE, TOSS THE BACON INTO A LARGE SKILLET OVER MEDIUM HEAT.

2 COOK, STIRRING OCCASIONALLY, UNTIL ALL THE FAT IS RENDERED AND THE BACON IS CRISPY, ABOUT 15 MINUTES.

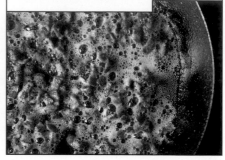

3 WITH A SLOTTED SPOON, TRANSFER THE CRUNCHY BACON BITS TO A PAPER TOWEL-LINED PLATE, RESERVING THE DRIPPINGS IN THE SKILLET.

4 USE A SPIRALIZER TO CUT THE SWEET POTATOES, CARROTS, AND ONION INTO NOODLE-LIKE RIBBONS.

5 SPREAD THE VEGETABLE NOODLES ON A RIMMED BAKING SHEET. TOSS THE NOODLES WITH 1½ TEASPOONS KOSHER SALT AND THE RESERVED BACON DRIPPINGS.

6 ROAST IN THE OVEN FOR 35 TO 45 MINUTES, STIRRING THE VEGGIES EVERY 10 TO 15 MINUTES TO ENSURE EVEN COOKING.

7 THESE CRISPY "SWOODLES" ARE DONE WHEN THEY'RE TENDER AND HAVE CRISPY BITS ALL OVER. WATCH THEM LIKE A HAWK IN THE LAST 10 MINUTES TO MAKE SURE THEY DON'T BURN!

8 ADD THE LIME JUICE, SEASON TO TASTE WITH SALT AND PEPPER, AND GARNISH WITH A SHOWER OF PARSLEY, CHIVES, AND CRISPY BACON BITS.

Per serving: 307 calories • 36 g carbohydrates • 8 g protein • 15 g fat • 6 g fiber

THIS SHEET PAN SUPPER HAS BEEN A SURE-FIRE WAY TO GET MY CHILDREN TO EAT MORE VEGETABLES. YES, I'M WELL AWARE THAT ADDING BACON IS THE ULTIMATE CHEAT CODE; AFTER ALL, SMOKY, SALTY, CRUNCHY BITS OF PORK MAKE EVERYTHING TASTE BETTER. BUT EVEN WITHOUT THEM, THE CRISPY COMBINATION OF ROASTED SWEET POTATOES, CARROTS, AND ONIONS WILL WIN OVER EVEN YOUR PICKIEST EATERS.

SHOYU RAMEN

MAKES 2 SERVINGS
◑ **30 MINUTES**

½   pound Char Siu (page 290), sliced

4   Holy Shiitake Mushrooms (page 72), thinly sliced

2   Ramen Eggs (page 88), cut in half

3   tablespoons All-Purpose Stir-Fry Sauce (page 29)

1   pound daikon radish, peeled

    Diamond Crystal kosher salt

3   cups low-sodium or unsalted bone broth or chicken broth

2   scallions, thinly sliced

> I'LL ADMIT IT: THIS RECIPE TITLE ISN'T VERY ACCURATE.

> IN JAPANESE, "SHOYU" MEANS SOY SAUCE, BUT YOU WON'T FIND ANY IN THIS DISH. FOR THAT MATTER, YOU WON'T FIND ANY ACTUAL WHEAT-FLOUR RAMEN NOODLES IN IT, EITHER!

1. IF YOU HAVEN'T YET, SLICE UP THE CHAR SIU, HOLY SHIITAKE MUSHROOMS, AND RAMEN EGGS. GRAB SOME ALL-PURPOSE STIR-FRY SAUCE, TOO.

2. BRING A LARGE POT OF WATER TO A BOIL OVER HIGH HEAT. WHILE YOU'RE WAITING, SPIRALIZE THE DAIKON.

3. ONCE THE WATER IS BOILING, ADD A LARGE PINCH OF SALT. THEN, DROP THE DAIKON "NOODLES" INTO THE BOILING WATER.

4. COOK, STIRRING OCCASIONALLY, FOR 1 TO 2 MINUTES OR UNTIL SLIGHTLY SOFTENED, BUT STILL FIRM.

5. DRAIN THE DAIKON NOODLES AND DIVIDE THEM INTO 2 SERVING BOWLS.

6. POUR THE BROTH AND ALL-PURPOSE STIR-FRY SAUCE IN A MEDIUM SAUCEPAN AND COOK OVER HIGH HEAT UNTIL BOILING.

7. TASTE FOR SEASONING AND ADJUST WITH MORE ALL-PURPOSE STIR-FRY SAUCE OR SALT AS NEEDED. THEN, LADLE THE HOT SOUP OVER THE NOODLES IN THE BOWLS.

8. TOP THE NOODLES WITH SLICED CHAR SIU, HOLY SHIITAKE MUSHROOMS, RAMEN EGGS, AND SCALLIONS. SERVE AND EAT!

Per serving: 610 calories • 36 g carbohydrates • 50 g protein • 30 g fat • 8 g fiber

FOR YEARS AFTER GOING PALEO, I LONGED FOR THE DEEP, COMPLEX FLAVORS OF SHOYU RAMEN, JAPANESE SOUP NOODLES IN A SOY SAUCE-BASED BROTH. SO WHEN I SAW SPIRALIZED DAIKON OFFERED AS A NOODLE ALTERNATIVE AT KAYO'S RAMEN BAR IN PORTLAND, OREGON, A SWITCH WAS FLIPPED IN MY HEAD: PALEO RAMEN ISN'T JUST POSSIBLE; IT'S THE ULTIMATE IN LOW-FUSS, SLURP-WORTHY FARE.

USE A HIGH-QUALITY LOW-SODIUM OR UNSALTED BROTH IN THIS RECIPE. THE ALL-PURPOSE STIR-FRY SAUCE WILL ALREADY ADD PLENTY OF SALTINESS!

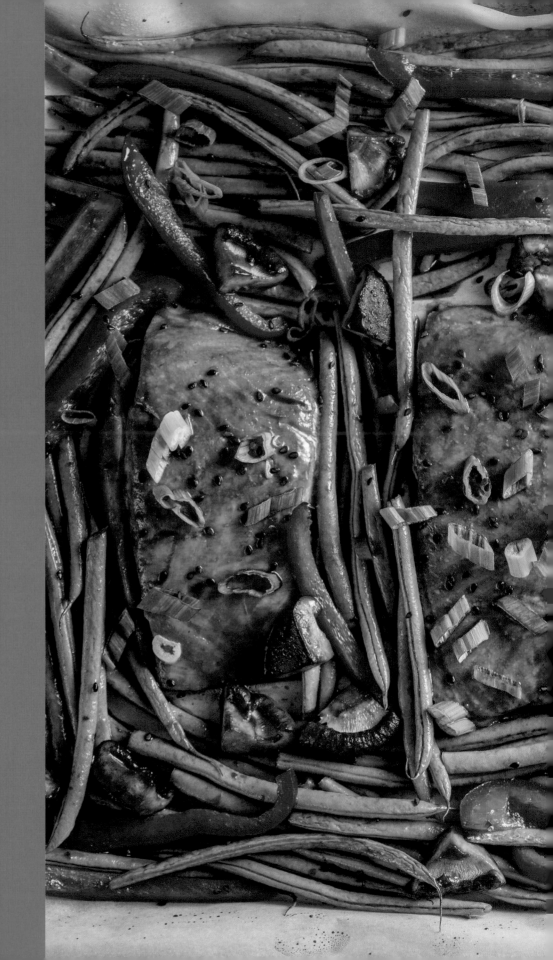

SEAFOOD

AHI AVOCADO POKE

MAKES 4 SERVINGS
◔ 15 MINUTES

WHOLE30®	KETO-FRIENDLY
NUT-FREE	EGG-FREE

¼ cup All-Purpose Stir-Fry Sauce (page 29)

2 teaspoons paleo-friendly sriracha or ½ teaspoon crushed red pepper flakes

1 pound sushi- or sashimi-grade ahi tuna steaks, cut into ½-inch cubes

1 medium Hass avocado, cut into ½-inch cubes

1 scallion, thinly sliced

2 teaspoons toasted sesame seeds

¼ cup microgreens (optional)

I STILL REMEMBER THE VERY FIRST TIME I ATE AT MAUI'S STAR NOODLE OVER A DECADE AGO. THIS POKE BOWL IS INSPIRED BY THE RESTAURANT'S PERFECTLY SEASONED AND ELEVATED AHI AVO!

1. POUR THE ALL-PURPOSE STIR-FRY SAUCE AND SRIRACHA INTO A MEASURING CUP.

2. STIR TOGETHER AND SET THE SAUCE ASIDE.

3. PLACE THE TUNA CUBES IN A LARGE BOWL.

4. ADD THE AVOCADO AND SCALLION.

5. POUR IN THE SAUCE.

6. CAREFULLY MIX THE INGREDIENTS, MAKING SURE THE SAUCE IS WELL DISTRIBUTED.

7. TOP WITH TOASTED SESAME SEEDS AND MICROGREENS IF DESIRED.

8. SERVE IMMEDIATELY.

Per serving: 269 calories • 8 g carbohydrates • 28 g protein • 13 g fat • 4 g fiber

I ABSOLUTELY ADORE HAWAIIAN POKE, A RAW SEAFOOD SALAD TRADITIONALLY TOSSED WITH SEA SALT OR SEASONED SOY SAUCE, CHOPPED KUKUI NUTS, SCALLIONS, SEAWEED, AND LIMU (A TYPE OF BROWN ALGAE). BUT I'VE FOUND IT NEXT-TO-IMPOSSIBLE TO FIND A PALEO-FRIENDLY VERSION, SO I MADE ONE MYSELF. THE RESULT? A SUPER-EASY, FLAVOR-PACKED POKE BOWL FEATURING SOME OF MY FAVORITE INGREDIENTS!

SALMON NIÇOISE SALAD

MAKES 6 SERVINGS
● **1 HOUR**

WHOLE30®	NUT-FREE

• VINAIGRETTE •

½ cup extra-virgin olive oil

⅓ cup lemon juice or red wine vinegar

2 tablespoons minced shallot

1 teaspoon Dijon-style mustard

¾ teaspoon Diamond Crystal kosher salt, plus more to taste

½ teaspoon freshly ground black pepper, plus more to taste

• SALAD •

4 Jammy Eggs (page 88)

1 pound small red potatoes, quartered or halved

Diamond Crystal kosher salt

Freshly ground black pepper

1 pound salmon fillet

1 tablespoon extra-virgin olive oil

½ pound French green beans, trimmed

1 large head Boston, Bibb, or romaine lettuce, torn into bite-sized pieces

1 cup cherry tomatoes, halved

½ small red onion, sliced thinly

¼ cup Niçoise or Kalamata olives, pitted

1 tablespoon chopped fresh basil

1 tablespoon chopped fresh chives

1 tablespoon chopped fresh oregano

1 WHISK ALL THE VINAIGRETTE INGREDIENTS TOGETHER IN A LIQUID MEASURING CUP. TASTE FOR SEASONING AND ADJUST WITH SALT AND PEPPER IF NEEDED.

2 YOU'LL NEED JAMMY EGGS TO MAKE THIS SALAD, SO GRAB OR QUICKLY MAKE SOME.

3 PUT THE POTATOES IN A LARGE POT AND FILL IT WITH COLD WATER UNTIL THEY'RE COVERED BY AT LEAST 2 INCHES OF WATER. STIR IN A LARGE PINCH OF SALT.

4 BRING THE POT TO A BOIL OVER HIGH HEAT. COOK FOR 6 TO 8 MINUTES OR UNTIL THE POTATOES ARE EASILY PIERCED WITH A KNIFE BUT NOT FALLING APART.

5 TRANSFER THE POTATOES TO A BOWL, LEAVING THE WATER IN THE POT. SEASON THE COOKED POTATOES WITH SALT AND PEPPER TO TASTE.

6 DRIZZLE ABOUT ¼ CUP OF THE VINAIGRETTE ONTO THE 'TATERS, TOSS, AND SET ASIDE.

7 TURN ON THE BROILER WITH THE TOP RACK POSITIONED 6 INCHES AWAY FROM THE HEATING ELEMENT.

8 PUT THE SALMON ON A GREASED RIMMED BAKING SHEET, AND PAT DRY WITH A PAPER TOWEL. BRUSH ON THE OLIVE OIL AND SPRINKLE ON SOME SALT AND PEPPER.

Per serving: 441 calories • 22 g carbohydrates • 23 g protein • 30 g fat • 5 g fiber

9 POP THE SALMON UNDER THE BROILER AND COOK FOR **7** TO **10** MINUTES . . .

10 . . . OR UNTIL THE TOP IS BROWNED AND THE TEMPERATURE IN THE THICKEST PART OF THE FISH IS 120°F TO 130°F (ABOUT MEDIUM-RARE OR MEDIUM). SET IT ASIDE.

11 PREPARE AN ICE BATH BY FILLING A LARGE BOWL WITH WATER AND ICE CUBES.

12 REMEMBER THE WATER YOU BOILED THE POTATOES IN? BRING THE WATER IN THE POT BACK TO A BOIL AND TOSS IN THE GREEN BEANS.

13 COOK UNTIL THEY'RE TENDER-CRISP AND BRIGHT GREEN, ABOUT **2** TO **3** MINUTES.

14 THEN, DUMP THE GREEN BEANS INTO THE ICE BATH TO STOP THE COOKING PROCESS.

15 TAKE THE GREEN BEANS OUT OF THE ICE BATH AND PAT DRY WITH PAPER TOWELS, AND SET ASIDE.

16 IN A LARGE MIXING BOWL, TOSS THE LET-TUCE LEAVES WITH ABOUT ¼ CUP OF THE VINAIGRETTE . . .

17 . . . AND TRANSFER THE DRESSED GREENS TO A LARGE SHALLOW SERVING PLATTER.

18 USE A FORK TO BREAK UP THE SALMON INTO LARGE CHUNKS AND DRIZZLE ¼ CUP OF THE VINAIGRETTE ON THE FISH. ARRANGE THE SALMON ATOP THE DRESSED GREENS.

19 IN THE MIXING BOWL, TOSS THE CHERRY TOMATOES AND ONIONS WITH **2** TABLE-SPOONS OF VINAIGRETTE. SEASON WITH SALT AND PEPPER TO TASTE.

20 ARRANGE THE TOMATOES AND ONIONS ON THE DRESSED GREENS.

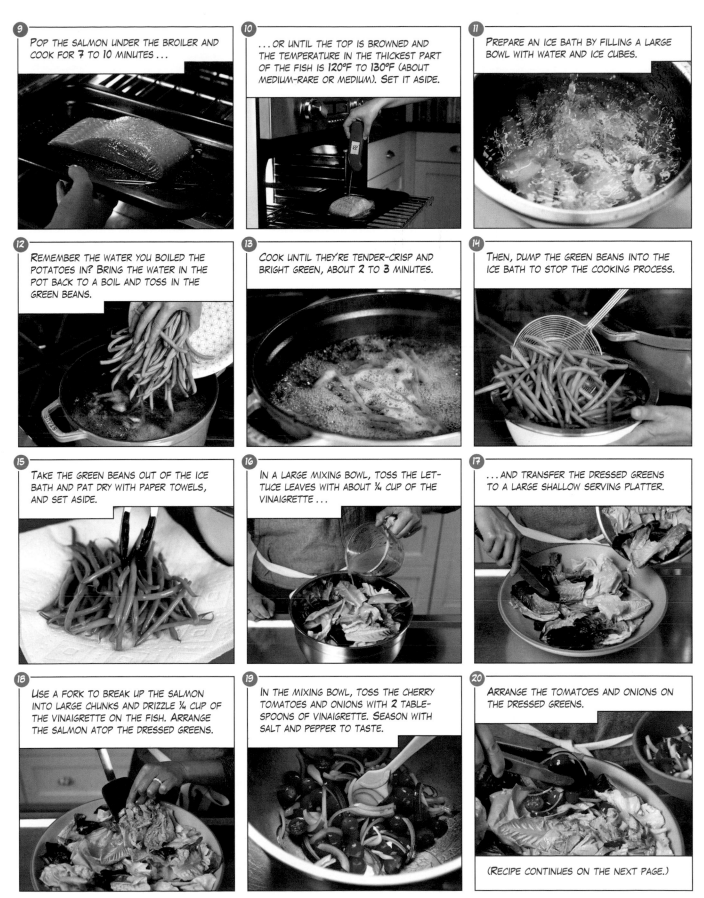

(RECIPE CONTINUES ON THE NEXT PAGE.)

21 DUMP THE GREEN BEANS INTO THE MIXING BOWL AND TOSS WITH 2 TABLESPOONS OF VINAIGRETTE. SEASON THE GREEN BEANS WITH SALT AND PEPPER TO TASTE, AND THEN TRANSFER THEM TO THE SALAD.

22 NEXT, PLOP THE SEASONED POTATOES ONTO THE LETTUCE, TOO.

23 CUT THE JAMMY EGGS IN HALF AND PLACE THEM ON THE SALAD WITH THE OLIVES.

24 GARNISH WITH 1 TABLESPOON EACH OF CHOPPED BASIL, CHIVES, AND OREGANO. ADD FRESHLY CRACKED BLACK PEPPER OVER THE TOP OF THE SALAD BEFORE SERVING.

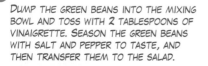

SWITCH IT UP: TUNA NIÇOISE SALAD

IF YOUR OVEN'S BROKEN BUT YOU HAVE SOME FANCY JARS OF OLIVE OIL-PACKED TUNA IN YOUR PANTRY (VENTRESCA OR TUNA BELLY'S MY FAVORITE), JUST DRAIN 12 OUNCES OF THE TUNA AND SUBSTITUTE IT IN PLACE OF THE COOKED SALMON.

THIS CLASSIC FRENCH COMPOSED SALAD IS THE PERFECT WEEKEND BRUNCH FARE, WITH BUTTERY SALMON IN PLACE OF TUNA, BRINY OLIVES, FRESH VEGETABLES, AND JAMMY EGGS SERVED OVER A BED OF GREENS TOSSED WITH A MUSTARDY VINAIGRETTE. ALL OF THE COMPONENTS CAN BE PREPARED AHEAD OF TIME AND ASSEMBLED INTO A STUNNING SALAD RIGHT BEFORE SERVING.

SHEET PAN TERIYAKI SALMON

MAKES 4 SERVINGS
🕐 **45 MINUTES**
(15 MINUTES HANDS-ON)

WHOLE30®	NUT-FREE
EGG-FREE	

4 (5-ounce) salmon fillets

¾ cup All-Purpose Stir-Fry Sauce (page 29), divided

1 tablespoon avocado oil

1 pound French green beans, trimmed

¼ pound fresh shiitake mushrooms, quartered

1 red bell pepper, cored and thinly sliced

1 tablespoon toasted sesame seeds

2 scallions, thinly sliced

LET'S NOT FORGET THE BEST THING ABOUT ONE-PAN SUPPERS: FEWER DISHES TO WASH!

1 SNUGLY ARRANGE THE SALMON FILLETS IN A HIGH-SIDED DISH. POUR IN ⅓ CUP OF ALL-PURPOSE STIR-FRY SAUCE.

2 COAT THE FILLETS WELL, KEEPING THEM SKIN-SIDE UP IN THE MARINADE UNTIL YOU'RE READY TO COOK. MARINATE FOR AS LITTLE AS 15 MINUTES, BUT NO LONGER THAN 8 HOURS IN THE REFRIGERATOR.

3 WHEN YOU'RE READY TO COOK, HEAT THE OVEN TO 400°F WITH THE RACK IN THE MIDDLE. THEN, IN A LARGE MIXING BOWL, WHISK TOGETHER ¼ CUP ALL-PURPOSE STIR-FRY SAUCE WITH THE AVOCADO OIL.

4 ADD THE GREEN BEANS, MUSHROOMS, AND BELL PEPPER, AND TOSS WELL.

5 PLACE THE MARINATED SALMON SKIN-SIDE DOWN IN THE CENTER OF A PARCHMENT-LINED RIMMED BAKING SHEET.

6 IN A SINGLE LAYER, ARRANGE THE VEGETABLES EVENLY AROUND THE SALMON.

7 BAKE FOR 10 TO 15 MINUTES OR UNTIL THE SALMON IS COOKED TO YOUR PREFERRED DONENESS. (I LIKE THE SALMON COOKED TO ABOUT MEDIUM, ABOUT 130°F TO 135°F IN THE THICKEST PART OF THE FILLET.)

8 BRUSH ON THE REMAINING 2 TABLESPOONS OF ALL-PURPOSE STIR-FRY SAUCE TO ADD A BRIGHT KICK OF FLAVOR. GARNISH WITH SESAME SEEDS AND SCALLIONS AND SERVE.

Per serving: 352 calories • 23 g carbohydrates • 33 g protein • 14 g fat • 5 g fiber

I LOVE SHEET PAN SUPPERS, BUT IT'S NOT ALWAYS EASY TO PAIR A PROTEIN WITH VEGETABLES THAT'LL COOK AT THE SAME TIME AND TASTE GOOD TOGETHER. LUCKY FOR US, THIS COMBO STICKS THE LANDING!

THIS EASY TERIYAKI SALMON HITS ALL THE FLAVOR NOTES OF A CLASSIC TERIYAKI SAUCE, BUT WITH ZERO BAD-FOR-YOU INGREDIENTS. TO BE SURE, MY SAUCE ISN'T AS SYRUPY-THICK OR CLOYINGLY SWEET AS RESTAURANT-STYLE TERIYAKI, BUT TASTE IS PARAMOUNT, AND WHEN IT COMES TO FLAVOR, I'LL HAVE YOU KNOW THAT EVEN MY PICKIEST CRITICS (A.K.A. MY FAMILY) HAPPILY GOBBLE THIS UP AND ASK FOR SECONDS!

HASH BROWN FISH

MAKES 4 SERVINGS
45 MINUTES

WHOLE30®	NUT-FREE
EGG-FREE	

2 teaspoons Umami Stir-Fry Powder (page 43), divided

1 pound russet potatoes, peeled

½ cup thinly sliced scallions

4 (5-ounce) skinless sea bass or cod fillets, each about ¾ inch thick (and no thicker than 1 inch)

4 tablespoons avocado oil or ghee, divided

1 lemon, cut into wedges

> I GAVE THIS DISH AN ASIAN TWIST BY INCORPORATING GREEN ONIONS AND UMAMI STIR-FRY POWDER, BUT IT'S ORIGINALLY INSPIRED BY ONE OF MY FAVORITE JACQUES PÉPIN RECIPES: SEA BASS IN SHREDDED POTATO SKIN!

NESTLED BETWEEN LAYERS OF CRISPITY-CRUNCHITY POTATOES, THESE TENDER FISH FILLETS ARE SEASONED TO PERFECTION. THERE'S NO BETTER MARRIAGE OF FLAVOR AND TEXTURE!

Per serving: 338 calories • 24 g carbohydrates • 28 g protein • 15 g fat • 3 g fiber

1 MAKE SURE YOU HAVE SOME *UMAMI STIR-FRY POWDER*. THEN, GRATE THE POTATOES WITH A FOOD PROCESSOR OR USING THE LARGE HOLES OF A BOX GRATER.

2 BUNDLE THE SHREDDED POTATOES IN A CLEAN KITCHEN TOWEL. THEN, WRING OUT THE POTATOES AND DISCARD THE LIQUID.

3 IN A LARGE BOWL, TOSS TOGETHER THE POTATOES, SCALLIONS, AND 1 TEASPOON OF *UMAMI STIR-FRY POWDER*.

4 PAT THE FISH DRY WITH PAPER TOWELS. SPRINKLE THE OTHER TEASPOON OF *UMAMI STIR-FRY POWDER* ON THE FISH FILETS.

5 HEAT A LARGE CAST-IRON OR NON-STICK SKILLET OVER MEDIUM HEAT, AND THEN ADD 2 TABLESPOONS OF OIL TO THE PAN. ADD TWO 1/3-CUP MOUNDS OF POTATOES . . .

6 . . . AND FLATTEN THEM INTO RECTANGLES APPROXIMATING THE SIZE AND SHAPE OF YOUR FISH FILLETS.

7 SMUSH A FILLET ON EACH POTATO LAYER . . .

8 . . . AND COVER EACH WITH A THIN LAYER OF SHREDDED POTATOES.

9 FRY FOR 5 TO 8 MINUTES OR UNTIL THE BOTTOM LATER OF POTATOES IS CRISP AND GOLDEN BROWN.

10 CAREFULLY FLIP THE FILLET PACKETS OVER WITH A FISH SPATULA AND COOK FOR 5 TO 8 MINUTES MORE ON THE OTHER SIDE.

11 ONCE THE OTHER POTATO LAYER IS NICELY BROWNED AND THE CENTER OF THE FISH REGISTERS 135°F ON AN INSTANT-READ THERMOMETER, TRANSFER TO A PLATE.

12 REPEAT STEPS 5 TO 11 WITH THE REMAINING FISH AND POTATOES, AND SERVE WITH LEMON WEDGES.

PATRA NI MACHHI (SPICY FISH IN BANANA LEAVES)

MAKES 4 SERVINGS
◗ **30 MINUTES**
(20 MINUTES HANDS-ON)

KETO-FRIENDLY	NUT-FREE
EGG-FREE	

1 cup packed fresh cilantro

½ cup unsweetened shredded coconut

¼ cup packed fresh mint leaves

6 garlic cloves, peeled and chopped

2 serrano peppers, roughly chopped

1 tablespoon chopped ginger

1 teaspoon ground cumin

Diamond Crystal kosher salt

½ teaspoon coconut sugar

2 teaspoons lemon juice

3 tablespoons water

4 (5-ounce) sea bass, cod, or other white fish fillets

4 (10-inch) thawed or fresh banana leaf squares, trimmed of any brown edges, washed, and wiped

NOT A FAN OF FIERY FOODS? LOWER THE HEAT BY REMOVING THE SPICY MEMBRANES FROM THE SERRANO PEPPERS!

1 ON THE STOVETOP, SET UP A STEAMER WITH 1 INCH OF WATER IN IT. (OR CREATE YOUR OWN STEAMER USING A LARGE LIDDED POT WITH A METAL STEAMER INSIDE.)

2 IN A FOOD PROCESSOR, ADD THE CILANTRO, COCONUT, MINT LEAVES, GARLIC, SERRANO PEPPERS, GINGER . . .

3 . . . CUMIN, 1 TEASPOON KOSHER SALT, SUGAR, AND LEMON JUICE.

4 PROCESS CHOP . . .

5 . . . AND SCRAPE DOWN THE SIDES.

6 THEN, ADD THE WATER.

7 CONTINUE TO PROCESS . . .

8 . . . UNTIL A THICK PASTE FORMS. TASTE IT (IT'S SPICY!) AND ADJUST THE SEASONING IF NECESSARY. SET THE CHUTNEY ASIDE.

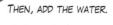

Per serving: 200 calories • 5 g carbohydrates • 27 g protein • 8 g fat • 2 g fiber

9 PAT THE FILLETS DRY WITH A PAPER TOWEL AND SPRINKLE SALT ALL OVER THEM.

10 PUT A SQUARE OF BANANA LEAF SHINY-SIDE DOWN ON A CLEAN, FLAT PREP SURFACE.

11 SPOON AND SMEAR SOME CHUTNEY ONTO THE MIDDLE OF THE LEAF.

12 PLACE A FISH FILLET ON TOP.

13 COVER THE TOP AND SIDES OF THE FISH WITH MORE CHUTNEY.

14 WRAP THE LEAF AROUND THE FISH . . .

15 . . . AND SECURE WITH TOOTHPICKS.

16 REPEAT WITH ALL THE BANANA LEAVES AND FISH UNTIL YOU HAVE 4 PACKETS.

17 PUT ALL THE PACKETS IN THE STEAMER . . .

18 . . . AND STEAM, COVERED, OVER MEDIUM HEAT FOR 7 TO 10 MINUTES. THE FISH IS DONE WHEN THE INTERNAL TEMPERATURE REACHES 130°F TO 135°F.

19 PLATE . . .

20 . . . AND UNWRAP. THE FISH SHOULD BE OPAQUE AND JUST BARELY FLAKING APART. SERVE IMMEDIATELY.

153

SPICY AND LIGHT, PATRA NI MACHHI IS MADE BY SLATHERING AN HERBY GREEN CHUTNEY ON CREAMY WHITE FISH FILLETS AND THEN GENTLY STEAMING THEM IN AROMATIC BANANA LEAVES. EACH PACKET IS THEN UNWRAPPED LIKE A PRESENT AT THE DINNER TABLE. IT'S NO WONDER PATRA NI MACHHI IS SO OFTEN FEATURED AT PARSI WEDDINGS AND NAVJOTE CELEBRATIONS!

THE MOST DIFFICULT PART OF MAKING PATRA NI MACHHI MIGHT BE TRACKING DOWN FRESH BANANA LEAVES. CHECK YOUR LOCAL ASIAN AND LATIN MARKETS; IF YOU CAN'T FIND FRESH LEAVES, THE FROZEN KIND WILL DO. AND IF ALL ELSE FAILS, YOU CAN JUST COOK THE FISH FILLETS IN PARCHMENT PAPER OR FOIL.

GINGER SCALLION FISH FILLETS

MAKES 6 SERVINGS
🕐 **15 MINUTES**
(5 MINUTES HANDS-ON)

WHOLE30®	KETO-FRIENDLY
NUT-FREE	EGG-FREE
NIGHTSHADE-FREE	

- ¼ cup Ginger Scallion Sauce (page 33), divided
- 2 (1-pound) barramundi (Asian sea bass) fillets or other white fish fillets, about 1 inch thick
- 1 teaspoon Diamond Crystal kosher salt
- ¼ teaspoon ground white pepper
- 2 tablespoons avocado oil

NATIVE TO THE INDO-PACIFIC, BARRAMUNDI IS DELICIOUS, PACKED WITH HEALTHY OMEGA-3S, AND ECO-FRIENDLY TO BOOT. IT'S BEEN NAMED A "BEST CHOICE" UNDER THE MONTEREY BAY AQUARIUM'S SEAFOOD WATCH SUSTAINABILITY PROGRAM!

1 IF YOU GUESSED FROM THE TITLE OF THIS RECIPE THAT YOU'LL NEED SOME GINGER SCALLION SAUCE TO PREPARE THIS DISH, YOU'RE CORRECT, SO GRAB OR MAKE SOME.

2 TURN ON THE BROILER WITH THE TOP RACK POSITIONED 6 INCHES AWAY FROM THE HEATING ELEMENT.

3 PAT DRY THE FISH FILLETS WITH PAPER TOWELS. SPRINKLE THE TOP AND BOTTOM WITH SALT AND WHITE PEPPER.

4 POUR THE AVOCADO OIL ON A RIMMED BAKING SHEET, AND RUB OR BRUSH THE OIL ON ALL SIDES OF THE FILLETS.

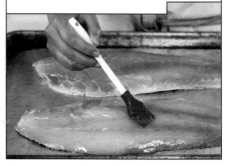

5 ARRANGE THE FISH SKIN-SIDE DOWN ON THE BAKING SHEET.

6 PLACE THE FILLETS UNDER THE BROILER . . .

7 . . . AND COOK FOR 8 TO 12 MINUTES OR UNTIL THE FISH REACHES 140°F. USE A FORK TO CHECK THAT THE THICKEST PARTS ARE OPAQUE AND FLAKE APART EASILY.

8 TAKE THE FISH OUT OF THE OVEN AND GENEROUSLY SPOON THE GINGER SCALLION SAUCE ON TOP OF THE FISH. SERVE IT UP!

Per serving: 207 calories • 1 g carbohydrates • 28 g protein • 10 g fat • 1 g fiber

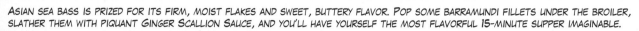

ASIAN SEA BASS IS PRIZED FOR ITS FIRM, MOIST FLAKES AND SWEET, BUTTERY FLAVOR. POP SOME BARRAMUNDI FILLETS UNDER THE BROILER, SLATHER THEM WITH PIQUANT GINGER SCALLION SAUCE, AND YOU'LL HAVE YOURSELF THE MOST FLAVORFUL 15-MINUTE SUPPER IMAGINABLE.

SEARED SCALLOPS WITH CHILI CRISP

MAKES 4 SERVINGS
⏱ **20 MINUTES**

WHOLE30®	KETO-FRIENDLY
NUT-FREE	EGG-FREE

¼ cup Nom Nom Chili Crisp (page 38)

1½ pounds dry-packed sea scallops (10 count per pound)

½ teaspoon Diamond Crystal kosher salt

3 tablespoons avocado oil or ghee

> TENDER AND SWEET-YET-BRINY, SEA SCALLOPS SHINE BRIGHTEST IN SIMPLE RECIPES THAT SHOW OFF THE DELICIOUSNESS OF THE SCALLOPS THEMSELVES.

🔄 **SWITCH IT UP: BROILED FISH WITH CHILI CRISP**

HEY! KNOW WHAT ALSO PAIRS PERFECTLY WITH NOM NOM CHILI CRISP BESIDES SCALLOPS? FISH! FOLLOW MY RECIPE FOR GINGER SCALLION FISH FILLETS (PAGE 156) AND FOLLOW STEPS 2 THROUGH 7. TOP WITH NOM NOM CHILI CRISP AND SERVE.

THERE ARE FEW THINGS IN LIFE AS UNCOMPLICATED YET STRIKINGLY APPETIZING AS SEARED SCALLOPS. PAIR THEM WITH A CRUNCHY SPOONFUL OF MY FIERY, SAVORY NOM NOM CHILI CRISP AND YOU'LL MANAGE TO WOW YOUR PALS IN JUST A MATTER OF MINUTES. THAT IS, UNLESS THEY HATE SPICY FOOD, IN WHICH CASE YOU SHOULD PROBABLY SKIP THIS DISH (AND ALSO GET YOURSELF SOME NEW FRIENDS).

Per serving: 334 calories • 7 g carbohydrates • 22 g protein • 24 g fat • 1 g fiber

1 GO GRAB YOUR NOM NOM CHILI CRISP. BRING IT TO ROOM TEMPERATURE IF IT'S BEEN CHILLING IN THE FRIDGE.

2 USING YOUR FINGERS, PULL OFF AND DISCARD THE TENDON ATTACHED TO THE SIDE OF EACH SCALLOP.

3 GENTLY BLOT THE SCALLOPS COMPLETELY DRY WITH PAPER TOWELS. (IF THEY'RE WET, YOUR EXPENSIVE MORSELS FROM THE SEA WON'T BROWN PROPERLY.)

4 SPRINKLE BOTH SIDES OF THE SCALLOPS LIGHTLY WITH SALT. WAIT 1 TO 2 MINUTES AND BLOT 'EM AGAIN WITH PAPER TOWELS.

5 HEAT A LARGE (12-INCH) HEAVY-BOTTOMED SKILLET OVER MEDIUM-HIGH HEAT. WHEN THE PAN IS HOT, SWIRL IN 2 TABLESPOONS AVOCADO OIL.

6 WHEN THE OIL IS SHIMMERING, CAREFULLY PLACE HALF OF THE SCALLOPS FLAT-SIDE DOWN IN THE SKILLET IN A SINGLE LAYER.

7 COOK UNDISTURBED (WITHOUT MOVING THE SCALLOPS) FOR 1½ TO 2 MINUTES OR UNTIL THE BOTTOMS ARE GOLDEN BROWN.

8 FLIP THE SCALLOPS.

9 USE A LARGE SPOON TO BASTE THEM WITH THE OIL. COOK UNDISTURBED FOR 1 MINUTE OR UNTIL THE CENTERS ARE OPAQUE AND THE SIDES ARE FIRM.

10 TRANSFER THE SCALLOPS TO A PLATE.

11 ADD ANOTHER TABLESPOON OF AVOCADO OIL TO THE PAN AND REPEAT STEPS 6 TO 10 WITH THE REMAINING SCALLOPS.

12 DRIZZLE NOM NOM CHILI CRISP ON TOP OF THE SCALLOPS AND SERVE.

SHRIMP SIMMERED IN GREEN MOLE

MAKES 4 SERVINGS
⏱ 15 MINUTES

WHOLE30®	KETO-FRIENDLY
NUT-FREE	EGG-FREE

- **2** cups Pipián Verde (page 36)
- **2** tablespoons raw pepitas
- **1½** pounds shrimp (21–25 count per pound), shelled and deveined
- **¾** teaspoon Diamond Crystal kosher salt
- **¼** teaspoon freshly ground black pepper
- **2** tablespoons fresh cilantro leaves

I ALWAYS KEEP FROZEN SHRIMP ON HAND 'CAUSE THEY'RE EASY TO COOK AND FULL OF FLAVOR. WHENEVER I HAVE A WEEKNIGHT DINNER EMERGENCY, I CAN QUICKLY THAW 'EM IN A COLANDER UNDER RUNNING WATER IN JUST 5 TO 10 MINUTES.

1 GOT SOME PIPIÁN VERDE? YOU'LL NEED IT, SO GO GRAB OR MAKE SOME ALREADY.

2 HEAT A LARGE SKILLET OVER MEDIUM HEAT. ONCE IT'S HOT, ADD THE PEPITAS IN A SINGLE LAYER.

3 TOAST THE SEEDS, STIRRING OCCASION-ALLY, FOR 3 TO 5 MINUTES OR UNTIL THE PEPITAS ARE FRAGRANT AND YOU CAN HEAR THEM POPPING.

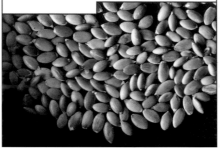

4 TRANSFER THE TOASTED PEPITAS TO A PLATE TO COOL.

5 POUR THE GREEN MOLE SAUCE INTO THE SKILLET. COOK UNTIL IT'S SIMMERING, ABOUT 1 TO 2 MINUTES.

6 WHILE THE GREEN MOLE SAUCE IS HEATING UP, TOSS THE SHRIMP IN A MEDIUM BOWL WITH SALT AND PEPPER.

7 ADD THE SHRIMP TO THE SIMMERING MOLE SAUCE.

8 COOK, STIRRING, FOR 3 TO 5 MINUTES OR UNTIL THE SHRIMP ARE COOKED THROUGH.

Per serving: 287 calories • 7 g carbohydrates • 39 g protein • 12 g fat • 2 g fiber

9 SEASON TO TASTE WITH EXTRA SALT AND PEPPER IF NEEDED. GARNISH WITH TOASTED PEPITAS AND CILANTRO BEFORE SERVING.

IF YOU HAVE SOME PIPIÁN VERDE IN THE FRIDGE, THIS'LL TAKE JUST 15 MINUTES TO PREPARE, BUT IT'LL LOOK AND TASTE LIKE SOMEONE LABORED FOR HOURS TO COOK UP THIS SPICY MEXICAN SEAFOOD FEAST!

SHRIMP AND SUGAR SNAP PEAS

MAKES 4 SERVINGS
◑ **30 MINUTES**

WHOLE30®	KETO-FRIENDLY
NUT-FREE	EGG-FREE

1½ pounds shrimp (21–25 count per pound), shelled and deveined

2 teaspoons Umami Stir-Fry Powder (page 43), divided

½ cup bone broth or chicken broth

2 teaspoons arrowroot powder

½ teaspoon toasted sesame oil

2 tablespoons avocado oil or ghee

½ pound sugar snap peas

2 medium carrots, cut diagonally into slices ¼ inch thick

½ medium yellow onion, thinly sliced

3 garlic cloves, minced

½ teaspoon crushed red pepper flakes

2 scallions, thinly sliced

PER CALORIE, SHRIMP IS ONE OF THE MOST PROTEIN-PACKED FOODS AROUND!

MIXING SEASONED SHRIMP WITH CRISP SUGAR SNAP PEAS, THIS TAKEOUT FAVORITE CAN BE COOKED AT HOME IN A FLASH. AS WITH ALL STIR-FRIES, A WOK ISN'T STRICTLY REQUIRED; JUST GRAB A BIG SKILLET AND YOU'RE GOOD TO GO!

Per serving: 293 calories • 12 g carbohydrates • 37 g protein • 10 g fat • 3 g fiber

1. IN A MEDIUM BOWL, TOSS TOGETHER THE SHRIMP AND 1 TEASPOON OF UMAMI STIR-FRY POWDER. SET ASIDE.

2. IN A SMALL MEASURING CUP, WHISK THE BROTH, ARROWROOT POWDER, AND SESAME OIL AND SET ASIDE.

3. HEAT A LARGE SKILLET OVER MEDIUM-HIGH HEAT. ONCE IT'S HOT, ADD THE OIL AND SWIRL THE PAN TO COAT IT.

4. ADD THE SUGAR SNAP PEAS, CARROTS, AND ONION TO THE PAN.

5. COOK THE VEGGIES, STIRRING FREQUENTLY, UNTIL THE SUGAR SNAP PEAS AND CARROTS ARE TENDER-CRISP, ABOUT 2 MINUTES.

6. SPRINKLE 1 TEASPOON OF UMAMI STIR-FRY POWDER ON THE VEGETABLES.

7. ADD THE GARLIC AND RED PEPPER FLAKES.

8. COOK, STIRRING, FOR ABOUT 30 SECONDS OR UNTIL FRAGRANT.

9. TOSS IN THE SHRIMP AND COOK, STIRRING, FOR 1 TO 2 MINUTES OR UNTIL THEY TURN ORANGE-PINK.

10. WHISK THE BROTH MIXTURE AGAIN. THEN, POUR IT INTO THE PAN.

11. COOK, STIRRING FREQUENTLY, UNTIL THE LIQUID THICKENS SLIGHTLY. AS SOON AS IT THICKENS, TAKE THE PAN OFF THE HEAT. (THE ARROWROOT POWDER WILL LOSE ITS THICKENING POWER WITH TOO MUCH HEAT.)

12. TASTE FOR SEASONING AND ADJUST WITH MORE UMAMI STIR-FRY POWDER OR SALT IF NEEDED. PLATE, GARNISH WITH SCALLIONS, AND SERVE.

UMAMI FRIED SHRIMP

MAKES 4 SERVINGS
◑ **30 MINUTES**

WHOLE30®	KETO-FRIENDLY
NUT-FREE	EGG-FREE
NIGHTSHADE-FREE (IF MODIFIED)	

2 teaspoons Umami Stir-Fry Powder (page 43)

1½ pounds shrimp (21–25 count per pound), shelled and deveined

½ cup potato starch (not nightshade-free) or tapioca flour

1 cup avocado oil

2 scallions, thinly sliced

¼ teaspoon freshly ground black pepper

THESE PRAWNS ARE SHRIMPLY AMAZING, SO IF YOU GOBBLE 'EM UP ALL BY YOURSELF, NO ONE WILL BLAME YOU FOR BEING SHELLFISH!

1 GO GRAB OR MAKE SOME UMAMI STIR-FRY POWDER, BECAUSE YOU'LL NEED IT.

2 BLOT THE SHRIMP DRY USING A PAPER TOWEL AND TOSS THEM IN A BOWL WITH UMAMI STIR-FRY POWDER.

3 PLACE THE POTATO STARCH IN A SHALLOW BOWL AND DREDGE THE SHRIMP IN IT UNTIL EVENLY COVERED.

4 SHAKE OFF THE EXCESS STARCH AND SET THE SHRIMP ASIDE ON A PARCHMENT-LINED SHEET PAN.

5 ADD ENOUGH OIL TO REACH ¼ INCH UP THE SIDES OF A 12-INCH CAST-IRON OR NON-STICK PAN. HEAT OVER MEDIUM HEAT UNTIL THE OIL IS SHIMMERING (OR WHEN IT REACHES ABOUT 375°F).

6 IN BATCHES, FRY THE SHRIMP IN A SINGLE LAYER IN THE OIL FOR 1 MINUTE PER SIDE OR UNTIL THEY TURN ORANGE-PINK.

7 TRANSFER ALL THE COOKED SHRIMP TO A WIRE RACK. CONTINUE FRYING BATCHES OF SHRIMP UNTIL FINISHED. TASTE A SHRIMP FOR SEASONING AND SPRINKLE ON MORE UMAMI STIR-FRY POWDER IF DESIRED.

8 TRANSFER THE SHRIMP TO A SERVING PLATTER AND TOP WITH SLICED SCALLIONS AND BLACK PEPPER. SERVE IMMEDIATELY.

Per serving: 307 calories • 4 g carbohydrates • 35 g protein • 16 g fat • 1 g fiber

THE LIGHT DUSTING OF STARCH GIVES THIS SHRIMP A LOVELY CRISPNESS, BUT TO SAVE TIME AND EFFORT, YOU CAN SKIP THE COATING AND JUST SEASON THE PRAWNS WITH UMAMI STIR-FRY POWDER BEFORE PAN-FRYING THEM IN A LITTLE OIL. BOTH TECHNIQUES YIELD DELECTABLE RESULTS BECAUSE UMAMI STIR-FRY POWDER IS A SINGULARLY AMAZING FLAVOR-BOOSTER. IT CERTAINLY BEATS PLAIN OLD SALT AND PEPPER!

BABY BOK CHOY WITH CRAB MEAT SAUCE

MAKES 4 SERVINGS
◑ 30 MINUTES

WHOLE30®	KETO-FRIENDLY
NUT-FREE	NIGHTSHADE-FREE

- **1** teaspoon Umami Stir-Fry Powder (page 43)
- **1½** cups bone broth or chicken broth
- **1½** tablespoons arrowroot powder
- **1½** teaspoons paleo-friendly fish sauce (use less if the broth is salty)
- **3** tablespoons avocado oil or ghee, divided
- **3** garlic cloves, peeled and smashed
- **1½** pounds baby bok choy, ends trimmed and cut in half or quartered
- **1** tablespoon minced ginger
- **1** pound lump crab meat
- **1** teaspoon rice vinegar
- **1** egg white, whisked
- **¼** teaspoon ground white pepper
- **2** scallions, thinly sliced

WITH SMALLER LEAVES AND JADE-GREEN STALKS, BABY BOK CHOY COOKS UP SLIGHTLY SWEETER THAN FULL-SIZE BOK CHOY.

1 MAKE SURE YOU HAVE SOME UMAMI STIR-FRY POWDER!

2 IN A MEASURING CUP OR BOWL, WHISK TOGETHER THE BROTH, ARROWROOT POWDER, AND FISH SAUCE. SET IT ASIDE.

3 HEAT A LARGE SKILLET OVER MEDIUM-HIGH HEAT. SWIRL IN 1 TABLESPOON OF OIL AND ADD THE SMASHED GARLIC.

4 COOK, STIRRING, FOR ABOUT 30 SECONDS OR UNTIL THE GARLIC IS FRAGRANT. DON'T LET THE GARLIC BURN!

5 ADD THE BOK CHOY AND COOK, STIRRING, FOR ABOUT 2 MINUTES . . .

6 . . . UNTIL THE LEAVES START TO WILT.

7 ADD THE UMAMI STIR-FRY POWDER AND STIR WELL TO EVENLY DISTRIBUTE.

8 COVER THE SKILLET AND DECREASE THE HEAT TO MEDIUM.

Per serving: 265 calories • 11 g carbohydrates • 26 g protein • 12 g fat • 2 g fiber

9 Cook for 2 to 3 minutes or until the baby bok choy is tender-crisp.

10 Taste and season with more Umami Stir-Fry Powder if needed. Transfer the bok choy to a serving platter.

11 Rinse and wipe the skillet. Then, heat the pan over medium-high and swirl in the remaining 2 tablespoons of avocado oil.

12 Stir in the minced ginger and cook until fragrant, about 30 seconds. Try not to burn the ginger!

13 Add the crab meat and rice vinegar.

14 Cook, stirring frequently, for about 1 minute or until the crab meat is heated through.

15 Whisk the reserved sauce and pour it into the pan.

16 Bring to a simmer and cook, stirring frequently, until the sauce thickens.

17 Add the egg white and cook, stirring, for about 30 seconds until the egg whites turn opaque.

18 Turn off the heat and add the white pepper. Stir well, taste for seasoning, and adjust with salt if needed.

19 Spoon the finished crab sauce over the bok choy on the serving platter.

20 Garnish with scallions and serve.

THE STIR-FRIES I WHIP UP AT HOME ARE
TYPICALLY WEEKNIGHT, CLEAN-OUT-THE-
FRIDGE MEALS ... BUT NOT THIS ONE!
THIS SAUCY STIR-FRY COMBINES TENDER,
SUBTLY GARLICKY GREENS AND A DELICATE
CRAB SAUCE TO CREATE AN ENTRÉE FIT
FOR A SPECIAL-OCCASION FEAST.

SNOW PEA SHOOTS ARE CLASSICALLY USED
IN PLACE OF (EASIER-TO-FIND) BOK CHOY,
SO IF YOU'RE A STICKLER FOR TRADITION,
FEEL FREE TO MAKE THE SUBSTITUTION.

LOBSTER TAILS WITH THAI RED CURRY

MAKES 2 SERVINGS
⏱ 45 MINUTES

KETO-FRIENDLY	NUT-FREE
EGG-FREE	

- **1** tablespoon coconut oil
- **2** tablespoons red Thai curry paste
- **1** (13.5-ounce) can full-fat coconut milk or coconut cream
- **2** teaspoons coconut sugar
- **1½** teaspoons paleo-friendly fish sauce
- **2** limes, divided
- **4** (4-ounce) lobster tails
- **2** tablespoons melted ghee
  Diamond Crystal kosher salt
  Freshly ground black pepper
- **2** scallions, finely sliced
- **2** tablespoons fresh basil, Thai basil, and/or cilantro, roughly chopped

MAKE THE SAUCE FIRST, 'CAUSE LOBSTER COOKS QUICKLY!

SWITCH IT UP: SEARED SCALLOPS WITH THAI RED CURRY

HERE'S ANOTHER QUICK SEAFOOD OPTION: SERVE YOUR LEFTOVER THAI RED CURRY SAUCE WITH SEARED SCALLOPS. FOLLOW STEPS 2 THROUGH 11 IN MY SEARED SCALLOPS WITH CHILI CRISP RECIPE (PAGE 158) AND LADLE THE CURRY SAUCE OVER THEM.

1 LET'S FIRST MAKE THE THAI CURRY SAUCE! HEAT THE OIL IN A SMALL SAUCEPAN OVER MEDIUM HEAT. ADD THE CURRY PASTE . . .

2 . . . AND COOK UNTIL FRAGRANT.

3 POUR IN THE COCONUT MILK.

4 STIR TO COMBINE AND BRING TO A BOIL OVER HIGH HEAT.

5 DECREASE THE HEAT TO MAINTAIN A VIGOROUS SIMMER FOR ABOUT 15 MINUTES, STIRRING OCCASIONALLY, UNTIL THE LIQUID IN THE SAUCEPAN HAS REDUCED BY A THIRD.

6 STIR IN THE COCONUT SUGAR AND FISH SAUCE.

7 REMOVE THE SAUCEPAN FROM THE HEAT AND ADD THE JUICE FROM 1 LIME (APPROXIMATELY 2 TABLESPOONS). TASTE AND ADJUST FOR SEASONING IF NEEDED. COVER AND SET ASIDE.

8 TURN ON THE BROILER WITH THE RACK IN THE MIDDLE, ABOUT 10 INCHES FROM THE HEAT SOURCE.

Per serving: 575 calories • 9 g carbohydrates • 46 g protein • 40 g fat • 3 g fiber

9 TIME TO BUTTERFLY EACH OF THE LOBSTER TAILS! USING SHARP KITCHEN SHEARS, CUT THE TOP PART OF THE SHELL LENGTHWISE UNTIL YOU REACH THE TAIL. DON'T CUT ALL THE WAY THROUGH.

10 FLIP THE LOBSTER TAIL OVER AND USE BOTH THUMBS TO GENTLY CRACK EACH OF THE RIBS ON THE UNDERSIDE. BE CAREFUL NOT TO STAB YOURSELF ON ANY SPINY PROTRUSIONS!

11 USING YOUR FINGERS, CAREFULLY SEPARATE THE LOBSTER FLESH FROM THE SHELL (EXCEPT FOR THE BIT ATTACHED AT THE END OF THE TAIL).

12 STARTING AT THE CUT END OF THE TAIL, GENTLY PULL THE LOBSTER FLESH UP THROUGH THE SHELL, STILL KEEPING THE TAIL END CONNECTED.

13 PROP THE LOBSTER MEAT ON TOP OF THE SHELL.

14 REPEAT UNTIL ALL THE TAILS ARE BUTTERFLIED.

15 PAT THE LOBSTER TAILS DRY AND TRANSFER THEM TO A RIMMED BAKING SHEET.

16 BRUSH THE MELTED GHEE ON TOP OF THE MEAT . . .

17 . . . AND LIGHTLY SEASON WITH SALT AND PEPPER.

18 BROIL THE TAILS! IT SHOULD TAKE ABOUT 5 MINUTES TO COOK, OR ROUGHLY 1 MINUTE PER OUNCE. START CHECKING AT THE 4-MINUTE MARK SO YOU DON'T OVERCOOK YOUR PRICEY TAILS.

19 YOU'LL KNOW THE TAILS ARE READY WHEN THE SHELLS ARE BRIGHT RED, THE MEAT IS NO LONGER TRANSLUCENT, AND THE INTERNAL TEMPERATURE IS BETWEEN 135° AND 140°F. TAKE THE COOKED LOBSTER TAILS OUT OF THE OVEN AND SET THEM ASIDE.

20 SPOON SOME OF THE CURRY SAUCE ONTO THE BOTTOM OF 2 SHALLOW BOWLS.

(RECIPE CONTINUES ON THE NEXT PAGE.)

171

21 PLACE 2 COOKED LOBSTER TAILS ON THE SAUCE IN EACH BOWL.

22 LADLE MORE CURRY ON THE TOP. (YOU'LL HAVE ENOUGH EXTRA SAUCE TO MAKE UP TO 4 MORE LOBSTER TAILS LATER.)

23 CUT THE REMAINING LIME INTO WEDGES TO SERVE WITH THE LOBSTER TAILS.

24 GARNISH WITH 2 FINELY SLICED SCALLIONS AND 2 TABLESPOONS CHOPPED BASIL, THAI BASIL, AND/OR CILANTRO BEFORE SERVING.

LOBSTER TAILS COME IN ALL SIZES, FROM 4 OUNCES TO 1½ POUNDS. I PREFER THE SMALLER TAILS BECAUSE THEY'RE QUICKER TO COOK AND EASIER TO SOURCE; IF YOU'RE LUCKY, YOU CAN EVEN FIND THEM FROZEN IN BULK AT YOUR NEARBY WAREHOUSE STORE.

SWITCH IT UP: AIR FRYER LOBSTER TAILS

I KNOW SOME OF YOU INSIST ON COOKING EVERYTHING YOU CAN IN THE AIR FRYER, SO HERE YOU GO: 4-OUNCE LOBSTER TAILS TAKE 4 TO 6 MINUTES IN AN AIR FRYER SET AT 400°F. THEY'RE DONE WHEN THE TEMPERATURE OF THE MEAT IS BETWEEN 135° AND 140°F. DON'T OVERCOOK THEM!

BUTTERFLYING SUCCULENT LOBSTER TAILS MAY SEEM INTIMIDATING, BUT IT'S WAY EASIER THAN IT LOOKS. BEST OF ALL, THIS METHOD RESULTS IN A BEAUTIFUL CELEBRATION MEAL AS ELEGANT AS IT IS EFFORTLESS. FOR THE BEST-TASTING RESULTS, A HIGH-QUALITY THAI RED CURRY PASTE IS MANDATORY. I LIKE AROY-D AND MAE PLOY BRANDS, WHICH ARE AVAILABLE AT MOST ASIAN MARKETS. THE RESULTING SAUCE IS FREAKISHLY VERSATILE AND CAN BE REPURPOSED TO MAKE ALL SORTS OF DISHES. JUST ADD PROTEIN AND/OR VEGGIES TO MAKE A THAI CURRY IN MINUTES!

POULTRY

CHICKEN VELVET AND SPINACH SOUP

MAKES 4 SERVINGS
⏱ **45 MINUTES**

WHOLE30®	KETO-FRIENDLY
NUT-FREE	NIGHTSHADE-FREE

1	pound boneless, skinless chicken breasts, cut into 1-inch cubes
2	teaspoons arrowroot powder
1	teaspoon Diamond Crystal kosher salt
2	teaspoons ice water
1	large egg white
1	tablespoon avocado oil, ghee, or fat of choice
1	large shallot, thinly sliced
¼	pound large shiitake mushrooms, stemmed and thinly sliced
1	(2-inch) piece fresh ginger, peeled and cut into thin coins
3	garlic cloves, peeled and smashed
6	cups bone broth or chicken broth
2	teaspoons coconut aminos
1	teaspoon paleo-friendly fish sauce or No-Fish Sauce (page 28)
6	cups baby spinach
½	teaspoon toasted sesame oil

=SLURP!=

THIS COMFORTING CHICKEN SOUP USES A TECHNIQUE I LEARNED FROM AN OLD KEN HOM COOKBOOK FOR MAKING A DELICATELY FLUFFY CHICKEN MIXTURE, OR VELVET, THAT DISPERSES THE FINELY CHOPPED CHICKEN THROUGHOUT THE BROTH. THIS DISH ALWAYS HITS THE SPOT WHEN THE WEATHER TURNS COLD OR I GET WISTFUL FOR CANTONESE SOUPS.

1 TOSS THE CHICKEN CUBES INTO THE BOWL OF A FOOD PROCESSOR . . .

2 . . . AND PULSE UNTIL THE CHICKEN IS CHOPPED UP.

Per serving: 318 calories • 8 g carbohydrates • 51 g protein • 9 g fat • 2 g fiber

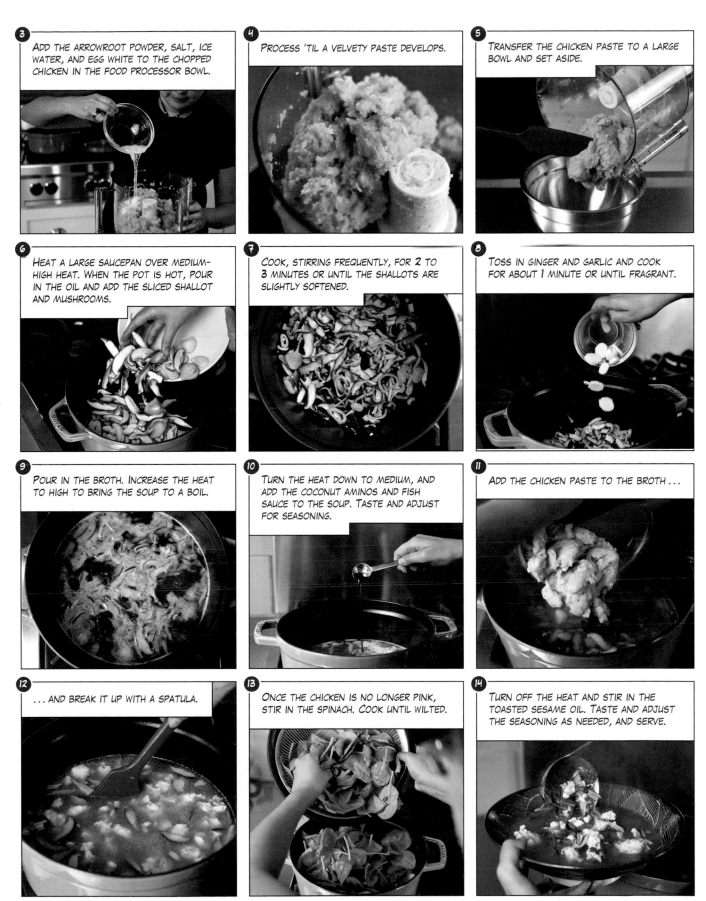

3 Add the arrowroot powder, salt, ice water, and egg white to the chopped chicken in the food processor bowl.

4 Process 'til a velvety paste develops.

5 Transfer the chicken paste to a large bowl and set aside.

6 Heat a large saucepan over medium-high heat. When the pot is hot, pour in the oil and add the sliced shallot and mushrooms.

7 Cook, stirring frequently, for 2 to 3 minutes or until the shallots are slightly softened.

8 Toss in ginger and garlic and cook for about 1 minute or until fragrant.

9 Pour in the broth. Increase the heat to high to bring the soup to a boil.

10 Turn the heat down to medium, and add the coconut aminos and fish sauce to the soup. Taste and adjust for seasoning.

11 Add the chicken paste to the broth . . .

12 . . . and break it up with a spatula.

13 Once the chicken is no longer pink, stir in the spinach. Cook until wilted.

14 Turn off the heat and stir in the toasted sesame oil. Taste and adjust the seasoning as needed, and serve.

TOM KHA GAI (THAI CHICKEN AND GALANGAL SOUP)

MAKES 6 SERVINGS
◑ **30 MINUTES
(10 MINUTES HANDS-ON)**

WHOLE30®	KETO-FRIENDLY
NUT-FREE	EGG-FREE

- **2** medium lemongrass stalks, peeled and trimmed
- **1** (2-inch) piece fresh galangal
- **6** makrut lime leaves, torn into large pieces (or zest from 2 limes shaved into strips with a vegetable peeler)
- **2** Thai chili peppers or 1 Fresno pepper, thinly sliced (optional)
- **2** teaspoons coconut oil or cooking fat of choice
- **2** large shallots, thinly sliced
- **¼** pound shiitake mushrooms, cut into quarters

  Diamond Crystal kosher salt
- **2** cups bone broth or chicken broth
- **2** (13.5-ounce) cans full-fat coconut milk, divided
- **1½** pounds boneless, skinless chicken thighs, cut into ½-inch strips
- **2** medium tomatoes, cut into wedges
- **1½** tablespoons paleo-friendly fish sauce or No-Fish Sauce (page 28)

  Juice from 2 medium limes
- **¼** cup chopped fresh cilantro leaves

1 LET'S START BY PREPPING SOME OF THE SPECIAL INGREDIENTS USED IN THIS RECIPE. FIRST, SMASH THE LEMONGRASS STALKS WITH A MEAT POUNDER.

2 THEN, TIE EACH STALK INTO A KNOT. THIS WILL BOTH HELP DRAW OUT AS MUCH FLAVOR AS POSSIBLE AND MAKE IT EASIER TO REMOVE FROM THE FINISHED SOUP.

3 THE "KHA" IN TOM KHA GAI MEANS GALANGAL, SO IT'S A CRUCIAL INGREDIENT. DON'T EVEN THINK ABOUT SUBSTITUTING SPICY GINGER FOR CITRUS-Y GALANGAL. THEY'RE COMPLETELY DIFFERENT IN FLAVOR.

4 SLICE THE GALANGAL INTO ¼-INCH COINS.

5 TEAR UP THE MAKRUT LIME LEAVES. (CAN'T FIND MAKRUT LIME LEAVES AT A NEARBY STORE? JUST SUBSTITUTE LIME ZEST CUT WITH A VEGETABLE PEELER INTO STRIPS.)

6 USING GLOVES, THINLY SLICE UP THE THAI CHILI PEPPERS. (IF YOU CAN'T HANDLE THE HEAT, YOU CAN LEAVE THEM OUT.)

7 HEAT A LARGE SAUCEPAN OVER MEDIUM HEAT, AND ADD THE OIL ONCE IT'S HOT. STIR IN THE SHALLOTS AND SHIITAKE MUSHROOMS WITH A SPRINKLE OF SALT.

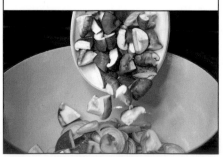

8 COOK, STIRRING, FOR **3** TO **5** MINUTES OR UNTIL THE SHALLOTS ARE SOFTENED BUT NOT BROWNED.

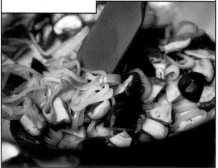

Per serving: 436 calories • 10 g carbohydrates • 26 g protein • 34 g fat • 1 g fiber

9 POUR IN THE BONE OR CHICKEN BROTH AND 1 CAN OF COCONUT MILK.

10 INCREASE THE HEAT TO MEDIUM-HIGH AND CONTINUE TO COOK, STIRRING FREQUENTLY, UNTIL THE CONTENTS START TO SIMMER.

11 ADD THE LEMONGRASS STALKS ...

12 ... GALANGAL COINS ...

13 ... AND TORN-UP MAKRUT LIME LEAVES.

14 MAINTAIN A SIMMER, DECREASING THE HEAT TO MEDIUM OR MEDIUM-LOW. COOK FOR 5 TO 10 MINUTES, STIRRING OCCASIONALLY, UNTIL THE AROMATICS HAVE INFUSED THE BROTH.

15 ADD THE CHICKEN. THEN, CRANK UP THE HEAT TO MEDIUM-HIGH.

16 BRING THE SOUP BACK TO A SIMMER AND COOK 'TIL THE CHICKEN'S NO LONGER PINK.

17 ADD THE REMAINING CAN OF COCONUT MILK ...

18 ... AND THE TOMATOES.

19 COOK, STIRRING OCCASIONALLY, UNTIL THE TOMATOES ARE HEATED THROUGH BUT NOT BROKEN DOWN.

20 FISH OUT AND DISCARD THE LEMONGRASS, LIME LEAVES, AND GALANGAL.

(RECIPE CONTINUES ON THE NEXT PAGE.)

21 TAKE THE POT OFF THE HEAT AND SEASON WITH 1½ TABLESPOONS FISH SAUCE, JUICE FROM 2 LIMES . . .

22 . . . AND ¼ CUP CHOPPED CILANTRO. TASTE THE SOUP AND ADJUST FOR SEASONING.

23 LADLE UP THE SOUP . . .

24 . . . AND ADD THAI CHILI PEPPERS TO THE BOWLS IF DESIRED. SERVE.

RICH AND INTENSE, THE AROMATIC AND COMPLEX FLAVORS OF THIS CHICKEN AND GALANGAL SOUP HAD ME CONVINCED FOR YEARS THAT IT'D BE FAR TOO COMPLICATED AND TIME-CONSUMING FOR ME TO MAKE MYSELF. BUT AFTER ATTENDING A COOKING CLASS IN CHIANG MAI, I SAW FIRSTHAND HOW EFFORTLESS IT IS TO PREPARE THIS THAI CLASSIC AT HOME. IT'S BECOME SUCH A FAVORITE IN OUR HOUSEHOLD THAT WE'VE EVEN SERVED IT AT THANKSGIVING DINNER!

TSUKUNE (JAPANESE CHICKEN MEATBALLS)

MAKES 24 MEATBALLS
●● 1¾ HOURS
(45 MINUTES HANDS-ON)

WHOLE30®	KETO-FRIENDLY
NUT-FREE	EGG-FREE
NIGHTSHADE-FREE	

⅓ cup All-Purpose Stir-Fry Sauce (page 29)

1½ pounds ground chicken thigh

1½ teaspoons Diamond Crystal kosher salt

½ teaspoon toasted sesame oil

2 scallions, minced

1 medium shallot, minced

1 dried shiitake mushroom

1 tablespoon avocado oil or ghee

2 tablespoons toasted sesame seeds (optional)

WHO DOESN'T LOVE CHICKEN BALLS?

MANY MOONS AGO, I FELL IN LOVE WITH TSUKUNE AT A BASEMENT-LEVEL YAKITORI JOINT IN TOKYO. OVER THE YEARS, I'VE STUFFED MY FACE WITH PLENTY OF CHICKEN DISHES, BUT MY HEART HAS ALWAYS BELONGED TO TSUKUNE: JUICY MEATBALLS GLAZED WITH A THIN LAYER OF TANGY-SWEET TARE SAUCE. LUCKILY, MY PALEO ALL-PURPOSE STIR-FRY SAUCE HITS THE SAME FLAVOR NOTES AS A CLASSIC TARE. (I TOLD YOU THAT SAUCE IS INSANELY VERSATILE!)

Per serving (6 meatballs): 332 calories • 7 g carbohydrates • 31 g protein • 20 g fat • 1 g fiber

1. GOT A BOTTLE OF ALL-PURPOSE STIR-FRY SAUCE? YOU'LL NEED IT FOR THIS RECIPE.

2. COMBINE THE GROUND CHICKEN, SALT, SESAME OIL, SCALLIONS, AND SHALLOT IN A LARGE BOWL. USE A RASP GRATER TO GRATE THE DRIED SHIITAKE INTO THE MEATBALL MIXTURE.

3. KNEAD THE MIXTURE VERY THOROUGHLY WITH YOUR HANDS. THE FINAL TEXTURE SHOULD BE STICKY AND TACKY.

4. IN A SKILLET, FRY UP A TINY PATTY AND TASTE IT FOR SEASONING. ADJUST WITH MORE SALT IF NEEDED.

5. COVER AND CHILL THE MEATBALL MIXTURE IN THE FRIDGE FOR AT LEAST 1 HOUR OR UP TO 1 DAY.

6. WHEN YOU'RE READY TO COOK, SET AN OVEN RACK 6 INCHES FROM THE HEATING ELEMENT AND TURN ON THE BROILER.

7. IN THE MEANTIME, BRUSH A RIMMED BAKING SHEET OR BROILER PAN WITH AVOCADO OIL. USING A 1½-TABLESPOON SCOOPER, SCOOP OUT 24 MEATBALLS . . .

8. . . . AND ROLL THEM INTO UNIFORM-SIZE BALLS WITH YOUR HANDS.

9. ARRANGE THE CHICKEN MEATBALLS EVENLY ON THE GREASED BAKING SHEET, AND BROIL FOR 2 MINUTES.

10. BRUSH THE CHICKEN MEATBALLS WITH ALL-PURPOSE STIR-FRY SAUCE. ROTATE THE TRAY 180 DEGREES AND BROIL FOR ANOTHER 2 MINUTES.

11. REPEAT STEP 10 TWICE MORE SO THAT THE MEATBALLS ARE BASTED 3 TIMES.

12. ONCE THE MEATBALLS ARE BROWNED AND COOKED THROUGH, PLATE THEM UP, SPRINKLE ON THE SESAME SEEDS, AND SERVE.

Refrigerate any leftover tsukune in an airtight container for up to 4 days or freeze 'em for up to 6 months. When you're ready to eat, reheat them in a 325°F oven or air fryer for about 5 minutes or until heated through.

SWITCH IT UP:
AIR FRYER TSUKUNE

Looking to make Tsukune in an air fryer? Set the temperature to 400°F and cook the chicken meatballs in batches for 10 to 12 minutes, basting every 2 to 3 minutes 'til they're done!

2-INGREDIENT CRISPY CHICKEN

MAKES 6 SERVINGS
● **1 HOUR**
(10 MINUTES HANDS-ON)

WHOLE30®	KETO-FRIENDLY
NUT-FREE	EGG-FREE
NIGHTSHADE-FREE	

3 pounds bone-in, skin-on chicken thighs

4 teaspoons Umami Stir-Fry Powder (page 43), Nomtastic Grilling Powder (page 44), or Diamond Crystal kosher salt

> THE RATIO OF EFFORT TO FLAVOR IS OFF THE CHARTS WITH THIS WEEKNIGHT CRISPY CHICKEN DINNER!

SWITCH IT UP: AIR FRYER 2-INGREDIENT CRISPY CHICKEN

WANNA MAKE THIS CHICKEN IN AN AIR FRYER INSTEAD? LAY THE CHICKEN SKIN-SIDE DOWN IN A SINGLE LAYER IN AN AIR FRYER BASKET, AND COOK AT 400°F FOR 20 TO 25 MINUTES, FLIPPING THE THIGHS SKIN-SIDE UP AT THE HALFWAY POINT.

1 HEAT THE OVEN TO 400°F ON CONVECTION MODE OR 425°F ON REGULAR MODE WITH THE RACK IN THE MIDDLE.

2 IN A LARGE BOWL, TOSS TOGETHER THE CHICKEN AND UMAMI STIR-FRY POWDER (OR NOMTASTIC GRILLING POWDER OR SALT).

3 MASSAGE THE POWDER ALL OVER THE CHICKEN. (COVER AND REFRIGERATE FOR UP TO A DAY IF NOT COOKING RIGHT AWAY.)

4 SET AN OVEN-SAFE WIRE RACK IN A RIMMED BAKING SHEET.

5 ARRANGE THE CHICKEN SKIN-SIDE DOWN IN A SINGLE LAYER ON THE RACK. DON'T OVERCROWD IT!

6 BAKE FOR 20 MINUTES. THEN, FLIP THE CHICKEN THIGHS SKIN-SIDE UP AND TURN THE TRAY AROUND.

7 BAKE FOR ANOTHER 20 TO 25 MINUTES OR UNTIL THE SKIN TURNS GOLDEN BROWN AND CRISPY AND THE THICKEST PARTS OF THE THIGHS REGISTER 165°F ON AN INSTANT-READ THERMOMETER.

8 SERVE IMMEDIATELY.

Per serving: 422 calories • 1 g carbohydrates • 31 g protein • 32 g fat • 0 g fiber

THIS IS THE SIMPLEST WAY TO GET CRISPY, JUICY, UMAMI-PACKED CHICKEN ON THE SUPPER TABLE. AND YES, YOU MUST USE SKIN-ON CHICKEN, PEOPLE. HOW ELSE DO YOU EXPECT TO GET YOUR CHICKEN TO CRISP UP PROPERLY?

CHICKEN KARAAGE (JAPANESE FRIED CHICKEN)

MAKES 6 SERVINGS
● 1 HOUR
(30 MINUTES HANDS-ON)

NUT-FREE

½ cup All-Purpose Stir-Fry Sauce (page 29)

2 pounds boneless, skinless chicken thighs

6 cups avocado oil for frying (or more, depending on the size of the cooking pot)

2 cups potato starch, divided

½ cup paleo-friendly mayonnaise

2 tablespoons honey

Shichimi togarashi (Japanese seven-spice blend) (optional)

Flake sea salt (optional)

2 lemons, cut into wedges (optional)

THE SAUCE TASTES LIKE PALEO KEWPIE MAYO!

1 I HOPE YOU HAVE SOME ALL-PURPOSE STIR-FRY SAUCE ON HAND, 'CAUSE YOU'LL NEED IT TO MAKE THIS CHICKEN KARAAGE.

2 PAT THE CHICKEN THIGHS DRY WITH A PAPER TOWEL AND CUT THEM INTO INCH-WIDE STRIPS OF ROUGHLY THE SAME SIZE.

3 PLACE THE CHICKEN PIECES IN A SHALLOW CONTAINER . . .

4 . . . AND THEN POUR IN THE ALL-PURPOSE STIR-FRY SAUCE.

5 TOSS TO MIX WELL.

6 COVER AND MARINATE IN THE FRIDGE FOR AT LEAST **30** MINUTES OR UP TO A DAY.

7 WHEN YOU'RE READY TO FRY THE CHICKEN, POUR AVOCADO OIL INTO A LARGE DUTCH OVEN OR HIGH-SIDED POT.

8 THE OIL SHOULD REACH ABOUT **2** INCHES UP THE SIDES OF THE POT.

Per serving: 490 calories • 14 g carbohydrates • 30 g protein • 36 g fat • 1 g fiber

9 HEAT THE OIL ON MEDIUM-HIGH UNTIL IT REACHES 350°F. (ONCE THE CHICKEN GOES IN, THE TEMPERATURE WILL DROP A BIT.)

10 WHILE THE OIL IS HEATING UP, DUMP 1 CUP OF POTATO STARCH INTO A LARGE, SHALLOW BOWL.

11 TAKE A FEW PIECES OF CHICKEN OUT OF THE MARINADE AND TOSS THEM INTO THE POTATO STARCH.

12 COAT THE PIECES WELL . . .

13 . . . SHAKING OFF ANY EXCESS STARCH.

14 PLACE THE COATED CHICKEN PIECES ON A WIRE RACK OVER A RIMMED BAKING SHEET.

15 REPEAT UNTIL ALL THE CHICKEN PIECES HAVE BEEN COATED IN POTATO STARCH. IF THE POTATO STARCH GETS TOO CLUMPY AFTER A WHILE, DUMP IT OUT AND ADD ANOTHER CUP OF FRESH POTATO STARCH.

16 WHEN THE OIL IS HOT, CAREFULLY ADD ABOUT A QUARTER OF THE CHICKEN PIECES TO THE OIL, MAKING SURE THEY'RE NOT OVERCROWDED.

17 FRY THE CHICKEN . . .

18 . . . UNTIL GOLDEN BROWN AND COOKED THROUGH, ABOUT 2 TO 3 MINUTES.

19 USE A SLOTTED SPOON OR SPIDER TO TRANSFER THE COOKED CHICKEN PIECES TO A PAPER TOWEL-LINED PLATE.

20 REPEAT WITH THE REMAINING CHICKEN PIECES, ADJUSTING THE HEAT TO MAINTAIN A COOKING OIL TEMPERATURE OF 350°F.

(RECIPE CONTINUES ON THE NEXT PAGE.)

191

21

TIME TO MAKE THE DIPPING SAUCE! MIX TOGETHER ½ CUP PALEO MAYONNAISE AND 2 TABLESPOONS HONEY TO MAKE A DIPPING SAUCE TO ACCOMPANY THE KARAAGE.

22

IF DESIRED, ADD A SPRINKLE OF SHICHIMI TOGARASHI . . .

23

. . . AND SEA SALT ON THE FRIED CHICKEN.

24

SERVE THE CHICKEN KARAAGE WITH LEMON WEDGES AND THE DIPPING SAUCE.

I DON'T KNOW IF IT'S THE CRISP, LIGHT COATING OR THE JUICY, FLAVORFUL NUGGETS OF MEAT, BUT THIS TRADITIONAL IZAKAYA (OR JAPANESE BAR) FOOD MAKES MY STOMACH RUMBLE IN THE BEST WAY POSSIBLE.

WHETHER YOU SERVE IT AS AN AFTERNOON SNACK OR AN ENTRÉE, I GUARANTEE THAT MY PALEO PLAY ON CHICKEN KARAAGE WILL MAKE A BELIEVER OUT OF YOU, TOO.

193

CHICKEN TIKKA MASALA

MAKES 6 SERVINGS
45 MINUTES

WHOLE30®	KETO-FRIENDLY
NUT-FREE	EGG-FREE

- **2** pounds boneless, skinless chicken thighs or breasts, cut into 1-inch cubes
- **1½** teaspoons Diamond Crystal kosher salt
- **2** tablespoons ghee
- **1** large onion, peeled and finely minced
- **2** tablespoons minced fresh ginger (or 2 teaspoons ground ginger)
- **4** garlic cloves, minced
- **2** teaspoons garam masala
- **2** teaspoons ground cumin
- **1** teaspoon turmeric powder
- **½** teaspoon cayenne pepper
- **1½** cups tomato purée
- **½** cup coconut cream
- **¼** cup minced fresh cilantro

I EAT THIS WITH BASMATI RICE, WHICH ISN'T PALEO, BUT I DON'T CARE!

TENDER CHICKEN SLOWLY SIMMERED IN A SPICED TOMATO-CREAM SAUCE, CHICKEN TIKKA MASALA IS A CLASSIC BRITISH-INDIAN FUSION DISH. SOME CLAIM THAT IT WAS INVENTED BY A PAKISTANI CHEF IN GLASGOW, OR PERHAPS A BANGLADESHI CHEF IN LONDON. OTHER CULINARY HISTORIANS TRACE IT BACK TO INDIA AS A VARIANT OF MURGH MAKHANI (A.K.A. BUTTER CHICKEN). NO ONE CAN PINPOINT CHIKEN TIKKA MASALA'S ORIGINS, BUT I CAN TELL YOU THAT MY SHORTCUT VERSION IS A CROWD-PLEASER NO MATTER WHERE YOU GO!

1 IN A MEDIUM BOWL, SEASON THE CHICKEN WITH 1½ TEASPOONS OF DIAMOND CRYSTAL KOSHER SALT AND SET ASIDE.

2 HEAT A LARGE SAUCEPAN OR SKILLET ON MEDIUM HEAT AND SWIRL IN 2 TABLESPOONS GHEE WHEN THE PAN IS HOT.

Per serving: 334 calories • 11 g carbohydrates • 32 g protein • 19 g fat • 3 g fiber

3 TOSS IN THE MINCED ONIONS . . .

4 . . . AND SAUTÉ FOR 5 TO 10 MINUTES, OR UNTIL SOFTENED.

5 NEXT, ADD THE GINGER, GARLIC, GARAM MASALA, CUMIN, TURMERIC, AND CAYENNE.

6 COOK, STIRRING, FOR 30 SECONDS OR UNTIL FRAGRANT.

7 MIX IN THE TOMATO PURÉE AND SCRAPE UP ANY BROWNED BITS.

8 ADD THE CHICKEN TO THE SAUCE AND STIR WELL.

9 INCREASE THE HEAT TO BRING THE SAUCE TO A BOIL.

10 LOWER THE HEAT TO MAINTAIN A SIMMER. COOK COVERED FOR 5 TO 10 MINUTES, STIRRING OCCASIONALLY, UNTIL THE CHICKEN IS FULLY COOKED THROUGH.

11 TASTE THE SAUCE FOR SEASONING. ADJUST WITH A LITTLE MORE SALT IF NECESSARY.

12 TURN OFF THE HEAT AND ADD THE COCONUT CREAM.

13 STIR WELL TO INCORPORATE THE CREAM.

14 TOP WITH MINCED CILANTRO. SERVE WITH CAULIFLOWER RICE (PAGE 107) IF DESIRED.

HOT AND STICKY CHICKEN

MAKES 6 SERVINGS
**1¼ HOURS
(15 MINUTES HANDS-ON)**

NUT-FREE	EGG-FREE

¾ cup coconut aminos

¼ cup honey

2 tablespoons Tabasco sauce or paleo-friendly pepper sauce

2 teaspoons Diamond Crystal kosher salt

3 large garlic cloves, minced

3 pounds chicken thighs

1 tablespoon toasted sesame seeds

WHAT'S HOT, STICKY, AND NEEDS TO GET IN YOUR MOUTH? THIS CHICKEN!

WITH THE SPICY TANG OF PEPPER SAUCE AND SWEETNESS OF HONEY, THIS CHICKEN DINNER'S DEFINITELY A WINNER. JUST MAKE SURE YOU HAVE PLENTY OF NAPKINS ON HAND!

BOOKMARK THIS PAGE, BECAUSE THIS IS WHAT YOU'LL COOK FOR DINNER THE NEXT TIME YOU FORGET TO GO GROCERY SHOPPING. MADE WITH COMMON PANTRY STAPLES, THIS SPICY, JUICY CHICKEN IS ASTONISHINGLY SIMPLE TO PREPARE.

Per serving: 506 calories • 19 g carbohydrates • 32 g protein • 33 g fat • 1 g fiber

1 HEAT THE OVEN TO 400°F ON CONVECTION MODE OR 425°F ON REGULAR MODE WITH THE RACK IN THE MIDDLE POSITION.

2 IN A MEASURING CUP, WHISK TOGETHER THE COCONUT AMINOS, HONEY, TABASCO SAUCE, SALT, AND GARLIC.

3 TOSS THE CHICKEN THIGHS INTO A LARGE BOWL AND POUR ABOUT ½ CUP OF THE SPICY MARINADE ON TOP. SET ASIDE THE REMAINING SAUCE.

4 TOSS THE CHICKEN WELL. MARINATE THE THIGHS FOR 30 MINUTES OR UP TO A DAY IN THE REFRIGERATOR.

5 WHILE THE CHICKEN IS MARINATING, POUR THE REMAINING ¾ CUP OF MARINADE INTO A SMALL SAUCEPAN. BRING TO A SIMMER OVER MEDIUM HEAT.

6 COOK THE LIQUID FOR 3 TO 5 MINUTES, STIRRING FREQUENTLY, UNTIL THICKENED. COVER AND SET ASIDE THE SAUCE.

7 PLACE THE CHICKEN THIGHS SKIN-SIDE DOWN ON A WIRE RACK SET IN A RIMMED BAKING SHEET.

8 ROAST FOR 20 MINUTES.

9 FLIP THE CHICKEN SKIN-SIDE UP AND COOK FOR ANOTHER 20 TO 25 MINUTES.

10 THE CHICKEN'S READY WHEN THE SKIN IS GOLDEN BROWN AND THE THICKEST PART OF THE THIGHS REGISTERS 165°F ON A MEAT THERMOMETER.

11 BRUSH ON THE REDUCED SAUCE.

12 GARNISH WITH SESAME SEEDS AND SERVE.

GREEK CHICKEN AND POTATOES

MAKES 6 SERVINGS
● **1 HOUR**
(20 MINUTES HANDS-ON)

WHOLE30®	NUT-FREE
EGG-FREE	

1 (4-pound) whole chicken

Diamond Crystal kosher salt

1 tablespoon lemon zest

⅓ cup extra-virgin olive oil

3 tablespoons lemon juice

6 garlic cloves, minced

1 tablespoon dried oregano or dried marjoram

¼ teaspoon freshly ground black pepper

1½ pounds Yukon Gold potatoes, cut into 1-inch cubes

¼ cup minced fresh Italian parsley (optional)

1 lemon, cut into wedges (optional)

1 START BY SPATCHCOCKING (BUTTERFLYING) THE CHICKEN. CUT OUT THE BACKBONE WITH A SHARP PAIR OF KITCHEN SHEARS.

2 OPEN UP THE BIRD LIKE A BOOK, LAYING IT BREAST-SIDE DOWN.

3 MAKE A ½-INCH INCISION IN THE CARTILAGE OF THE BREAST BONE...

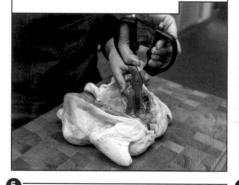

4 ...AND FIRMLY PRESS DOWN ON THE BREAST TO FLATTEN THE BIRD.

5 FLIP THE BIRD OVER, AND USE YOUR FINGERS TO GENTLY SEPARATE THE SKIN OF THE CHICKEN FROM THE MEAT TO CREATE POCKETS. TRY NOT TO TEAR ANY HOLES!

6 SEASON THE CHICKEN WITH 1 TABLESPOON SALT, BOTH OVER AND UNDER THE SKIN.

7 SET THE BIRD ASIDE OR REFRIGERATE IT UP TO 3 DAYS UNTIL YOU'RE READY TO ROAST.

8 WHEN YOU'RE READY TO COOK, HEAT THE OVEN TO 400°F ON CONVECTION MODE (OR 425°F ON REGULAR MODE) WITH THE RACK IN THE MIDDLE POSITION.

Per serving: 520 calories • 24 g carbohydrates • 30 g protein • 34 g fat • 4 g fiber

9 TO PREPARE THE LEMON ZEST, PEEL THE OUTERMOST LAYER FROM A LEMON...

10 ...AND MINCE IT. MEASURE OUT 1 TABLE-SPOON OF THE ZEST.

11 IN A MEASURING CUP, ADD THE LEMON ZEST, OLIVE OIL, LEMON JUICE, MINCED GARLIC CLOVES, AND DRIED OREGANO.

12 WHISK IT ALL TOGETHER.

13 SEASON WITH SALT AND PEPPER TO TASTE. (I LIKE TO USE ABOUT 1 TEASPOON KOSHER SALT AND ¼ TEASPOON BLACK PEPPER.)

14 PLACE THE CHICKEN ON A RIMMED BAKING SHEET, AND POUR ⅓ OF THE MARINADE ALL OVER THE TOP AND BOTTOM OF THE BIRD.

15 MASSAGE THE MARINADE INTO THE MEAT.

16 PLACE THE CHICKEN FLAT AGAINST THE BAKING SHEET WITH THE WINGS TUCKED BEHIND THE SHOULDERS.

17 IN A LARGE BOWL, TOSS THE CUBED POTA-TOES WITH THE REMAINING MARINADE.

18 SCATTER THEM AROUND THE CHICKEN...

19 ...MAKING SURE THE POTATOES ARE IN A SINGLE LAYER.

20 ROAST IN THE OVEN FOR 45 MINUTES...

(RECIPE CONTINUES ON THE NEXT PAGE.)

21 ...ROTATING THE TRAY AT THE HALFWAY POINT. IF THE CHICKEN IS BROWNING TOO FAST, PUT A BIT OF FOIL OVER THE SKIN.

22 THIS SHEET PAN SUPPER IS DONE WHEN THE CHICKEN TURNS GOLDEN BROWN, THE INTERNAL TEMPERATURE REACHES 150°F IN THE BREAST AND 165°F IN THE THICKEST PART OF THE THIGHS, AND THE POTATOES ARE BROWNED AND TENDER.

23 SPRINKLE ON ¼ CUP MINCED PARSLEY...

24 ...AND SERVE WITH LEMON WEDGES.

WITH THE BRIGHTNESS OF OREGANO, OLIVE OIL, LEMON, AND GARLIC, THIS SIMPLE MARINATED ROAST CHICKEN VIVIDLY EVOKES THE VIBRANT FLAVORS OF THE MEDITER-RANEAN. BEST OF ALL, THIS FAMILY-SIZE SHEET PAN SUPPER FEELS LIKE A FEAST!

SHEET PAN ITALIAN CHICKEN

MAKES 4 SERVINGS
◑ 30 MINUTES
(10 MINUTES HANDS-ON)

WHOLE30®	NUT-FREE
EGG-FREE	

- **2** teaspoons Magic Mushroom Powder (page 45) or Diamond Crystal kosher salt
- **1½** pounds boneless, skinless chicken thighs, cut into 1½-inch cubes
- **1** pound French green beans, trimmed
- **2** cups cherry tomatoes
- **½** cup Castelvetrano olives, pitted
- **1** small red onion, cut into ½-inch wedges
- **2** garlic cloves, minced
- **3** tablespoons extra-virgin olive oil
- **2** tablespoons aged balsamic vinegar
- **¼** cup minced fresh Italian parsley and/or basil

> THIS IS SO EASY EVEN I COULD MAKE IT! BUT I WON'T, 'CAUSE IF I JUST WAIT, SOMEONE ELSE'LL DO IT FOR ME.

1 GRAB SOME MAGIC MUSHROOM POWDER. HEAT THE OVEN TO 425°F ON CONVECTION MODE OR 450°F ON REGULAR MODE WITH THE RACK IN THE MIDDLE POSITION.

2 PUT THE CHICKEN, GREEN BEANS, CHERRY TOMATOES, OLIVES, ONIONS, AND GARLIC ON A SHEET PAN.

3 SEASON THE INGREDIENTS WITH THE MAGIC MUSHROOM POWDER AND OIL.

4 COMBINE EVERYTHING, MAKING SURE THE CHICKEN AND VEGGIES ARE WELL COATED.

5 SPREAD ALL THE INGREDIENTS IN A SINGLE LAYER ON THE SHEET PAN.

6 POP THE SHEET PAN IN THE OVEN AND ROAST FOR 15 TO 25 MINUTES, ROTATING THE TRAY HALFWAY THROUGH COOKING.

7 CHECK TO MAKE SURE THE CHICKEN PIECES ARE COOKED THROUGH (AN INSERTED MEAT THERMOMETER SHOULD REGISTER 165°F) AND THE GREEN BEANS ARE BLISTERED.

8 DRIZZLE ON THE AGED BALSAMIC VINEGAR, SPRINKLE ON FRESH HERBS, AND SERVE.

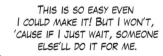

Per serving: 515 calories • 18 g carbohydrates • 27 g protein • 42 g fat • 5 g fiber

THIS SUPPER REMINDS ME OF SUMMER-
TIME IN ITALY, AND IT'S AS SIMPLE AND
DELICIOUS AS IT GETS: TOSS CHICKEN AND
VEGGIES ON A SHEET PAN, BAKE, AND EAT.
CLEAN-UP IS EASY-PEASY, TOO!

SHEET PAN "PEANUT" SAUCE CHICKEN AND BROCCOLINI

MAKES 4 SERVINGS
● **1 HOUR**
(30 MINUTES HANDS-ON)

WHOLE30®	NUT-FREE
EGG-FREE	

- **¼** cup Sunbutter Hoisin Sauce (page 32)
- **¼** cup sunflower seed butter
- **2** tablespoons rice vinegar
- **2** tablespoons water
- **½** cup full-fat coconut milk
- **2** tablespoons paleo-friendly fish sauce or No-Fish Sauce (page 28)
- **1** tablespoon Thai red curry paste
- **1** large Medjool date, pitted and chopped
- **3** garlic cloves, peeled and roughly chopped
- **½** teaspoon ground turmeric
- **1½** pounds boneless, skinless chicken breasts or thighs, cut into ½-inch strips
- **1** pound broccolini, ends trimmed
- **2** tablespoons avocado oil
- **¾** teaspoon Umami Stir-Fry Powder (page 43) or Diamond Crystal kosher salt
- **2** scallions, thinly sliced
- **1** tablespoon toasted black sesame seeds

LOVE CHICKEN SATAY, BUT HATE STABBING SLIPPERY PIECES OF RAW CHICKEN ONTO THE POINTY ENDS OF SKEWERS? THEN POP THIS ALL-IN-ONE SHEET PAN MEAL INTO THE OVEN AND DRIZZLE ON THE PEANUT-FREE SAUCE AT THE END. IF YOU MARINATE THE CHICKEN AHEAD OF TIME, DINNER CAN BE ON THE TABLE IN JUST 30 MINUTES!

1 FIRST, MAKE THE "PEANUT" SAUCE. PUT THE HOISIN SAUCE, SUNFLOWER SEED BUTTER, VINEGAR, AND WATER IN A BLENDER.

2 BLITZ UNTIL SMOOTH. POUR THE SAUCE INTO A CONTAINER AND SET IT ASIDE. (THIS SAUCE WILL KEEP IN THE FRIDGE FOR UP TO 4 DAYS.)

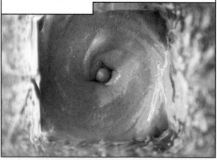

Per serving: 502 calories • 28 g carbohydrates • 45 g protein • 23 g fat • 2 g fiber

3 IN THE NOW-EMPTY BLENDER CUP, ADD THE COCONUT MILK, FISH SAUCE, THAI CURRY PASTE, DATE, GARLIC, AND TURMERIC.

4 BLITZ UNTIL SMOOTH TO FORM A MARINADE FOR THE CHICKEN.

5 PUT THE CHICKEN IN A LARGE BOWL, AND POUR THE MARINADE OVER IT.

6 MIX WELL. COVER AND MARINATE IN THE FRIDGE FOR AT LEAST 30 MINUTES OR UP TO 12 HOURS.

7 WHEN YOU'RE READY TO COOK, HEAT THE OVEN TO 400°F ON CONVECTION MODE OR 425°F ON REGULAR MODE WITH THE RACK IN THE MIDDLE POSITION.

8 ON A RIMMED BAKING SHEET, TOSS THE BROCCOLINI WITH AVOCADO OIL AND UMAMI STIR-FRY POWDER.

9 THEN, NUDGE THE BROCCOLINI TO EITHER SIDE OF THE SHEET PAN TO MAKE SPACE FOR THE CHICKEN IN THE MIDDLE.

10 ARRANGE THE CHICKEN IN A SINGLE LAYER IN THE MIDDLE OF THE SHEET PAN.

11 COOK IN THE OVEN FOR 15 TO 20 MINUTES, ROTATING THE TRAY AND TOSSING THE INGREDIENTS AT THE HALFWAY POINT.

12 THE SHEET PAN SUPPER'S READY WHEN THE CHICKEN'S COOKED THROUGH AND THE BROCCOLINI IS TENDER-CRISP.

13 TAKE IT OUT OF THE OVEN AND GARNISH WITH SCALLIONS AND SESAME SEEDS.

14 DRIZZLE ON THE SAUCE AND SERVE.

SHEET PAN PINEAPPLE CHICKEN

MAKES 4 SERVINGS
● **1 HOUR**
(40 MINUTES HANDS-ON)

NUT-FREE	EGG-FREE

1 (13.5-ounce) can pineapple rings in pineapple juice

½ cup paleo-friendly ketchup

½ cup coconut aminos

2 tablespoons rice vinegar or apple cider vinegar

2 tablespoons honey

1 tablespoon paleo-friendly fish sauce or No-Fish Sauce (page 28)

1 teaspoon sesame oil

1 teaspoon ground ginger

5 garlic cloves, minced

1½ pounds boneless, skinless chicken thighs

¾ teaspoon Diamond Crystal kosher salt

1 teaspoon toasted sesame seeds

2 scallions, thinly sliced

> DON'T SUBSTITUTE FRESH PINEAPPLE AND GINGER FOR CANNED PINEAPPLE AND GROUND GINGER! THE FRESH STUFF CONTAINS ENZYMES THAT WILL BREAK DOWN PROTEINS, MAKING YOUR CHICKEN UNPALATABLY MUSHY.

1 OPEN UP THE PINEAPPLE CAN AND SET ASIDE THE PINEAPPLE RINGS.

2 POUR ½ CUP OF THE PINEAPPLE JUICE FROM THE CAN INTO A LARGE MEASURING CUP. (WE WON'T BE USING THE REST.)

3 ADD THE KETCHUP, COCONUT AMINOS, RICE VINEGAR, HONEY, FISH SAUCE, AND SESAME OIL TO THE JUICE IN THE MEASURING CUP.

4 TOSS IN THE GROUND GINGER . . .

5 . . . AND MINCED GARLIC.

6 WHISK IT ALL TOGETHER TO FORM A MARINADE.

7 PLACE THE CHICKEN IN A MEDIUM BOWL AND SPRINKLE WITH THE SALT. POUR IN ½ CUP OF THE MARINADE. SET ASIDE THE REST OF THE MARINADE.

8 TOSS THE CHICKEN WELL.

Per serving: 421 calories • 40 g carbohydrates • 29 g protein • 16 g fat • 2 g fiber

9 COVER AND MARINATE FOR **30** MINUTES OR UP TO A DAY IN THE FRIDGE.

10 IN THE MEANTIME, POUR THE REMAINING MARINADE INTO A SMALL SAUCEPAN AND BRING IT TO A BOIL OVER HIGH HEAT.

11 THEN, DECREASE THE HEAT TO MAINTAIN A SIMMER FOR ABOUT **20** MINUTES . . .

12 . . . UNTIL THE LIQUID HAS THICKENED INTO A SAUCE. REMOVE FROM THE HEAT AND SET ASIDE. YOU SHOULD NOW HAVE ABOUT **1** CUP OF SAUCE.

13 SET ASIDE ABOUT ¼ CUP OF THE SAUCE TO BASTE THE CHICKEN, AND SAVE THE REST TO SERVE WITH THE FINISHED DISH.

14 HEAT THE OVEN TO 400°F ON CONVECTION MODE OR 425°F ON REGULAR MODE WITH THE RACK IN THE MIDDLE.

15 ARRANGE THE CHICKEN THIGHS AND THE PINEAPPLE RINGS IN A SINGLE LAYER ON A RIMMED, GREASED, OR PARCHMENT-LINED BAKING SHEET.

16 BAKE FOR 15 MINUTES.

17 THEN, ROTATE THE TRAY AND BRUSH THE RESERVED ¼ CUP OF COOKED SAUCE ONTO THE CHICKEN AND PINEAPPLE RINGS.

18 BAKE FOR AN ADDITIONAL 5 TO 10 MINUTES OR UNTIL THE THICKEST PART OF THE THIGHS REGISTERS 165°F ON A MEAT THERMOMETER.

19 GARNISH THE CHICKEN AND PINEAPPLE WITH SESAME SEEDS AND SCALLIONS.

20 SERVE WITH THE RESERVED SAUCE!

This easy sheet pan meal is my riff on Huli Huli Chicken, a classic Hawaiian barbecue staple featuring a sweet and savory sauce made with pineapple juice, ketchup, and soy sauce. Believe me: no one can resist a pan of sticky chicken and pineapple, especially when it's re-imagined with healthier, paleo-friendly ingredients.

POACHED CHICKEN WITH GINGER SCALLION SAUCE

MAKES 6 SERVINGS
● **1 HOUR**
(15 MINUTES HANDS-ON)

WHOLE30®	KETO-FRIENDLY
NUT-FREE	EGG-FREE
NIGHTSHADE-FREE	

¼ cup Ginger Scallion Sauce (page 33)

4 (12-ounce) chicken breasts, skin-on and bone-in

2 scallions, root end trimmed

4 (¼-inch) slices fresh ginger, peeled and smashed

3 garlic cloves, peeled and smashed

I USUALLY PREFER USING CHICKEN THIGHS OVER BREASTS, BUT THIS RECIPE IS AN EXCEPTION 'CAUSE THE WHITE MEAT ACTUALLY STAYS JUICY AND TENDER. YOU CAN'T OVERCOOK THIS CHICKEN 'CAUSE IT'S POACHED OFF THE HEAT SOURCE!

A VERSION OF THIS CHICKEN DISH IS SERVED AT CHINESE WEDDING BANQUETS AND LUNAR NEW YEAR CELEBRATIONS, BUT IT'S NOT JUST FOR SPECIAL OCCASIONS: IT'S ANYTIME FOOD!

WHETHER IT'S SERVED HOT OR COLD, THIS IS CANTONESE HOME COOKING AT ITS FINEST, WITH MINIMAL INGREDIENTS AND CLEAN, BRIGHT FLAVORS. GIVEN THE UTTER SIMPLICITY OF THE PREPARATION, YOU'LL BE SURPRISED BY HOW MUCH TASTINESS THIS CHICKEN DELIVERS.

Per serving: 305 calories • 2 g carbohydrates • 49 g protein • 11 g fat • 1 g fiber

1 GRAB SOME GINGER SCALLION SAUCE, AND TAKE THE CHICKEN OUT OF THE REFRIGERATOR 30 MINUTES BEFORE COOKING. (YOU DON'T WANT IT TO BE SUPER COLD!)

2 FILL A LARGE SAUCEPAN OR STOCKPOT WITH ENOUGH WATER TO REACH 4 INCHES UP THE SIDES.

3 ADD THE SCALLIONS, GINGER, AND GARLIC.

4 COVER THE POT AND BRING THE WATER TO A ROLLING BOIL OVER HIGH HEAT.

5 SLIP THE BREASTS INTO THE HOT WATER IN A SINGLE LAYER, SUBMERGING THEM COMPLETELY. COVER AND BRING THE CONTENTS OF THE POT BACK UP TO A BOIL.

6 ONCE THE WATER'S BOILING AGAIN, SLIDE THE COVERED POT OFF THE HEAT.

7 LEAVE THE BREASTS IN THE COVERED POT TO POACH FOR 30 TO 45 MINUTES WHILE OFF THE HEAT SOURCE.

8 USE A MEAT THERMOMETER TO CHECK THAT THE THICKEST PART OF THE BREASTS REGISTER BETWEEN 150° AND 165°F.

9 FISH OUT THE BREASTS AND PAT 'EM DRY.

10 REMOVE THE BONES AND THE SKIN (IF DESIRED). THIS CHICKEN CAN BE SERVED HOT OR COLD, SO REFRIGERATE THE BREASTS IF YOU'RE NOT EATING RIGHT AWAY.

11 SLICE THE CHICKEN AGAINST THE GRAIN.

12 PLATE THE CHICKEN AND DRIZZLE GENEROUSLY WITH GINGER SCALLION SAUCE.

CHEESY CHICKEN AND KALE CASSEROLE

MAKES 6 SERVINGS
⏱ 45 MINUTES
(30 MINUTES HANDS-ON)

WHOLE30®	EGG-FREE

1 cup Cashew Cheese Sauce (page 34)

2 teaspoons Magic Mushroom Powder (page 45) or Diamond Crystal kosher salt, divided

1¼ pounds boneless, skinless chicken thighs, cut into 1-inch cubes

4 tablespoons extra-virgin olive oil, divided

1 small onion, diced

3 garlic cloves, minced

2 tablespoons water

1 bunch curly kale, stems removed and leaves roughly torn

1 medium cauliflower head, riced (or 16 ounces fresh or frozen riced cauliflower) (page 107)

> DON'T HAVE ANY RICED CAULIFLOWER ON HAND? YOU CAN USE 1 POUND OF RICED BROCCOLI OR SHREDDED HANNAH WHITE-FLESHED SWEET POTATOES INSTEAD!

① YOU'LL NEED CASHEW CHEESE SAUCE FOR THIS RECIPE, SO GRAB OR MAKE SOME.

② IF YOU HAVE MAGIC MUSHROOM POWDER, GRAB THAT, TOO. (OTHERWISE, JUST USE SALT FOR THIS RECIPE.)

③ THEN, HEAT THE OVEN TO 400°F WITH THE RACK IN THE MIDDLE.

④ TOSS THE CHICKEN WITH 1 TEASPOON MAGIC MUSHROOM POWDER OR SALT.

⑤ HEAT A 12-INCH OVEN-SAFE SKILLET OVER MEDIUM HEAT. SWIRL IN 2 TABLESPOONS OF OLIVE OIL.

⑥ ADD THE CHICKEN TO THE SKILLET . . .

⑦ . . . AND COOK FOR **3** TO **5** MINUTES . . .

⑧ . . . OR UNTIL THE CHICKEN CUBES ARE NO LONGER PINK.

Per serving: 398 calories • 16 g carbohydrates • 26 g protein • 27 g fat • 3 g fiber

9 Transfer to a plate and set it aside.

10 Add the remaining 2 tablespoons of olive oil to the skillet and toss in the diced onion.

11 Cook, stirring, for 5 minutes or until the onions are translucent.

12 Stir in the minced garlic and cook for about a minute or so until fragrant.

13 Add 2 tablespoons of water to deglaze the pan, and then add the kale.

14 Cook the kale for 3 to 5 minutes or until wilted. Then, turn off the heat.

15 Add the riced cauliflower . . .

16 . . . as well as the remaining teaspoon of Magic Mushroom Powder or salt.

17 Stir to incorporate.

18 Then, add in the reserved chicken . . .

19 . . . and the Cashew Cheese Sauce.

20 Mix well.

(Recipe continues on the next page.)

21 Use a spatula to smooth the top of the casserole.

22 Pop the skillet into the oven . . .

23 . . . and cook for 15 minutes or until the casserole is bubbly.

24 Serve immediately.

OH, KALE YEAH!

ON LAZY EVENINGS WHEN YOU JUST WANT TO SPRAWL IN FRONT OF THE TV, THERE'S NOTHING BETTER THAN A HOMEY MEAL OF CHEESY, COMFORTING CHICKEN CASSEROLE. WHO'S WITH ME?

CHICKEN AND BROCCOLI HAND PIES

MAKES 6 HAND PIES
●● 1¾ HOURS
(45 MINUTES HANDS-ON)

• FILLING •

2   cups diced cooked chicken

1   cup roughly chopped cooked broccoli florets

½   cup Cashew Cheese Sauce (page 34)

   Diamond Crystal kosher salt

   Freshly ground black pepper

• DOUGH •

2   cups (256 grams) cassava flour

½   cup (72 grams) tapioca flour

1½   teaspoons Diamond Crystal kosher salt

1   teaspoon ground turmeric

¾   cup (168 grams) ghee, coconut oil, or palm shortening, chilled solid and coarsely chopped

3   large eggs, divided

½   cup ice water, plus more if needed

> HAND PIES SHOULD BE SHAPED LIKE ACTUAL HANDS SO YOU CAN BITE THE HAND THAT FEEDS YOU!

1. LET'S START BY MAKING THE FILLING. PUT THE CHICKEN, BROCCOLI, AND CASHEW CHEESE SAUCE IN A LARGE BOWL.

2. MIX WELL TO COAT. TASTE FOR SEASONING AND ADJUST WITH SALT AND PEPPER.

3. COVER AND REFRIGERATE UNTIL YOU'RE READY TO ASSEMBLE THE HAND PIES.

4. TIME TO MAKE THE DOUGH! ADD THE CASSAVA FLOUR, TAPIOCA FLOUR, SALT, TURMERIC, GHEE, AND 2 EGGS TO THE WORK BOWL OF A FOOD PROCESSOR.

5. PULSE UNTIL THE DRY INGREDIENTS RESEMBLE COARSE BREADCRUMBS.

6. TRANSFER THE CONTENTS FROM THE FOOD PROCESSOR TO A LARGE MIXING BOWL.

7. DRIZZLE IN SOME ICE WATER, 2 TABLESPOONS AT A TIME . . .

8. . . . FOLDING IT IN WITH A SPATULA . . .

Per hand pie: 599 calories • 46 g carbohydrates • 19 g protein • 38 g fat • 2 g fiber

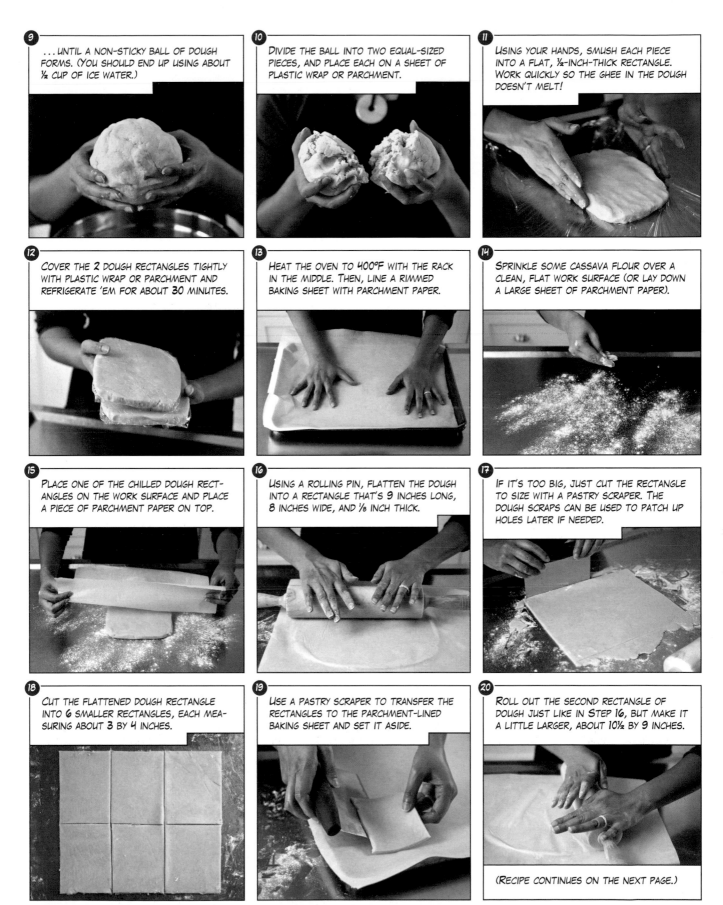

9 ...UNTIL A NON-STICKY BALL OF DOUGH FORMS. (YOU SHOULD END UP USING ABOUT ½ CUP OF ICE WATER.)

10 DIVIDE THE BALL INTO TWO EQUAL-SIZED PIECES, AND PLACE EACH ON A SHEET OF PLASTIC WRAP OR PARCHMENT.

11 USING YOUR HANDS, SMUSH EACH PIECE INTO A FLAT, ½-INCH-THICK RECTANGLE. WORK QUICKLY SO THE GHEE IN THE DOUGH DOESN'T MELT!

12 COVER THE 2 DOUGH RECTANGLES TIGHTLY WITH PLASTIC WRAP OR PARCHMENT AND REFRIGERATE 'EM FOR ABOUT 30 MINUTES.

13 HEAT THE OVEN TO 400°F WITH THE RACK IN THE MIDDLE. THEN, LINE A RIMMED BAKING SHEET WITH PARCHMENT PAPER.

14 SPRINKLE SOME CASSAVA FLOUR OVER A CLEAN, FLAT WORK SURFACE (OR LAY DOWN A LARGE SHEET OF PARCHMENT PAPER).

15 PLACE ONE OF THE CHILLED DOUGH RECTANGLES ON THE WORK SURFACE AND PLACE A PIECE OF PARCHMENT PAPER ON TOP.

16 USING A ROLLING PIN, FLATTEN THE DOUGH INTO A RECTANGLE THAT'S 9 INCHES LONG, 8 INCHES WIDE, AND ⅛ INCH THICK.

17 IF IT'S TOO BIG, JUST CUT THE RECTANGLE TO SIZE WITH A PASTRY SCRAPER. THE DOUGH SCRAPS CAN BE USED TO PATCH UP HOLES LATER IF NEEDED.

18 CUT THE FLATTENED DOUGH RECTANGLE INTO 6 SMALLER RECTANGLES, EACH MEASURING ABOUT 3 BY 4 INCHES.

19 USE A PASTRY SCRAPER TO TRANSFER THE RECTANGLES TO THE PARCHMENT-LINED BAKING SHEET AND SET IT ASIDE.

20 ROLL OUT THE SECOND RECTANGLE OF DOUGH JUST LIKE IN STEP 16, BUT MAKE IT A LITTLE LARGER, ABOUT 10½ BY 9 INCHES.

(RECIPE CONTINUES ON THE NEXT PAGE.)

21 CUT THIS BIG DOUGH SHEET INTO 6 RECTANGLES THAT MEASURE ABOUT 3½ INCHES BY 4½ INCHES. SET ASIDE.

22 EVENLY DISTRIBUTE THE CHICKEN FILLING ONTO EACH OF THE 6 DOUGH RECTANGLES ON THE BAKING SHEET.

23 BEAT THE REMAINING EGG IN A SMALL BOWL.

24 BRUSH THE EGG WASH ON THE EDGES OF THE DOUGH PIECES.

25 PLACE THE 6 RESERVED DOUGH RECTANGLES ON TOP OF THE CHICKEN FILLING.

26 SEAL THE EDGES UP WITH YOUR FINGERS (OR CRIMP 'EM WITH A FORK). GOT CRACKS IN THE DOUGH? JUST USE A BIT OF WATER OR DOUGH SCRAPS TO PATCH THEM UP.

27 BRUSH THE EGG WASH ON TOP OF THE HAND PIES.

28 USE A SHARP PARING KNIFE TO CUT 3 SLITS ON THE TOP OF EACH PIE.

29 POP THE TRAY OF PIES IN THE OVEN.

30 BAKE FOR 25 TO 30 MINUTES, ROTATING AT THE HALFWAY POINT.

31 THE HAND PIES ARE DONE WHEN THE TOPS ARE GOLDEN BROWN.

32 TRANSFER THE HAND PIES TO A WIRE RACK TO COOL TO ROOM TEMPERATURE. EAT!

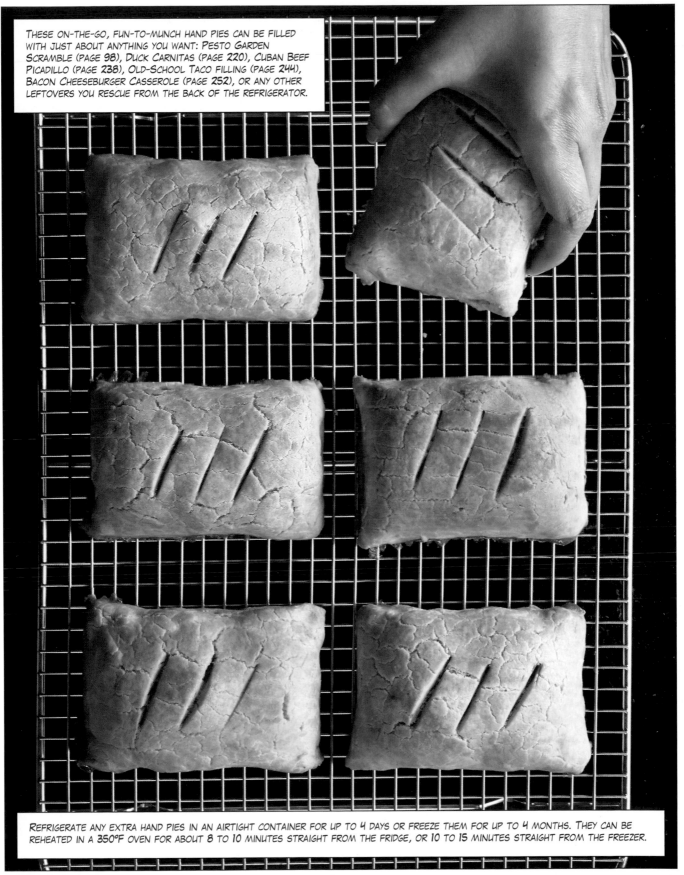

These on-the-go, fun-to-munch hand pies can be filled with just about anything you want: Pesto Garden Scramble (page 98), Duck Carnitas (page 220), Cuban Beef Picadillo (page 238), Old-School Taco Filling (page 244), Bacon Cheeseburger Casserole (page 252), or any other leftovers you rescue from the back of the refrigerator.

Refrigerate any extra hand pies in an airtight container for up to 4 days or freeze them for up to 4 months. They can be reheated in a 350°F oven for about 8 to 10 minutes straight from the fridge, or 10 to 15 minutes straight from the freezer.

INSTANT POT DUCK CARNITAS

MAKES 4 SERVINGS
●● 2 HOURS
(30 MINUTES HANDS-ON)

WHOLE30®	KETO-FRIENDLY
NUT-FREE	EGG-FREE

• CARNITAS •

2 teaspoons ground cumin

1½ teaspoons Diamond Crystal kosher salt

1 teaspoon dried Mexican oregano

½ teaspoon crushed red pepper flakes

4 duck legs

1 large yellow onion, peeled and quartered

6 garlic cloves, peeled

1 medium orange

1 dried bay leaf

2 tablespoons duck fat, ghee, or avocado oil

• GARNISH •

1 small white onion, finely diced (optional)

2 tablespoons minced fresh cilantro (optional)

1 cup tomato salsa (optional)

2 limes, cut into wedges (optional)

8 Grain-Free Tortillas (page 48) (not Whole30), butter lettuce leaves, or thinly sliced jicama (optional)

1 FIRST, LET'S PREP THE DUCK FOR COOKING. COMBINE THE CUMIN, SALT, OREGANO, AND RED PEPPER FLAKES IN A SMALL BOWL.

2 MASSAGE THE SPICE BLEND ALL OVER THE DUCK LEGS.

3 PLOP THE ONION AND GARLIC CLOVES INTO THE INSERT OF AN INSTANT POT.

4 PLACE THE DUCK LEGS SKIN-SIDE UP IN A SINGLE LAYER ON TOP OF THE ONION AND GARLIC IN THE INSTANT POT INSERT.

5 USING A VEGETABLE PEELER, PEEL WIDE STRIPS OF ZEST OFF THE ENTIRE ORANGE. STAY CLOSE TO THE SURFACE, MAKING SURE TO AVOID DIGGING INTO THE BITTER WHITE PITH.

6 PLACE THE STRIPS OF ORANGE ZEST INTO THE INSTANT POT.

7 JUICE THE ORANGE. YOU SHOULD END UP WITH ABOUT ½ CUP JUICE.

8 POUR THE JUICE INTO THE INSTANT POT INSERT. DROP IN THE BAY LEAF.

Per serving: 478 calories • 9 g carbohydrates • 47 g protein • 27 g fat • 2 g fiber

9 COVER AND SEAL THE INSTANT POT, AND PROGRAM IT TO COOK UNDER HIGH PRESSURE FOR 45 MINUTES.

10 AFTER THE DUCK IS DONE COOKING, LET THE PRESSURE DROP NATURALLY. IF YOU'RE IMPATIENT, MANUALLY RELEASE THE PRESSURE AFTER 20 MINUTES HAS PASSED.

11 CAREFULLY REMOVE THE DUCK LEGS. THE MEAT SHOULD BE FORK-TENDER, SO DON'T MANHANDLE THE COOKED LEGS OR THE DUCK MEAT MIGHT FALL APART ON YOU.

12 AT THIS POINT, IF YOU'RE NOT PLANNING TO EAT THE CARNITAS RIGHT AWAY, YOU CAN STORE THE DUCK IN A SEALED CONTAINER IN THE FRIDGE FOR UP TO 4 DAYS.

13 CAREFULLY REMOVE THE DUCK SKIN AND SHRED UP THE MEAT. DISCARD THE BONES.

14 HEAT THE DUCK FAT IN A LARGE PAN OVER MEDIUM HEAT AND CAREFULLY ADD THE RESERVED DUCK SKIN.

15 COOK THE SKIN FOR 5 TO 10 MINUTES, FLIPPING HALFWAY THROUGH, UNTIL DEEP GOLDEN BROWN AND CRISP ON BOTH SIDES.

16 TRANSFER THE CRISPY DUCK SKINS TO PAPER TOWELS TO DRAIN.

17 CRUMBLE UP THE SKIN INTO SMALL PIECES AND SET ASIDE.

18 ADD THE MEAT TO THE SKILLET AND COOK ABOUT 7 TO 10 MINUTES, STIRRING OCCASIONALLY TO ENSURE EVEN BROWNING.

19 ONCE THE MEAT REACHES YOUR DESIRED CRISPNESS, TRANSFER IT TO A SERVING PLATE OR BOWL.

20 LET'S PREPARE THE GARNISH. IN A BOWL, MIX TOGETHER THE ONIONS AND CILANTRO.

(RECIPE CONTINUES ON THE NEXT PAGE.)

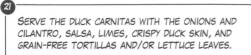

21 SERVE THE DUCK CARNITAS WITH THE ONIONS AND CILANTRO, SALSA, LIMES, CRISPY DUCK SKIN, AND GRAIN-FREE TORTILLAS AND/OR LETTUCE LEAVES.

I'M A DIE-HARD PORK CARNITAS SUPERFAN. BUT CARNITAS IS A MICHOACÁNO DISH THAT LITERALLY MEANS "LITTLE MEATS," SO THERE'S NO REASON IT HAS TO BE MADE WITH PORK, OR ANY OTHER FOUR-LEGGED LAND ANIMAL FOR THAT MATTER. IN FACT, MY FAVORITE MEAT FOR CARNITAS COMES FROM WATERFOWL. SUCCULENT, EARTHY, AND FRIED CRISPY AROUND THE EDGES, DUCK CARNITAS IS MELTINGLY TENDER AND OFFERS UP FRAGRANT NOTES OF CITRUS AND SPICES. SERVE THE CARNITAS IN GRAIN-FREE TORTILLAS WITH A SPRINKLE OF CRACKLY DUCK SKIN AND YOU'LL SOON BE A CONVERT, TOO.

SWITCH IT UP:
SLOW COOKER
DUCK CARNITAS

NO INSTANT POT? IF YOU HAVE A SLOW COOKER, DON'T SWEAT IT. JUST TOSS ALL OF THE CARNITAS INGREDIENTS IN THE COOKER (PUT THE DUCK LEGS IN FIRST, AND THEN PUT ALL THE OTHER STUFF ON TOP) AND COOK ON LOW FOR 8 HOURS!

CANTONESE PIPA DUCK

MAKES 4 SERVINGS
⚠ **2 DAYS**
(45 MINUTES HANDS-ON)

WHOLE30®	NUT-FREE
EGG-FREE	NIGHTSHADE-FREE

- **1** cup All-Purpose Stir-Fry Sauce (page 29)
- **1** (5-pound) Pekin duck, innards removed
- **6** cups boiling water
- **1** teaspoon Chinese five-spice powder
- **2** tablespoons avocado oil or avocado oil spray
- **½** cup Sunbutter Hoisin Sauce (page 32) (optional)

THIS DISH GOT ITS NAME 'CAUSE WHEN A DUCK IS ROASTED FLAT WITH ITS LONG NECK INTACT, IT RESEMBLES A CHINESE LUTE GUITAR CALLED A PIPA (PRONOUNCED "PEI PA").

BUTTERFLIED TO ENSURE QUICKER AND MORE EVEN COOKING, THIS DUCK IS MUSIC TO MY MOUTH!

1 GOT SOME ALL-PURPOSE STIR-FRY SAUCE? IF NOT, MAKE SOME ALREADY.

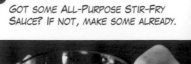

2 PLACE THE DUCK IN A COLANDER IN THE SINK, AND POUR THE BOILING WATER ALL OVER THE DUCK.

3 FLIP THE BIRD (HA!) WITH A PAIR OF TONGS TO MAKE SURE THE BOILING WATER HITS EVERY INCH OF SKIN.

4 PAT THE DUCK DRY WITH PAPER TOWELS. TRIM OFF ANY LUMPS OF EXCESS FAT AND EXTRA SKIN.

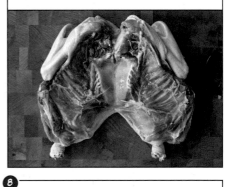

5 CUT OUT THE DUCK'S BACKBONE WITH A SHARP PAIR OF KITCHEN SHEARS. THEN, FLIP THE DUCK BREAST-SIDE DOWN AND MAKE A SMALL INCISION IN THE CARTILAGE OF THE BREASTBONE.

6 FIRMLY PRESS DOWN WITH YOUR HANDS TO FLATTEN OUT (SPATCHCOCK) THE DUCK.

7 FLIP THE DUCK OVER AND USE A SHARP PARING KNIFE TO STAB LITTLE HOLES ALL OVER THE SURFACE OF THE SKIN. PLACE THE DUCK IN A LARGE BOWL.

8 WHISK TOGETHER THE ALL-PURPOSE STIR-FRY SAUCE AND CHINESE FIVE-SPICE POWDER TO FORM A MARINADE.

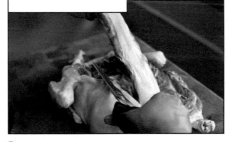

Per serving: 814 calories • 28 g carbohydrates • 38 g protein • 63 g fat • 5 g fiber

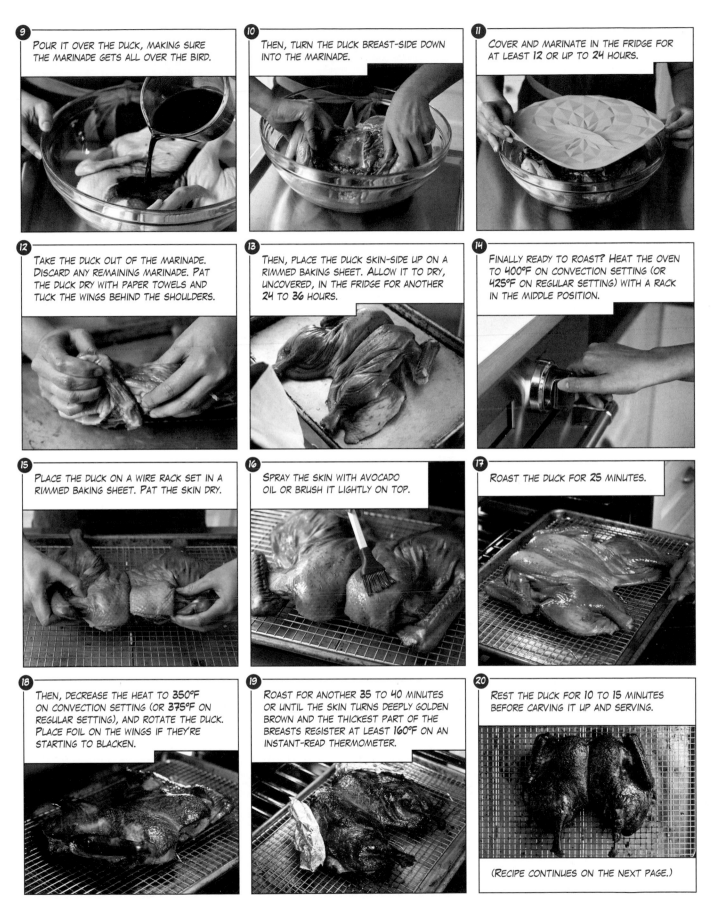

9 POUR IT OVER THE DUCK, MAKING SURE THE MARINADE GETS ALL OVER THE BIRD.

10 THEN, TURN THE DUCK BREAST-SIDE DOWN INTO THE MARINADE.

11 COVER AND MARINATE IN THE FRIDGE FOR AT LEAST 12 OR UP TO 24 HOURS.

12 TAKE THE DUCK OUT OF THE MARINADE. DISCARD ANY REMAINING MARINADE. PAT THE DUCK DRY WITH PAPER TOWELS AND TUCK THE WINGS BEHIND THE SHOULDERS.

13 THEN, PLACE THE DUCK SKIN-SIDE UP ON A RIMMED BAKING SHEET. ALLOW IT TO DRY, UNCOVERED, IN THE FRIDGE FOR ANOTHER 24 TO 36 HOURS.

14 FINALLY READY TO ROAST? HEAT THE OVEN TO 400°F ON CONVECTION SETTING (OR 425°F ON REGULAR SETTING) WITH A RACK IN THE MIDDLE POSITION.

15 PLACE THE DUCK ON A WIRE RACK SET IN A RIMMED BAKING SHEET. PAT THE SKIN DRY.

16 SPRAY THE SKIN WITH AVOCADO OIL OR BRUSH IT LIGHTLY ON TOP.

17 ROAST THE DUCK FOR 25 MINUTES.

18 THEN, DECREASE THE HEAT TO 350°F ON CONVECTION SETTING (OR 375°F ON REGULAR SETTING), AND ROTATE THE DUCK. PLACE FOIL ON THE WINGS IF THEY'RE STARTING TO BLACKEN.

19 ROAST FOR ANOTHER 35 TO 40 MINUTES OR UNTIL THE SKIN TURNS DEEPLY GOLDEN BROWN AND THE THICKEST PART OF THE BREASTS REGISTER AT LEAST 160°F ON AN INSTANT-READ THERMOMETER.

20 REST THE DUCK FOR 10 TO 15 MINUTES BEFORE CARVING IT UP AND SERVING.

(RECIPE CONTINUES ON THE NEXT PAGE.)

225

IF DESIRED, SERVE THE DUCK WITH SOME SUNBUTTER HOISIN SAUCE.

IN CASE YOU'RE WONDERING, THIS ISN'T THE SAME AS PEKING DUCK, WHICH IS PRIZED FOR ITS PUFFED-UP, PERFECTLY CRISP SKIN. IN CONTRAST, CANTONESE PIPA DUCK IS FAMOUS INSTEAD FOR ITS WELL-SEASONED, JUICY MEAT. SO WHILE ITS SKIN DOES GET CRISPIER THAN THAT OF A STANDARD ROAST DUCK, DON'T EXPECT IT TO BE AS ULTRA-CRISPY AS THAT OF A PEKING DUCK.

MEATS

ALBÓNDIGAS SOUP

MAKES 6 SERVINGS
● **1 HOUR**
(30 MINUTES HANDS-ON)

WHOLE30®	NUT-FREE

• MEATBALLS •

1 medium zucchini

1 pound ground beef (15% fat)

¼ cup chopped fresh cilantro

2 tablespoons chopped fresh mint

2 garlic cloves, minced

1½ teaspoons Diamond Crystal kosher salt

1 teaspoon ground cumin

¼ teaspoon freshly ground pepper

1 large egg, beaten

• SOUP •

2 tablespoons avocado oil

1 large yellow onion, diced

3 medium carrots, peeled and sliced at an angle into ½-inch pieces

1 large russet potato, peeled and cut into 1-inch cubes

Diamond Crystal kosher salt

Freshly ground black pepper

2 tablespoons tomato paste

3 garlic cloves, minced

2 teaspoons dried Mexican oregano

2 teaspoons ground cumin

2 bay leaves

6 cups bone broth or chicken broth

1 cup canned tomato sauce

½ pound green beans, cut into pieces

Juice from 1 medium lime

¼ cup fresh cilantro, roughly chopped

1 TRIM ONE END OF THE ZUCCHINI. THEN, SHRED THE ZUCCHINI USING THE LARGE HOLES OF A GRATER.

2 PUT THE SHREDDED ZUCCHINI IN A CLEAN KITCHEN TOWEL . . .

3 . . . AND SQUEEZE OUT THE EXCESS LIQUID, LEAVING ABOUT 1 PACKED CUP OF ZUCCHINI.

4 IN A LARGE BOWL, COMBINE THE SHREDDED ZUCCHINI WITH THE REST OF THE MEATBALL INGREDIENTS.

5 MIX WELL WITH YOUR HANDS.

6 NERVOUS ABOUT HOW THE MEATBALLS WILL TASTE? FRY UP A TINY PATTY OF THE MIXTURE IN A SKILLET TO TASTE AND ADJUST FOR SEASONING.

7 SHAPE THE MIXTURE INTO APPROXIMATELY 24 1-INCH-DIAMETER BALLS.

8 SET 'EM ASIDE WHILE YOU HEAT A LARGE STOCKPOT OVER MEDIUM-HIGH HEAT.

Per serving: 338 calories • 20 g carbohydrates • 27 g protein • 17 g fat • 4 g fiber

9 ADD THE OIL WHEN THE POT IS HOT.

10 TOSS THE DICED ONION, SLICED CARROTS, POTATO CUBES, ½ TEASPOON SALT, AND ¼ TEASPOON PEPPER INTO THE STOCKPOT.

11 COOK, STIRRING OCCASIONALLY, UNTIL THE VEGETABLES HAVE SOFTENED SLIGHTLY, ABOUT 5 MINUTES.

12 DECREASE THE HEAT TO MEDIUM AND ADD THE TOMATO PASTE, GARLIC, OREGANO, CUMIN, AND BAY LEAVES.

13 COOK, STIRRING, FOR 1 TO 2 MINUTES OR UNTIL THE GARLIC IS FRAGRANT.

14 POUR IN THE BROTH AND TOMATO SAUCE . . .

15 . . . AND BRING THE SOUP TO A SIMMER OVER HIGH HEAT.

16 CAREFULLY ADD THE MEATBALLS . . .

17 . . . AND ADJUST THE HEAT TO MAINTAIN A SIMMER. COOK FOR 10 MINUTES.

18 ADD THE GREEN BEANS TO THE SOUP.

19 COOK FOR ANOTHER 5 TO 10 MINUTES OR UNTIL THE MEATBALLS ARE FULLY COOKED AND THE VEGETABLES ARE FORK-TENDER. STIR IN THE LIME JUICE.

20 TASTE AND ADJUST FOR SEASONING WITH SALT AND PEPPER. LADLE INTO BOWLS AND GARNISH WITH SOME CILANTRO IF DESIRED.

With tender beef meatballs cooked in a bubbling broth, this homey Mexican-style soup is herby, tomato-y, and packed with vegetables. It's one of my rainy-day favorites!

234

SWITCH IT UP:
INSTANT POT ALBÓNDIGAS SOUP

Follow my Albóndigas Soup recipe up through Step 8. Then, in place of Steps 9 to 13, sauté the veggies and spices in an Instant Pot for about 2 minutes. Plop the meatballs and soup ingredients (except the lime and cilantro) into the pot. Cook the soup under high pressure for 3 minutes. Release the pressure immediately. Add the lime juice, garnish, and serve.

SONORAN HOT DOGS

MAKES 4 SERVINGS
◑ 30 MINUTES
(10 MINUTES HANDS-ON)

WHOLE30®	KETO-FRIENDLY
NUT-FREE	EGG-FREE

4   slices bacon

4   grass-fed all-beef hot dogs

1   large onion, thinly sliced

1   red bell pepper, thinly sliced

    Diamond Crystal kosher salt

• OPTIONAL TOPPINGS •

8   butter lettuce leaves

½   cup pico de gallo (tomato salsa)

1   large Hass avocado, peeled and sliced

THINK HOT DOGS ARE GARBAGE FOOD? ONLY IF YOU'RE EATING HOT DOGS LOADED WITH LOW-QUALITY MEATS AND PRESERVATIVES. TRY TO BUY SUGAR-FREE GRASS-FED ALL-BEEF DOGS INSTEAD.

1 WRAP A STRIP OF BACON AROUND EACH HOT DOG . . .

2 . . . TUCKING THE END OF EACH BACON STRIP UNDERNEATH SO IT WON'T UNRAVEL DURING COOKING.

3 HEAT A 12-INCH SKILLET ON MEDIUM HEAT. ONCE IT'S HOT, PLACE BACON-WRAPPED HOT DOGS IN A SINGLE LAYER IN THE MIDDLE OF THE PAN.

4 COOK UNDISTURBED UNTIL THE BACON IS BROWNED ON ONE SIDE. THEN, FLIP THE HOT DOGS OVER AND FRY UNTIL BROWNED ON THE OTHER SIDE.

5 ADD THE ONIONS AND PEPPERS TO THE SPACE IN THE PAN AROUND THE HOT DOGS AND SPRINKLE SALT ON THE VEGETABLES.

6 CONTINUE BROWNING THE HOT DOGS WHILE STIRRING THE ONIONS AND PEPPERS TO ENSURE EVEN COOKING.

7 ONCE THE BACON-WRAPPED HOT DOGS ARE BROWNED ON ALL SIDES AND THE PEPPERS AND ONIONS ARE TENDER AND CARAMELIZED, YOU'RE DONE.

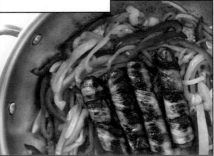

8 SERVE AS-IS . . .

Per serving: 237 calories • 14 g carbohydrates • 7 g protein • 19 g fat • 5 g fiber

9 ...OR ON BUTTER LETTUCE LEAVES AND GARNISHED WITH YOUR FAVORITE TOPPINGS, LIKE FRESH SALSA AND SLICED AVOCADOS.

I FIRST ENCOUNTERED THESE MEXICAN-INSPIRED BACON-WRAPPED HOT DOGS BACK WHEN I WAS A COLLEGE STUDENT WANDERING AROUND SAN FRANCISCO'S MISSION DISTRICT. OR RATHER, MY NOSE FOUND THEM. I FOLLOWED THE INTOXICATING SCENT OF SIZZLING BACON, HOT DOGS, GRILLED PEPPERS, AND ONIONS TO A SIDEWALK VENDOR COOKING UP SONORAN HOT DOGS. A FEW BUCKS AND A BIG BITE LATER, I WAS IN HEAVEN. YEARS (DECADES!) LATER, I FINALLY MODIFIED THE RECIPE TO BE PALEO-FRIENDLY, AND IT'S SO TASTY I DON'T EVEN MISS THE BUN!

CUBAN BEEF PICADILLO

MAKES 6 SERVINGS

⏱ **45 MINUTES**

WHOLE30®	NUT-FREE
EGG-FREE	

THIS IS CLASSIC CUBAN COMFORT FOOD, MADE FROM GROUND MEAT COOKED WITH A DELICIOUS COMBINATION OF CAPERS, OLIVES, AND RAISINS. THIS SIMPLE ONE-PAN MEAL TASTES JUST AS GREAT SPOONED OVER A BOWL OF CAULIFLOWER RICE (PAGE 107) OR TUCKED INSIDE SCRAMBLES OR WRAPS.

¼	cup raisins
2	tablespoons avocado oil or ghee
1	red bell pepper, stemmed, seeded, and diced
1	large onion, diced
	Diamond Crystal kosher salt
6	garlic cloves, minced
2	tablespoons tomato paste
1	pound lean ground beef
1	pound ground pork
1	tablespoon dried oregano
1	tablespoon ground cumin
1	(14.5-ounce) can diced fire-roasted tomatoes, drained
½	cup bone broth or chicken broth
2	dried bay leaves
½	cup pitted green olives, chopped
2	tablespoon capers, drained
1	tablespoon red wine vinegar
	Freshly ground black pepper

GOT EXTRA PICADILLO? USE IT AS AN ALTERNATIVE FILLING FOR THE HAND PIES ON PAGE 216!

Per serving: 517 calories • 14 g carbohydrates • 28 g protein • 38 g fat • 3 g fiber

1 IN A SMALL BOWL, SOAK THE RAISINS IN HOT WATER FOR AT LEAST 10 MINUTES OR UNTIL PLUMPED. DRAIN AND SET ASIDE.

2 HEAT A LARGE SKILLET OVER MEDIUM HEAT AND SWIRL IN THE OIL WHEN THE PAN IS HOT. ADD THE BELL PEPPERS, ONIONS, AND A SPRINKLE OF SALT.

3 COOK UNTIL THE VEGETABLES ARE SOFTENED, ABOUT 5 MINUTES.

4 STIR IN THE GARLIC AND TOMATO PASTE. COOK UNTIL FRAGRANT, AROUND 30 SECONDS.

5 ADD THE BEEF AND PORK TO THE SKILLET, BREAKING UP THE MEAT WITH A SPATULA.

6 WHEN THE MEAT IS NO LONGER PINK, STIR IN THE OREGANO, CUMIN, AND 1 TEASPOON OF KOSHER SALT.

7 MIX IN THE TOMATOES, BROTH, AND PLUMPED RAISINS.

8 TUCK THE BAY LEAVES INTO THE MEAT. THEN, INCREASE THE HEAT TO BRING THE CONTENTS OF THE SKILLET UP TO A BOIL.

9 THEN, DECREASE THE HEAT TO MAINTAIN A GENTLE SIMMER FOR ABOUT 10 MINUTES.

10 PICK OUT THE BAY LEAVES AND TOSS IN THE OLIVES AND CAPERS.

11 INCREASE THE HEAT TO MEDIUM-HIGH AND COOK, STIRRING OCCASIONALLY, UNTIL THE SAUCE IS THICKENED, ABOUT 5 MINUTES.

12 STIR IN VINEGAR AND TASTE FOR SEASONING. ADJUST WITH SALT, PEPPER, AND VINEGAR IF NECESSARY. SERVE OVER CAULIFLOWER RICE.

239

INDIAN-SPICED SHEPHERD'S PIE

MAKES 8 SERVINGS
◐ 1½ HOURS
(1 HOUR HANDS-ON)

WHOLE30®	NUT-FREE
EGG-FREE	

• SWEET POTATO MASH •

2   pounds sweet potatoes, peeled and cut into 1-inch cubes

2   garlic cloves, minced

½   cup full-fat coconut milk

1   teaspoon Diamond Crystal kosher salt

2   teaspoons garam masala

• FILLING •

2   tablespoons ghee

1   large onion, finely chopped

3   large garlic cloves, minced

2   tablespoons minced fresh ginger

2   jalapeño peppers, finely diced

2   pounds lean ground beef, lamb, or goat

2½ teaspoons Diamond Crystal kosher salt

1   teaspoon ground turmeric

½   cup full-fat coconut milk

2   cups frozen peas, thawed

1   tablespoon garam masala

2   tablespoons lemon juice

¼   cup minced fresh cilantro

1 MAKE THE MASH FIRST. DUMP THE SWEET POTATOES, GARLIC, COCONUT MILK, AND SALT IN A LARGE SAUCEPAN.

2 BRING TO A BOIL OVER MEDIUM HEAT, STIRRING OCCASIONALLY. THEN, TURN DOWN THE HEAT TO MAINTAIN A SIMMER.

3 COVER AND COOK FOR 40 TO 50 MINUTES OR UNTIL THE SWEET POTATO PIECES ARE EASILY PIERCED WITH A FORK.

4 ADD IN THE GARAM MASALA.

5 BLITZ THE SWEET POTATOES WITH AN IMMERSION BLENDER OR MASH WITH A POTATO MASHER UNTIL SMOOTH. TASTE AND ADD MORE SALT IF NEEDED.

6 WHILE THE SWEET POTATOES ARE STILL COOKING, LET'S MAKE THE FILLING. HEAT A 12-INCH BROILER-SAFE SKILLET OVER MEDIUM HEAT.

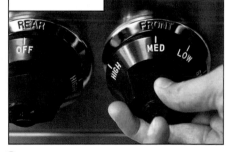

7 WHEN THE PAN IS HOT, ADD THE GHEE. SWIRL IT AROUND, AND THEN TOSS THE ONIONS IN THE PAN.

8 COOK, STIRRING, FOR 10 MINUTES OR UNTIL THE ONIONS ARE TRANSLUCENT AND TENDER. (GOT EXTRA TIME? COOK FOR ANOTHER 10 MINUTES, UNTIL THE ONIONS ARE BROWNED, FOR EVEN DEEPER FLAVOR.)

Per serving: 521 calories • 32 g carbohydrates • 24 g protein • 33 g fat • 6 g fiber

9 Toss the garlic, ginger, and peppers into the pan. Sauté for 30 seconds or until fragrant.

10 Crumble in the ground meat.

11 Cook for 3 to 5 minutes or until the meat is mostly no longer pink, breaking up the pieces with your spatula.

12 Stir in the salt, turmeric, and coconut milk, and bring to a simmer.

13 Cover the pan and reduce the heat to medium-low. Cook for 20 minutes, stirring occasionally.

14 Stir in the peas. Cook uncovered on medium heat for another 3 to 5 minutes or until the liquid in the skillet has mostly evaporated.

15 Remove the pan from the heat and mix in the garam masala, lemon juice, and minced cilantro.

16 Adjust the seasoning to taste with additional salt, garam masala, or lemon juice. Smooth the top of the meat in the pan.

17 Heat the broiler on high with the rack about 6 inches from the oven's heating element.

18 Dollop the sweet potato mash all over the top and carefully smooth it to the edges with a silicone spatula.

19 Rake the tines of a fork across the top if you want to make your shepherd's pie look even more awesome!

20 Broil for 10 to 14 minutes or 'til the crust is golden brown and the filling is bubbly. Let the shepherd's pie cool for 5 to 10 minutes before garnishing with minced cilantro. Serve and eat.

241

WANT TO SPEED THIS RECIPE UP? MAKE THE MASH IN AN INSTANT POT. COOK THE SWEET POTATOES, GARLIC, COCONUT MILK, AND SALT IN AN INSTANT POT UNDER HIGH PRESSURE FOR 10 MINUTES. RELEASE THE PRESSURE IMMEDIATELY, AND PICK UP THE RECIPE STARTING WITH STEP 4.

OLD-SCHOOL TACOS

MAKES 4 SERVINGS
◑ 30 MINUTES

WHOLE30®	KETO-FRIENDLY
NUT-FREE	EGG-FREE

• TACOS •

1 tablespoon avocado oil

1 small onion, finely diced

1 pound lean ground beef, dark meat turkey, or chicken thigh

3 medium garlic cloves, minced

1½ tablespoons chili powder

1 teaspoon ground cumin

½ teaspoon dried oregano

¼ teaspoon cayenne pepper (optional)

1 teaspoon Diamond Crystal kosher salt

½ cup roasted tomato salsa

8 Grain-Free Tortillas (page 48) (not Whole30), butter lettuce leaves, or thinly sliced jicama

• OPTIONAL TOPPINGS •

1 cup shredded iceberg lettuce

1 cup cherry tomatoes, sliced

½ cup guacamole

½ cup Cashew Cheese Sauce (page 34) (not nut-free)

I LOVE TACO TUESDAYS, AND WEDNESDAYS, AND THURSDAYS ...

1 HEAT A LARGE SKILLET OVER MEDIUM HEAT. WHEN THE SKILLET IS HOT, SWIRL IN THE OIL AND ADD THE CHOPPED ONION.

2 COOK, STIRRING OCCASIONALLY, UNTIL THE ONIONS HAVE SOFTENED, ABOUT 3 TO 5 MINUTES.

3 ADD THE GROUND MEAT TO THE SKILLET, BREAKING IT UP WITH A SPATULA.

4 COOK THE MEAT FOR 5 TO 7 MINUTES OR UNTIL IT'S MOSTLY NO LONGER PINK.

5 ADD THE MINCED GARLIC AND COOK UNTIL FRAGRANT, ABOUT 30 SECONDS.

6 MIX IN THE CHILI POWDER, CUMIN, DRIED OREGANO, CAYENNE PEPPER, AND SALT. STIR TO COMBINE.

7 ONCE EVERYTHING'S COMBINED, POUR IN THE SALSA AND MIX WELL.

8 BRING THE MEATY FILLING TO A SIMMER AND COOK FOR 5 TO 10 MINUTES OR UNTIL MOST OF THE EXTRA LIQUID IS COOKED OFF. YOU MAY HAVE TO LOWER THE HEAT IF THE SAUCE IS BOILING TOO VIGOROUSLY.

Per serving (of taco meat): 354 calories • 7 g carbohydrates • 21 g protein • 27 g fat • 2 g fiber

9 SCOOP THE GROUND BEEF FILLING INTO GRAIN-FREE TACO SHELLS OR LETTUCE WRAPS AND TOP WITH YOUR FAVORITE TACO TOPPINGS.

I LIKE TO THINK I'VE DEVELOPED A SOPHISTICATED PALATE OVER THE YEARS, BUT I STILL HAVE A SOFT SPOT FOR AMERICANIZED GROUND BEEF TACOS FROM MY CHILDHOOD. MY GRADE SCHOOL DIDN'T HAVE A CAFETERIA, BUT ONCE A MONTH, PARENT VOLUNTEERS WOULD HOST A "HOT FOOD DAY" OFFERING BURGERS, TACOS, OR PIZZA. STUFFED WITH SEASONED GROUND MEAT, ICEBERG LETTUCE, CHEESE, AND TOMATOES, THE OLD-SCHOOL TACOS WERE MY HANDS-DOWN FAVORITE. NOW, I CAN SERVE UP A PALEO-FIED, NOSTALGIA-FILLED VERSION TO MY OWN FAMILY.

INSTANT POT GROUND BEEF CHILI

MAKES 6 SERVINGS
🕐 **45 MINUTES**
(20 MINUTES HANDS-ON)

WHOLE30®	KETO-FRIENDLY
NUT-FREE	EGG-FREE

• CHILI •

1 tablespoon avocado oil

1 large yellow onion, diced

1 small red bell pepper, diced

Diamond Crystal kosher salt

2 tablespoons tomato paste

4 garlic cloves, minced

2 pounds lean ground beef

3 tablespoons chili powder

1 tablespoon dried oregano

1 tablespoon ground cumin

¼ teaspoon cayenne pepper (optional)

1 (14.5-ounce) can diced fire-roasted tomatoes, drained

½ cup bone broth or chicken broth

2 teaspoons paleo-friendly fish sauce or No-Fish Sauce (page 28)

1 tablespoon apple cider vinegar (optional)

• OPTIONAL TOPPINGS •

2 avocados, sliced

4 scallions, sliced

1 small white onion, finely diced

½ cup fresh cilantro, minced

3 limes, cut into wedges

1 PRESS "SAUTÉ" ON THE INSTANT POT AND WAIT FOR THE METAL INSERT TO HEAT UP.

2 ONCE THE INSERT IS HOT, ADD THE OIL.

3 AS SOON AS THE OIL STARTS SHIMMERING, TOSS IN THE ONION AND BELL PEPPER.

4 ADD A SPRINKLE OF SALT.

5 COOK, STIRRING, FOR **3** MINUTES OR UNTIL THE VEGETABLES SOFTEN.

6 STIR IN THE TOMATO PASTE AND GARLIC.

7 COOK FOR ABOUT **30** SECONDS OR UNTIL EVERYTHING'S FRAGRANT.

8 ADD IN THE GROUND BEEF . . .

Per serving: 445 calories • 8 g carbohydrates • 28 g protein • 34 g fat • 3 g fiber

9 ...ALONG WITH 1 TEASPOON KOSHER SALT.

10 BROWN THE GROUND BEEF AND BREAK IT UP WITH A SPATULA.

11 COOK FOR 5 TO 7 MINUTES OR UNTIL THE MEAT IS NO LONGER PINK. THEN, STIR IN THE CHILI POWDER, OREGANO, CUMIN, AND (IF DESIRED) CAYENNE PEPPER.

12 STIR WELL TO DISTRIBUTE THE SPICES.

13 ADD THE DRAINED DICED TOMATOES, BROTH, AND FISH SAUCE.

14 STIR EVERYTHING WELL, MAKING SURE THE LIQUID REACHES THE BOTTOM OF THE POT.

15 LOCK THE LID AND COOK UNDER HIGH PRESSURE FOR 15 MINUTES.

16 WHEN THE CHILI'S DONE COOKING, RELEASE THE PRESSURE MANUALLY IF YOU'RE ITCHING TO EAT RIGHT AWAY. OTHERWISE, LET THE PRESSURE COME DOWN NATURALLY.

17 TASTE THE CHILI...

18 ...SPRINKLE ON MORE SALT IF NEEDED.

19 STIR IN THE APPLE CIDER VINEGAR IF DESIRED. TASTE THE CHILI AGAIN TO SEE IF YOU NEED TO PUNCH UP THE FLAVORS.

20 LADLE UP THE CHILI. SERVE IT WITH YOUR FAVORITE TOPPINGS, LIKE SLICED AVOCADO, SCALLIONS, DICED ONION, CILANTRO, AND LIME WEDGES.

I'M SURE I'LL HEAR FROM HARDCORE CHILI
AFICIONADOS ABOUT WHAT BELONGS IN A
BOWL OF CHILI . . . AND WHAT DOESN'T. SO
IF YOU'RE A CHILI SNOB WHO TURNS UP
YOUR NOSE AT MY INSTANT POT GROUND
BEEF CHILI BECAUSE IT INCLUDES TOMA-
TOES AND FISH SAUCE (GASP!) AND OMITS
LEGUMES ALTOGETHER, FEEL FREE TO CALL
THIS SOMETHING OTHER THAN CHILI, OKAY?

NO MATTER WHAT YOU DECIDE TO NAME IT,
THIS BEEFY STEW IS COMFORTING, CRAZY
DELICIOUS, HEARTY, AND WON'T BREAK THE
BANK. PLUS, YOU CAN EASILY WHIP UP A
POT OF THIS STUFF ON A BUSY WEEKNIGHT!

SWITCH IT UP:
SLOW COOKER
GROUND BEEF CHILI

USE THE SAME RECIPE FOR INSTANT POT GROUND BEEF CHILI, BUT DO ALL THE SAUTÉING IN A POT ON THE STOVE BEFORE TRANSFERRING EVERYTHING TO A SLOW COOKER. SET THE SLOW COOKER ON LOW AND COOK THE CHILI FOR 6 TO 8 HOURS.

SWITCH IT UP:
STOVETOP
GROUND BEEF CHILI

USE THE SAME RECIPE FOR INSTANT POT GROUND BEEF CHILI, BUT INSTEAD OF USING ½ CUP CHICKEN BROTH OR BONE BROTH, USE 1 CUP. ALSO, RATHER THAN COOKING THE CHILI UNDER PRESSURE, SIMMER IT IN A PARTIALLY COVERED STOCKPOT OR DUTCH OVEN OVER MEDIUM-LOW HEAT FOR 1 HOUR OR UNTIL THE FLAVORS MELD.

PALEO PATTY MELTS

MAKES 2 SERVINGS
◑ 30 MINUTES

| WHOLE30® (IF MODIFIED) |
| KETO-FRIENDLY (IF MODIFIED) |
| EGG-FREE (IF MODIFIED) |

¼ cup Cashew Cheese Sauce (page 34), divided

2 tablespoons ghee or avocado oil, divided

4 slices Paleo Sandwich Bread (page 46) or butter lettuce leaves (to make this Whole30, keto-friendly, and egg-free)

½ pound ground beef (15% fat)

Diamond Crystal kosher salt

1 small yellow onion, thinly sliced lengthwise

3 tablespoons water

Freshly ground black pepper

CAN SOMEONE EXPLAIN WHY WE'RE PUTTING VEGAN CHEESE ON MEAT?

I THINK WE CAN ALL AGREE THAT NOTHING BEATS A WELL-SEASONED BURGER SMOTHERED WITH GRILLED ONIONS AND MELTY CHEESE, TUCKED BETWEEN SLICES OF GRIDDLED BREAD. I CAN'T EAT TOASTED RYE OR MELTED CHEESE ANYMORE, BUT JUST ONE BITE OF THIS PALEO PATTY MELT INSTANTLY TRANSPORTS ME BACK TO MY FAVORITE GREASY SPOON.

1 TAKE SOME CASHEW CHEESE SAUCE OUT OF THE FRIDGE AND BRING IT TO ROOM TEMPERATURE.

2 HEAT A 12-INCH PAN OVER MEDIUM-LOW HEAT. SWIRL IN 1 TABLESPOON GHEE AND PLACE 2 SLICES OF BREAD IN THE SKILLET.

Per serving (on bread): 833 calories • 38 g carbohydrates • 31 g protein • 62 g fat • 6 g fiber

3 TOAST ABOUT 3 MINUTES PER SIDE OR UNTIL GOLDEN BROWN. TRANSFER THE BREAD TO A WIRE RACK. TOAST THE 2 REMAINING SLICES OF BREAD.

4 FORM THE GROUND BEEF INTO 2 PATTIES AND SPRINKLE SALT ON BOTH SIDES.

5 INCREASE THE HEAT TO MEDIUM-HIGH AND PLACE THE PATTIES IN THE PAN.

6 USE A SPATULA TO SMUSH THE PATTIES UNTIL THEY'RE ABOUT ½ INCH THICK.

7 COOK THE PATTIES UNDISTURBED FOR ABOUT 1 TO 2 MINUTES OR UNTIL THEY'RE NICELY BROWNED. FLIP 'EM AND COOK FOR AN ADDITIONAL MINUTE (OR TO YOUR DESIRED DONENESS) ON THE OTHER SIDE.

8 TRANSFER THE PATTIES TO A PLATE. THEN, REDUCE THE HEAT TO MEDIUM AND ADD THE ONIONS TO THE NOW-EMPTY SKILLET.

9 SEASON THE ONIONS WITH SALT AND ADD 3 TABLESPOONS OF WATER TO THE ONIONS. SCRAPE UP ANY BROWNED BITS FROM THE PAN.

10 COOK FOR ABOUT 5 MINUTES, STIRRING FREQUENTLY, UNTIL THE ONIONS ARE SOFT AND GOLDEN BROWN. SEASON WITH PEPPER. TRANSFER THE ONIONS TO A PLATE.

11 NOW, IT'S TIME TO ASSEMBLE THE PATTY MELTS! FOR EACH SANDWICH, TOP A SLICE OF TOASTED BREAD WITH A PATTY AND A PILE OF ONIONS.

12 SPOON ON SOME CASHEW CHEESE SAUCE.

13 TOP WITH ANOTHER SLICE OF BREAD.

14 CUT IN HALF AND DIG IN!

BACON CHEESEBURGER CASSEROLE

MAKES 8 SERVINGS
◗ **45 MINUTES**
(25 MINUTES HANDS-ON)

WHOLE30®	KETO-FRIENDLY
EGG-FREE	

1¼ cups Cashew Cheese Sauce (page 34)

2 teaspoons avocado oil, extra-virgin olive oil, or ghee

1 small onion, diced

2½ teaspoons Magic Mushroom Powder (page 45) or Diamond Crystal kosher salt, divided

2 pounds lean ground beef

4 garlic cloves, minced

1 medium cauliflower head, riced (or 16 ounces fresh or frozen riced cauliflower) (page 107)

6 slices bacon (about 6 ounces) cut crosswise into ¼-inch pieces

> THIS RIB-STICKING ONE-DISH WONDER IS A FAMILY FAVORITE!

1 GRAB OR MAKE CASHEW CHEESE SAUCE.

2 HEAT THE OVEN TO 400°F WITH THE RACK IN THE MIDDLE.

3 HEAT A 12-INCH OVEN-SAFE SKILLET OVER MEDIUM HEAT.

4 WHEN THE PAN IS HOT, ADD THE OIL AND DICED ONIONS. ADD ½ TEASPOON OF MAGIC MUSHROOM POWDER OR KOSHER SALT.

5 COOK UNTIL THE ONIONS ARE SLIGHTLY SOFTENED, ABOUT 3 TO 5 MINUTES.

6 ADD THE GROUND BEEF. USE A SPATULA OR WOODEN SPOON TO BREAK UP THE MEAT.

7 INCREASE THE HEAT TO MEDIUM-HIGH AND COOK, STIRRING FREQUENTLY, UNTIL THE MEAT IS NO LONGER PINK.

8 ADD THE MINCED GARLIC, RICED CAULIFLOWER . . .

Per serving: 591 calories • 12 g carbohydrates • 28 g protein • 49 g fat • 2 g fiber

9 ...AND 2 TEASPOONS OF MAGIC MUSHROOM POWDER OR SALT.

10 STIR WELL.

11 POUR IN ALL THE CASHEW CHEESE SAUCE.

12 MIX WELL, TASTE, AND ADJUST FOR SEASONING.

13 THEN, SMOOTH THE TOP WITH A SPATULA.

14 STICK THE PAN IN THE OVEN AND BAKE FOR 15 TO 20 MINUTES OR UNTIL BUBBLY.

15 WHILE THE CASSEROLE IS BAKING, COOK UP THE CRISPY BACON BITS. TOSS THE SLICED BACON INTO A MEDIUM SKILLET.

16 COOK ON MEDIUM HEAT, STIRRING THE PORKY BITS FREQUENTLY, FOR 10 TO 15 MINUTES OR UNTIL THE BACON IS CRISPY.

17 REMOVE THE BACON BITS WITH A SLOTTED SPOON AND DRAIN ON A PAPER TOWEL-LINED PLATE.

18 TAKE THE CASSEROLE OUT OF THE OVEN ...

19 ...AND SPRINKLE THE BACON BITS ON TOP.

20 SCOOP AND SERVE.

When a chaotic weeknight demands a quick and satisfying meal, my Bacon Cheeseburger Casserole is your life-saver! Refrigerate any leftovers in an airtight container for up to 4 days, or freeze them for up to 4 months.

KALBI (KOREAN BARBECUE SHORT RIBS)

MAKES 6 SERVINGS
⚠ **5 HOURS**
(30 MINUTES HANDS-ON)

WHOLE30®	NUT-FREE
EGG-FREE	

• SHORT RIBS •

1 cup All-Purpose Stir-Fry Sauce (page 29)

4 pounds Korean-style short ribs (galbi or flanken-style)

1 kiwi, peeled and coarsely chopped

4 garlic cloves, minced

2 scallions, coarsely chopped

1 tablespoon minced fresh ginger

2 teaspoons toasted sesame oil

• GARNISHES•

2 scallions, thinly sliced

2 tablespoons toasted sesame seeds

• OPTIONAL SIDES•

1 butter lettuce head, separated into leaves

4 cups Cauliflower Rice (page 107)

1 cup kimchi

MARK MY WORDS: THESE THINLY SLICED, MARINATED BARBECUE SHORT RIBS WILL BE THE HIT OF YOUR SUMMER COOKOUTS. KALBI, SWEET AND SAVORY THIN STRIPS OF SHORT RIBS THAT ARE QUICKLY COOKED ON A HOT GRILL, IS ONE OF MY FAVORITE KOREAN GRILLED DISHES FROM MY PRE-PALEO DAYS. TRADITIONALLY, THE MARINADE HAS A SWEETENED SOY SAUCE BASE, BUT THIS VERSION USES MY PALEO-FRIENDLY ALL-PURPOSE STIR-FRY SAUCE INSTEAD. AS A RESULT, MY KALBI-MUNCHING DAYS ARE FAR FROM OVER!

NO GRILL? NO PROBLEM. POSITION YOUR OVEN RACK SO THAT IT'S 6 INCHES FROM THE HEATING ELEMENT AND SWITCH ON THE BROILER. ARRANGE THE KALBI IN A SINGLE LAYER ON A STAINLESS STEEL WIRE RACK SET IN A RIMMED BAKING SHEET AND POP THE SHORT RIBS UNDER THE BROILER. BROIL FOR ABOUT 3 TO 5 MINUTES PER SIDE UNTIL COOKED THROUGH.

Per serving: 475 calories • 14 g carbohydrates • 45 g protein • 25 g fat • 1 g fiber

1. YOU'LL NEED ALL-PURPOSE STIR-FRY SAUCE FOR THIS RECIPE, SO IF YOU DON'T ALREADY HAVE IT ON HAND, MAKE SOME.

2. SOAK THE SHORT RIBS IN COLD WATER FOR 15 MINUTES.

3. RINSE THE RIBS OF ANY BONE FRAGMENTS AND PAT THE SHORT RIBS DRY WITH PAPER TOWELS BEFORE SETTING THEM ASIDE.

4. IN A HIGH-SPEED BLENDER, COMBINE THE KIWI, GARLIC, SCALLIONS, AND GINGER.

5. POUR IN THE ALL-PURPOSE STIR-FRY SAUCE AND TOASTED SESAME OIL. BLITZ UNTIL SMOOTH.

6. POUR THE MARINADE OVER THE RIBS AND TOSS WELL TO COAT. COVER AND MARINATE THE SHORT RIBS FOR AT LEAST 4 HOURS OR UP TO 24 HOURS IN THE REFRIGERATOR.

7. WHEN YOU'RE READY TO COOK, HEAT YOUR GAS OR CHARCOAL GRILL TO MEDIUM-HIGH. THROW THE SHORT RIBS ON THE GRILL . . .

8. . . . AND COOK FOR 3 TO 4 MINUTES PER SIDE OR UNTIL THEY'RE COOKED THROUGH.

9. TRANSFER THE SHORT RIBS TO A PLATTER.

10. GARNISH WITH THINLY SLICED SCALLIONS AND TOASTED SESAME SEEDS.

11. SERVE WHOLE GRILLED KALBI PIECES AS A MAIN COURSE OR USE KITCHEN SHEARS TO CUT THE MEAT INTO SMALLER PIECES TO SERVE AS A STARTER OR PARTY NIBBLE.

12. SERVE THE KALBI WITH BUTTER LETTUCE LEAVES, CAULIFLOWER RICE, AND KIMCHI, AND HAVE EVERYONE ASSEMBLE THEIR OWN LETTUCE WRAPS.

INSTANT POT BALSAMIC BEEF STEW

MAKES 6 SERVINGS
◑◔ 1 HOUR 45 MINUTES
(45 MINUTES HANDS-ON)

WHOLE30®	NUT-FREE
EGG-FREE	

3 pounds boneless beef short ribs or chuck roast, cut into 4 x 2-inch pieces

Magic Mushroom Powder (page 45) or Diamond Crystal kosher salt

1 tablespoon extra-virgin olive oil

2 yellow onions, chopped

1 large carrot, peeled and diced

10 garlic cloves, smashed and peeled

2 tablespoons tomato paste

½ cup balsamic vinegar

5 fresh thyme sprigs

2 dried bay leaves

1 (14.5-ounce) can diced tomatoes, drained

Freshly ground black pepper

¼ cup chopped fresh basil and/or Italian parsley (optional)

1 SEASON THE BONELESS SHORT RIBS WITH 2 TEASPOONS MAGIC MUSHROOM POWDER (OR KOSHER SALT).

2 TURN ON THE SAUTÉ FUNCTION ON THE INSTANT POT.

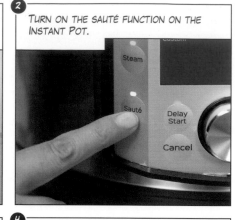

3 WHEN THE POT IS HOT, POUR IN THE OIL.

4 SEAR THE SHORT RIBS IN BATCHES, ABOUT 2 MINUTES PER SIDE.

5 THERE'S NO NEED TO BROWN ALL SIDES. JUST 2 SIDES PER PIECE WILL DO.

6 TRANSFER THE SHORT RIBS TO A PLATTER.

7 TOSS IN THE ONIONS, CARROT, GARLIC CLOVES, AND ½ TEASPOON MAGIC MUSHROOM POWDER.

8 SAUTÉ FOR 3 TO 5 MINUTES OR UNTIL THE ONIONS ARE SOFTENED.

Per serving: 479 calories • 14 g carbohydrates • 45 g protein • 26 g fat • 2 g fiber

9 Add the tomato paste and stir until fragrant, about 30 seconds.

10 Turn off the sauté function. Pour in the balsamic vinegar and scrape up any browned bits on the bottom.

11 Add the seasoned short ribs on top of the vegetables.

12 Add the thyme sprigs and bay leaves.

13 Pour the diced tomatoes on top of the short ribs. Don't stir them in.

14 Cover and cook in the Instant Pot for 35 minutes under high pressure.

15 When the short ribs are done cooking, let the pressure drop naturally. Impatient? Wait 15 minutes, and manually release the remaining pressure.

16 Fish out and discard the thyme sprigs and bay leaves.

17 Transfer the short ribs to a platter. Skim the excess fat from the surface of the cooking liquid.

18 Use an immersion blender to purée the cooking liquid.

19 Taste and adjust for seasoning with salt and pepper.

20 Pour the sauce over the short ribs, garnish with fresh herbs, and serve.

THIS COMFORTING BEEF SUPPER IS MADE WITH HUMBLE PANTRY BASICS, BUT THE FINAL PRODUCT IS HEAVENLY. MAKE IT AHEAD OF TIME, AND IT'LL TASTE EVEN BETTER THE NEXT DAY! (A TIP: IF YOU'RE REHEATING THIS STEW STRAIGHT OUT OF THE FRIDGE, REMOVE THE HARDENED FAT CAP TO AVOID AN OVERLY FATTY DISH.)

SWITCH IT UP:
SLOW COOKER
BALSAMIC BEEF STEW

TO MAKE THIS IN A SLOW COOKER, FOLLOW
THE RECIPE FOR INSTANT POT BALSAMIC
BEEF STEW, COOKING STEPS 1 TO 10 IN
A LARGE SKILLET. NEXT, DUMP ALL THE
INGREDIENTS INTO A SLOW COOKER. COOK
ON LOW FOR 8 TO 10 HOURS OR UNTIL
TENDER. FINISH UP WITH STEPS 16 TO 20.

SHAKING BEEF

MAKES 6 SERVINGS
◑ **30 MINUTES**

WHOLE30®	KETO-FRIENDLY
NUT-FREE	EGG-FREE

½ cup All-Purpose Stir-Fry Sauce (page 29)

1½ pounds filet mignon or top sirloin, cut into 1-inch cubes

1 teaspoon Diamond Crystal kosher salt

½ teaspoon freshly ground black pepper

3 tablespoons avocado oil, divided

4 cups watercress, arugula, or salad greens, lightly packed

1 cup cherry tomatoes, sliced in half

1 cup thinly sliced red onion

3 scallions, trimmed and cut into 1-inch segments

1 tablespoon minced garlic

2 tablespoons ghee

IT'S STEAK AND ONIONS, VIETNAMESE STYLE!

Per serving: 417 calories • 9 g carbohydrates • 22 g protein • 32 g fat • 1 g fiber

1 IF YOU HAVEN'T ALREADY, WHIP UP SOME ALL-PURPOSE STIR-FRY SAUCE. SET ASIDE ½ CUP OF IT.

2 IN A LARGE BOWL, TOSS TOGETHER THE BEEF CUBES, SALT, PEPPER, AND 1 TABLE-SPOON OF AVOCADO OIL.

3 MIX IT ALL TOGETHER, AND MARINATE AT ROOM TEMPERATURE FOR 20 MINUTES.

4 SPREAD THE WATERCRESS AND CHERRY TOMATOES ON A PLATTER. SET IT ASIDE.

5 HEAT A LARGE SKILLET OVER HIGH HEAT UNTIL HOT. POUR IN 2 TABLESPOONS OF AVOCADO OIL.

6 ADD THE STEAK IN A SINGLE LAYER IN THE HOT SKILLET.

7 SEAR THE MEAT FOR 3 TO 5 MINUTES, SHAKING THE SKILLET TO FLIP THE BEEF ...

8 ...UNTIL ALL THE SIDES ARE BROWNED AND THE CENTER IS MEDIUM-RARE.

9 TOSS IN THE RED ONION AND SCALLIONS. COOK, STIRRING, FOR ABOUT 30 SECONDS.

10 POUR IN THE ALL-PURPOSE STIR-FRY SAUCE AND STIR TO COAT THE BEEF.

11 ADD THE MINCED GARLIC AND GHEE, AND STIR TO INCORPORATE. TAKE THE SKILLET OFF THE HEAT.

12 SPOON THE BEEF AND ONIONS ON TOP OF THE WATERCRESS AND CHERRY TOMATOES, AND SERVE IMMEDIATELY.

IN VIETNAMESE, THIS STEAK DISH IS KNOWN AS BO LUC LAC, BUT IN ENGLISH, IT'S CALLED SHAKING BEEF DUE TO THE CONSTANT SHAKING OF THE PAN WHILE COOKING. SIZZLING AND SAVORY-SWEET, THESE PEPPERY, CARAMELIZED CUBES OF FILET MIGNON CAN BE ON YOUR DINNER TABLE IN 30 MINUTES FLAT.

INSTANT POT PIPIÁN PORK

MAKES 6 SERVINGS
● **1 HOUR**
(15 MINUTES HANDS-ON)

WHOLE30®	KETO-FRIENDLY
NUT-FREE	EGG-FREE

2   cups Pipián Verde (page 36), divided

3½   pounds boneless pork shoulder, cut into 1½-inch cubes

2   teaspoons Diamond Crystal kosher salt

2   tablespoons raw pepitas

2   radishes, cut into thin matchsticks (optional)

2   tablespoons fresh cilantro leaves (optional)

> PORK SHOULDER IS ALSO CALLED PORK BUTT, WHICH IS CONFUSING BECAUSE PIGS DON'T FART FROM THEIR SHOULDERS.

1 GOT PIPIÁN VERDE? YOU'LL NEED IT, SO GRAB OR MAKE SOME. THEN, IN A LARGE BOWL, TOSS THE PORK WITH THE SALT.

2 ADD THE PORK CUBES AND ½ CUP OF PIPIÁN VERDE TO AN INSTANT POT.

3 LOCK THE LID ON THE INSTANT POT. COOK UNDER HIGH PRESSURE FOR **35** MINUTES.

4 WHILE THE PORK IS COOKING, TOAST THE PEPITAS IN A LARGE SKILLET OVER MEDIUM HEAT FOR **3** TO **5** MINUTES OR UNTIL FRAGRANT. SET ASIDE.

5 ONCE THE PORK IS DONE COOKING, MANUALLY RELEASE THE PRESSURE.

6 POUR THE REMAINING 1½ CUPS OF PIPIÁN VERDE INTO THE INSTANT POT AND TURN ON THE SAUTÉ FUNCTION.

7 COOK FOR **5** TO **10** MINUTES OR UNTIL THE SAUCE THICKENS SLIGHTLY.

8 PLATE AND GARNISH WITH THE RADISHES, CILANTRO, AND TOASTED PEPITAS.

Per serving: 568 calories • 4 g carbohydrates • 50 g protein • 39 g fat • 2 g fiber

This is my simplified take on a satisfying green stew I always order at our local Oaxacan restaurant. It's an absolute breeze to make in a pressure cooker, especially if you already have some Pipián Verde on hand. I like to serve it over Cauliflower Rice (page 107), but it's just as tasty served in warm Grain-Free Tortillas (page 48) or with A Nice Green Salad (page 68).

SWITCH IT UP: SLOW COOKER PIPIÁN PORK

Want to make this in a slow cooker? Cook the salted pork with 2 cups of Pipián Verde on low in a slow cooker for 8 to 10 hours or until tender.

SWITCH IT UP: STOVETOP PIPIÁN PORK

In a 6-quart pot over high heat, bring the salted pork, 2 cups of Pipián Verde, and 1 cup of chicken broth to a boil. Lower the heat, cover, and simmer for 3 to 4 hours or until tender.

PESTO POTATO MEATZA

MAKES 4 SERVINGS
◐ **45 MINUTES**
(15 MINUTES HANDS-ON)

WHOLE30®	KETO-FRIENDLY
EGG-FREE	

- **4** tablespoons Basil Pesto (page 42) or store-bought pesto, divided
- **1** pound bulk mild Italian sausage
- **1** medium Yukon Gold potato, sliced very thin
- **2** teaspoons extra-virgin olive oil
- **¼** teaspoon Diamond Crystal kosher salt
- **¼** cup thinly sliced red onion
- **½** cup almond milk ricotta cheese or other dairy-free nut cheese (optional)
- **¼** teaspoon freshly ground black pepper

Meatza's like an upside-down pizza, with a crust made of meat. Top it with anything you like: marinara, mushrooms, olives, pepperoni, the works!

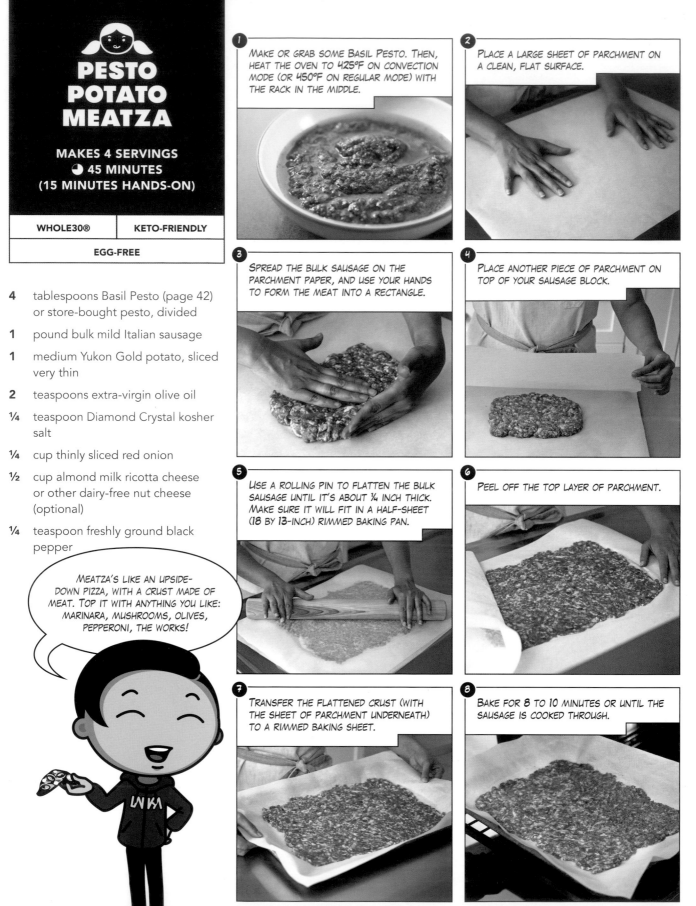

1 Make or grab some Basil Pesto. Then, heat the oven to 425°F on convection mode (or 450°F on regular mode) with the rack in the middle.

2 Place a large sheet of parchment on a clean, flat surface.

3 Spread the bulk sausage on the parchment paper, and use your hands to form the meat into a rectangle.

4 Place another piece of parchment on top of your sausage block.

5 Use a rolling pin to flatten the bulk sausage until it's about ¼ inch thick. Make sure it will fit in a half-sheet (18 by 13-inch) rimmed baking pan.

6 Peel off the top layer of parchment.

7 Transfer the flattened crust (with the sheet of parchment underneath) to a rimmed baking sheet.

8 Bake for 8 to 10 minutes or until the sausage is cooked through.

Per serving (not including cheese): 453 calories • 12 g carbohydrates • 21 g protein • 36 g fat • 2 g fiber

9 TAKE THE PAN OUT OF THE OVEN.

10 AT THIS POINT, YOU MAY NOTICE A LOT OF ACCUMULATED SAUSAGE JUICE. BLOT THE CRUST WELL WITH PAPER TOWELS.

11 CAREFULLY TRANSFER THE CRUST TO A CLEAN PIECE OF PARCHMENT. PUT THE CRUST (WITH THE NEW PARCHMENT) BACK ONTO THE BAKING SHEET.

12 SLATHER 3 TABLESPOONS OF PESTO IN A THIN LAYER ON THE MEATZA CRUST.

13 ADD THE POTATOES IN A SINGLE LAYER ON TOP OF THE PESTO.

14 BRUSH THE OIL ON THE POTATOES, AND SPRINKLE SALT EVENLY OVER THE TOP.

15 TOP WITH RED ONION SLICES.

16 IF DESIRED, ADD SOME SMALL DOLLOPS OF ALMOND MILK RICOTTA CHEESE ON TOP.

17 RETURN THE MEATZA TO THE OVEN, AND BAKE FOR 8 TO 12 MORE MINUTES OR UNTIL THE POTATOES ARE COOKED THROUGH AND BROWNED ON THE EDGES.

18 TAKE THE MEATZA OUT OF THE OVEN AND LET IT REST FOR 5 MINUTES.

19 DOLLOP ON THE REMAINING TABLESPOON OF PESTO AND ADD FRESHLY GROUND BLACK PEPPER.

20 SLICE AND EAT.

HENRY AND I USED TO BE PIZZA FREAKS,
FLYING ALL OVER THE WORLD IN SEARCH
OF THE PERFECT SLICE OF PIE. BUT
ONCE WE WENT PALEO, OUR NEVEREND-
ING PIZZAFEST ABRUPTLY ENDED . . . THAT
IS, UNTIL WE DISCOVERED THE WONDERS
OF MEATZA, A GRAIN-FREE PIZZA THAT
USES SAUSAGE IN PLACE OF THE CRUST!

YOU CAN TOP THIS SATISFYINGLY MEATY PIE WITH ANY NUMBER OF CLASSIC TOP-PINGS, BUT THIS PARTICULAR COMBINATION OF THINLY SLICED POTATOES, PESTO, AND SAUSAGE IS AT THE VERY TOP OF MY LIST. IT MAKES ME NOSTALGIC FOR THE POTATO PIZZA I USED TO IMPATIENTLY LINE UP TO BUY AT BERKELEY'S CHEESEBOARD PIZZA.

POT STICKERS

MAKES 48 POT STICKERS

●●●◐ 3½ HOURS
(2 HOURS HANDS-ON)

NUT-FREE	EGG-FREE
NIGHTSHADE-FREE	

• FILLING •

½ ounce dried shiitake mushrooms

1 small (1-pound) head Napa cabbage

3 teaspoons Diamond Crystal kosher salt, divided

1 pound ground pork

¼ cup bone broth or chicken broth

½ cup minced scallions

1 tablespoon minced fresh garlic

½ teaspoon ground ginger

½ teaspoon ground white pepper

1 tablespoon coconut aminos

1 teaspoon toasted sesame oil

• WRAPPERS •

3 cups (384 grams) cassava flour

¾ cup (96 grams) arrowroot powder

1½ teaspoons Diamond Crystal kosher salt

2¼ cups boiling water

• FOR COOKING •

4 tablespoons avocado oil for pan-frying, divided

2 cups boiling water for pan-steaming, divided

• FOR DIPPING •

½ cup Dumpling Dipping Sauce (page 30) (optional, not nightshade-free)

1 START BY MAKING THE FILLING. IN A BOWL, SOAK THE DRIED SHIITAKE MUSHROOMS IN WATER FOR AT LEAST 30 MINUTES OR UP TO 8 HOURS IN THE REFRIGERATOR UNTIL THEY'RE COMPLETELY REHYDRATED.

2 WHILE THE MUSHROOMS ARE SOAKING, FINELY CHOP UP THE NAPA CABBAGE HEAD. ALTERNATIVELY, YOU CAN PULSE IT IN A FOOD PROCESSOR.

3 COMBINE THE FINELY CHOPPED CABBAGE AND 2 TEASPOONS OF KOSHER SALT IN A LARGE BOWL AND TOSS WELL.

4 TRANSFER THE SALTED CABBAGE TO A FINE-MESH STRAINER OR COLANDER AND SET IT OVER A BOWL.

5 LET IT STAND AT ROOM TEMPERATURE FOR AT LEAST 30 MINUTES OR IN THE FRIDGE FOR UP TO 8 HOURS.

6 WHEN YOU'RE READY TO MAKE THE FILLING, GRAB THE SOAKED SHIITAKE MUSHROOMS AND SQUEEZE OUT THE EXCESS LIQUID.

7 REMOVE AND DISCARD THE TOUGH STEMS AND FINELY DICE THE CAPS.

8 DUMP THE SALTED CABBAGE ONTO A LARGE CHEESECLOTH OR CLEAN DISH TOWEL.

Per pot sticker: 74 calories • 9 g carbohydrates • 2 g protein • 3 g fat • 1 g fiber

9 GATHER UP THE EDGES...

10 ...AND SQUEEZE AND TWIST THE CABBAGE BUNDLE TO WRING OUT AS MUCH LIQUID AS POSSIBLE.

11 YOU SHOULD END UP WITH ABOUT 1 CUP OF CABBAGE.

12 IN A LARGE BOWL, ADD THE GROUND PORK AND CHICKEN BROTH.

13 USE YOUR HANDS TO MIX THE PORK WITH THE BROTH UNTIL THE LIQUID IS INCORPORATED INTO THE MEAT.

14 TOSS IN THE DRAINED CABBAGE, MUSHROOMS, MINCED SCALLIONS, MINCED GARLIC, GROUND GINGER, WHITE PEPPER, AND THE REMAINING TEASPOON OF SALT.

15 ADD THE COCONUT AMINOS AND SESAME OIL.

16 USE YOUR HANDS TO KNEAD THE FILLING UNTIL EVERYTHING IS WELL MIXED AND STARTS TO FEEL TACKY AND STICKY.

17 TO CHECK THE SEASONING, FRY UP A TINY PATTY OF THE MEAT MIXTURE IN A PAN AND TASTE IT. ADD MORE SALT IF NEEDED. IF YOU'RE NOT COOKING RIGHT AWAY, YOU CAN STORE THE FILLING IN A SEALED CONTAINER IN THE FRIDGE FOR UP TO 2 DAYS.

18 NOW, LET'S MAKE THE DOUGH FOR THE WRAPPERS. IN A LARGE BOWL, COMBINE ALL THE INGREDIENTS FOR THE WRAPPERS EXCEPT THE BOILING WATER.

19 POUR IN ABOUT 2 CUPS OF BOILING WATER AND STIR IT IN. ONCE THE WATER COOLS DOWN JUST ENOUGH TO TOUCH, USE YOUR HANDS TO KNEAD THE DOUGH.

20 CONTINUE ADDING A LITTLE BOILING WATER AT A TIME AND KNEAD IT UNTIL YOU FORM A SPRINGY, NOT-STICKY DOUGH.

(RECIPE CONTINUES ON THE NEXT PAGE.)

21 IF IT SEEMS EXTRA DRY, ADD A TOUCH MORE WATER, BUT WATCH OUT: YOU DON'T WANT A WET, SOFT DOUGH, OR YOU'LL HAVE TROUBLE WORKING WITH IT.

22 IF IT GETS TOO WET, KNEAD IN A LITTLE MORE CASSAVA FLOUR. WHEN IN DOUBT, ERR ON THE SIDE OF BEING A BIT STICKIER THAN DRIER.

23 DIVIDE THE DOUGH BALL INTO THIRDS, AND THEN DIVIDE EACH SMALLER BALL IN HALF TO PRODUCE 6 DOUGH BALLS. NEXT, DIVIDE EACH OF THE 6 DOUGH BALLS IN HALF, THEN IN HALF TWO MORE TIMES. GOT IT?

24 IF YOU FOLLOWED STEP 23 CORRECTLY, YOU SHOULD HAVE 48 EQUAL-SIZED BALLS.

25 COVER THE DOUGH BALLS WITH A DAMP KITCHEN TOWEL TO KEEP THEM FROM DRYING OUT.

26 NOW, IT'S TIME TO GATHER YOUR FRIENDS AND FAMILY TO HELP ASSEMBLE THE WRAPPERS AND POT STICKERS!

27 ASSIGN SOMEONE TO PORTION OUT THE FILLINGS. THIS STEP WILL ENSURE THAT YOU HAVE EXACTLY ENOUGH FILLING FOR THE WRAPPERS. SCOOP OUT A SCANT TABLESPOON OF FILLING AND PLACE THE OVAL-SHAPED FILLING ON A PLATE.

28 REPEAT UNTIL YOU HAVE 48 EQUAL OVAL-SHAPED PORTIONS.

29 NEXT, LET'S FORM THE WRAPPERS. GRAB A TORTILLA PRESS, SOME PARCHMENT, A RIMMED BAKING SHEET, A DAMP KITCHEN TOWEL, AND A SMALL BOWL OF WATER.

30 TAKE ONE OF THE DOUGH BALLS AND DAB IT WITH A LITTLE WATER IF IT FEELS DRY. THEN, USE YOUR HANDS TO ROLL IT INTO A ROUND BALL.

31 PLACE THE DOUGH BALL ON THE TORTILLA PRESS IN BETWEEN PIECES OF PARCHMENT PAPER, AND SMUSH IT FLAT.

32 THE RESULTING WRAPPER SHOULD BE VERY THIN, ABOUT 3½ INCHES IN DIAMETER.

33 PUT THE PRE-SCOOPED FILLING INTO THE MIDDLE OF THE WRAPPER. MAKE SURE YOUR FINGERS ARE CLEAN OR IT'LL BE HARD TO FOLD PROPERLY!

34 FOLD UP THE SIDES OF THE WRAPPER AROUND THE FILLING LIKE A TACO.

35 USE YOUR THUMB TO KEEP THE FILLING IN PLACE . . .

36 . . . WHILE USING YOUR OTHER HAND TO CAREFULLY PLEAT AND CRIMP ONE SIDE OF THE POT STICKER . . .

37 . . . AS YOU PRESS TOGETHER THE WRAPPER'S EDGES TO SEAL THE FILLING INSIDE.

38 CONTINUE PLEATING ONLY ONE SIDE OF THE WRAPPER AND SEALING THE TOP EDGE OF THE POT STICKER UNTIL YOU REACH THE OTHER SIDE.

39 USE YOUR FINGERS TO SECURELY SEAL THE TOP OF THE POT STICKER, DABBING ON A LITTLE WATER IF THE EDGES FEEL DRY.

40 THE POT STICKER SHOULD FORM A PLUMP CRESCENT WITH PLEATS ACROSS THE TOP.

41 ARRANGE THE FINISHED POT STICKERS ON A PARCHMENT-LINED RIMMED BAKING SHEET. KEEP THEM COVERED WITH A DAMP KITCHEN TOWEL TO KEEP THEM FROM DRYING OUT. CONTINUE MAKING AND STUFFING WRAPPERS UNTIL YOU HAVE 48 DUMPLINGS.

42 AT THIS POINT, YOU CAN EITHER FREEZE THE UNCOOKED POT STICKERS (IN A SINGLE LAYER IN A FOOD-SAFE FREEZER BAG) FOR UP TO 2 MONTHS OR COOK THEM UP RIGHT AWAY. YOU CAN FRY THEM DIRECTLY FROM THE FREEZER WHEN YOU'RE READY TO EAT.

43 NOW, LET'S FRY UP SOME POT STICKERS! HEAT A 10-INCH HEAVY-BOTTOMED SKILLET OVER MEDIUM-HIGH HEAT. WHEN THE PAN IS HOT, ADD A TABLESPOON OF AVOCADO OIL. PLACE AS MANY POT STICKERS INTO THE PAN THAT'LL FIT IN A SINGLE LAYER.

44 FRY THE DUMPLINGS UNTIL THE BOTTOMS ARE GOLDEN-BROWN, ABOUT 2 MINUTES.

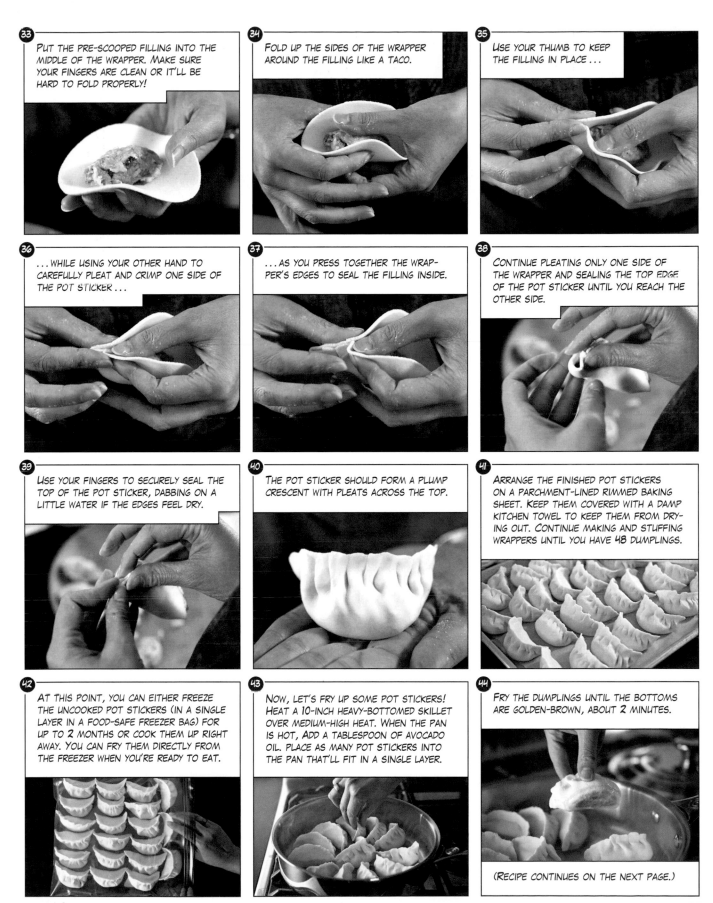

(RECIPE CONTINUES ON THE NEXT PAGE.)

45 CAREFULLY POUR IN A ½ CUP OF BOILING WATER . . .

46 . . . AND QUICKLY COVER THE SKILLET WITH A TIGHT-FITTING LID. REDUCE THE HEAT TO MEDIUM AND STEAM-FRY THE DUMPLINGS FOR 5 MINUTES (7 MINUTES IF COOKING FROM FROZEN).

47 WHEN THE TIMER GOES OFF, REMOVE THE LID. CONTINUE COOKING FOR 1 TO 2 MINUTES TO COOK OFF ANY REMAINING LIQUID AND TO RE-CRISP THE BOTTOM OF THE POTSTICKERS.

48 TRANSFER THE COOKED POT STICKERS TO A PLATE AND REPEAT THE PROCESS UNTIL YOU'RE DONE. IF DESIRED, SERVE THE POT STICKERS WITH DUMPLING DIPPING SAUCE (PAGE 30). EAT 'EM WHILE THEY'RE HOT!

HOMEMADE DUMPLINGS ARE THE PHYSICAL EMBODIMENT OF THE LOVE ASIAN MOMS HAVE FOR THEIR CHILDREN. I STILL REMINISCE ABOUT WRAPPING DUMPLINGS WITH MY MOM AND GRANDMA AT OUR KITCHEN TABLE AND HAPPILY GOBBLING 'EM UP (THE DUMPLINGS, NOT MY FAMILY) AS SOON AS THEY LEFT THE FRYING PAN. WHO COULD RESIST THESE DELICATELY WRAPPED PURSES FILLED WITH TENDER MEAT, SIZZLED TO GOLDEN PERFECTION AND DIPPED IN A VINEGARY SAUCE?

I KNOW THIS RECIPE FOR POT STICKERS REQUIRES MORE TIME
AND ELBOW GREASE THAN MY TYPICAL CREATIONS, BUT I CAN'T
OFFER YOU ANY OF MY USUAL SHORTCUTS. SOMETIMES, YOU
JUST NEED TO PUT IN THE WORK. BUT TRUST ME, PEOPLE:
THESE PAN-FRIED DUMPLINGS ARE WELL WORTH THE EFFORT.

WONTON MEATBALLS

MAKES 12 MEATBALLS
● **1 HOUR**
(20 MINUTES HANDS-ON)

WHOLE30®	KETO-FRIENDLY
NUT-FREE	EGG-FREE
NIGHTSHADE-FREE	

• MEATBALLS •

¼ ounce dried shiitake mushrooms, soaked in water until rehydrated

½ pound shrimp, shelled and deveined

1 pound ground pork

2 scallions, finely chopped

¼ cup fresh cilantro, minced

1 tablespoon coconut aminos

½ teaspoon Diamond Crystal kosher salt

½ teaspoon paleo-friendly fish sauce

¼ teaspoon ground white pepper

¼ teaspoon toasted sesame oil

Avocado oil

• OPTIONAL GARNISHES •

1 scallion, thinly sliced

½ cup Dumpling Dipping Sauce (page 30) (not nightshade-free)

¼ cup Nom Nom Chili Crisp (page 38) (not nightshade-free)

⟳ SWITCH IT UP: AIR FRYER WONTON MEATBALLS

YOU CAN COOK WONTON MEATBALLS A HALF BATCH AT A TIME IN AN AIR FRYER SET AT AT **375°F** FOR **10** TO **12** MINUTES.

① IF YOU HAVEN'T ALREADY, REHYDRATE YOUR DRIED MUSHROOMS. (PRO TIP: SOAK THEM IN A BOWL OF WATER IN THE MORNING SO THEY'LL BE PLUMP AND TENDER BY THE TIME YOU'RE READY TO MAKE DINNER.)

② ONCE YOU'RE READY TO COOK, HEAT THE OVEN TO 400°F, AND SQUEEZE THE WATER OUT OF THE MUSHROOMS. CUT OFF THE HARD STEMS, AND FINELY MINCE THE CAPS.

③ FINELY CHOP THE SHRIMP UNTIL IT TURNS INTO A CHUNKY PASTE.

④ TRANSFER THE CHOPPED SHRIMP TO A LARGE BOWL. ADD THE PORK, MUSHROOMS, SCALLIONS, CILANTRO, COCONUT AMINOS, SALT, FISH SAUCE, WHITE PEPPER, AND SESAME OIL.

⑤ USE YOUR HANDS TO SQUEEZE AND MIX THE MEATBALL MIXTURE UNTIL A STICKY AND TACKY MASS IS FORMED.

(ALTERNATIVELY, USE A FOOD PROCESSOR TO CHOP AND COMBINE THE INGREDIENTS.)

⑥ FORM A LITTLE PATTY AND COOK IT IN A SMALL SKILLET OVER MEDIUM HEAT. TASTE IT AND SEASON WITH MORE SALT IF NEEDED. (NOT READY TO COOK JUST YET? YOU CAN REFRIGERATE THE MEAT MIXTURE FOR UP TO 12 HOURS.)

⑦ USE A 3-TABLESPOON SCOOPER TO PORTION OUT 12 BLOBS OF THE MIXTURE.

⑧ RUB A LITTLE OIL ON YOUR PALMS, AND ROLL THE MEAT INTO 1½-INCH BALLS.

Per serving (3 meatballs): 370 calories • 3 g carbohydrates • 31 g protein • 25 g fat • 1 g fiber

9 ARRANGE THE MEATBALLS IN A SINGLE LAYER ON A GREASED OR PARCHMENT-LINED RIMMED BAKING SHEET. (OR ARRANGE THE BALLS IN A GREASED OVEN-SAFE SKILLET.)

10 BAKE THE BALLS IN THE OVEN FOR 15 TO 20 MINUTES OR UNTIL COOKED THROUGH.

11 IF DESIRED, GARNISH WITH SCALLIONS AND SERVE WITH DUMPLING DIPPING SAUCE OR NOM NOM CHILI CRISP IF DESIRED.

THESE BOUNCY, FLAVOR-PACKED MEATBALLS REMIND ME OF MY MOM'S PORK AND SHRIMP WONTON FILLING. EVEN OLLIE GAVE THIS RECIPE HIS ENTHUSIASTIC SEAL OF APPROVAL. (IN OTHER WORDS, HE FINISHED HIS SUPPER IN A MATTER OF MINUTES RATHER THAN HOURS.)

MOO SHU PORK

MAKES 4 SERVINGS
● ◐ 1¼ HOURS
(45 MINUTES HANDS-ON)

WHOLE30®	NUT-FREE
NIGHTSHADE-FREE	

¼   cup All-Purpose Stir-Fry Sauce (page 29)

½   ounce dried shiitake mushrooms

1   pound pork tenderloin, cut into thin matchsticks

     Diamond Crystal kosher salt

3   tablespoons avocado oil, divided

3   large eggs

¾   teaspoon paleo-friendly fish sauce or No-Fish Sauce (page 28)

4   cups thinly sliced Napa cabbage

1   large carrot, julienned

2   teaspoons arrowroot powder

½   teaspoon toasted sesame oil

3   scallions, thinly sliced

8   Grain-Free Tortillas (page 48) (not Whole30), butter lettuce leaves, or thinly sliced jicama (optional)

½   cup Sunbutter Hoisin Sauce (page 32) (optional)

WANNA EAT YOUR MOO SHU PORK WITH A FORK? SERVE IT OVER CAULIFLOWER RICE (PAGE 107)!

1   TAKE NOTE: YOU'LL NEED SOME ALL-PURPOSE STIR-FRY SAUCE FOR THIS RECIPE.

2   IN A MEDIUM BOWL, SUBMERGE THE DRIED SHIITAKE MUSHROOMS IN WATER FOR AT LEAST 30 MINUTES OR UNTIL REHYDRATED.

3   THEN, SQUEEZE OUT THE EXTRA LIQUID, CUT OFF THE STEMS, AND THINLY SLICE THE MUSHROOMS. SET THEM ASIDE WITH THE REST OF THE PREPPED VEGETABLES.

4   IN A LARGE BOWL, TOSS THE SLICED PORK WITH ¾ TEASPOON SALT AND 1 TEASPOON AVOCADO OIL. SET ASIDE.

5   IN A MEDIUM BOWL, WHISK TOGETHER THE EGGS AND FISH SAUCE.

6   HEAT A SMALL NON-STICK OR CAST-IRON SKILLET OVER MEDIUM HEAT. WHEN THE PAN IS HOT, ADD 2 TEASPOONS OF AVOCADO OIL. THEN, POUR IN THE EGGS.

7   STIR AND SCRAPE THE PAN CONSTANTLY TO SOFTLY SCRAMBLE THE EGGS. TRANSFER THE EGGS TO A PLATTER.

8   HEAT A LARGE 12-INCH SKILLET OVER MEDIUM-HIGH HEAT AND ADD 1 TABLESPOON OF AVOCADO OIL ONCE IT'S HOT. THEN, ADD THE SEASONED PORK.

Per serving (of filling only): 321 calories • 18 g carbohydrates • 37 g protein • 11 g fat • 3 g fiber

9 COOK, STIRRING FREQUENTLY...

10 ...UNTIL IT IS NO LONGER PINK. TRANSFER THE COOKED PORK TO A PLATE.

11 DISCARD ANY LIQUID IN THE PAN AND ADD ANOTHER TABLESPOON OF AVOCADO OIL. THEN, ADD THE CHOPPED MUSHROOMS, CABBAGE, AND CARROT.

12 SPRINKLE ½ TEASPOON OF KOSHER SALT ON THE VEGGIES. COOK, STIRRING, UNTIL TENDER CRISP, ABOUT 2 TO 3 MINUTES.

13 WHILE THE VEGETABLES ARE COOKING, ADD THE ALL-PURPOSE STIR-FRY SAUCE, ARROWROOT POWDER, AND SESAME OIL TO A SMALL MEASURING CUP.

14 WHISK WELL, AND SET THE SAUCE ASIDE.

15 WHEN THE VEGETABLES ARE READY, STIR IN THE RESERVED COOKED PORK...

16 ...AND POUR THE SAUCE OVER EVERYTHING.

17 COOK, STIRRING FREQUENTLY, UNTIL THE SAUCE HAS THICKENED SLIGHTLY.

18 TURN OFF THE HEAT AND STIR IN THE SCRAMBLED EGGS AND SCALLIONS. TASTE AND ADJUST FOR SEASONING IF NEEDED.

19 IF DESIRED, SLATHER SUNBUTTER HOISIN SAUCE ON A WARM TORTILLA OR LETTUCE WRAP AND FILL WITH MOO SHU PORK.

20 WRAP AND EAT. THE MESS IS WORTH IT!

Originally a dish from northern China, Moo Shu Pork has been adapted many times over in American Chinese restaurants and households. This delicious stir-fry isn't usually strongly flavored because it's supposed to be tucked into a thin pancake wrapper slathered with sweet-and-savory hoisin sauce. But personally, I like to flavor it up as much as possible!

My mom's version contains pork, Napa cabbage, and fluffy scrambled eggs, but she also includes more difficult-to-source components like wood ear mushrooms, dried daylily buds, and julienned bamboo shoots. I left them out to avoid having to make a special trip to the local Asian grocery store, but feel free to include them if you want.

INSTANT POT BUTA NO KAKUNI (BRAISED PORK BELLY)

MAKES 8 SERVINGS
◐◑ **1½ HOURS**
(20 MINUTES HANDS-ON)

WHOLE30®	KETO-FRIENDLY
NUT-FREE	EGG-FREE
NIGHTSHADE-FREE	

¾ cup All-Purpose Stir-Fry Sauce (page 29)

2 pounds pork belly, skin removed and cut into 2-inch cubes

5 scallions, divided

1 (2-inch) piece fresh ginger, peeled and cut into thin coins

THIS PORK BELLY IS SUPER SAVORY AND RICH, SO A LITTLE GOES A LONG WAY. I LIKE TO SERVE IT WITH CAULIFLOWER RICE (PAGE 107)!

SWITCH IT UP: SLOW COOKER BUTA NO KAKUNI

SAUTÉ THE PORK BELLY IN A SKILLET OVER MEDIUM-HIGH HEAT, AND THEN TRANSFER ALL THE INGREDIENTS INTO A SLOW COOKER. COOK IT ON LOW FOR 8 TO 10 HOURS. TRANSFER TO A PLATTER AND SERVE.

1 GRAB OR MAKE SOME ALL-PURPOSE STIR-FRY SAUCE, 'CAUSE YOU'LL NEED IT.

2 SWITCH ON THE INSTANT POT'S SAUTÉ FUNCTION. IN BATCHES, SEAR THE PORK BELLY PIECES ON 2 SIDES (TOP AND BOTTOM), ABOUT 3 TO 4 MINUTES PER SIDE. TRANSFER ALL THE PORK TO A PLATTER.

3 TURN OFF THE SAUTÉ FUNCTION. DISCARD ALL BUT ABOUT 1 TABLESPOON OF THE FAT LEFT IN THE INSTANT POT. PUT ALL THE PORK CUBES BACK INTO THE INSTANT POT.

4 CUT 3 OF THE SCALLIONS INTO 2-INCH PIECES, AND TOSS THEM INTO THE INSTANT POT ALONG WITH THE GINGER.

5 ADD THE ALL-PURPOSE STIR-FRY SAUCE.

6 SEAL AND COOK FOR 35 MINUTES UNDER HIGH PRESSURE. WAIT FOR THE PRESSURE TO RELEASE NATURALLY.

7 TRANSFER THE PORK TO A SERVING BOWL AND LADLE THE SAUCE ON TOP.

8 THINLY SLICE THE REMAINING SCALLIONS AND USE THEM TO GARNISH THE PORK.

Per serving: 464 calories • 4 g carbohydrates • 7 g protein • 45 g fat • 1 g fiber

Buta no Kakuni, which literally means "square-cut simmered pork" in Japanese, is actually derived from a thousand-year-old Chinese dish called Dong Po Rou. According to legend, a brilliant but absentminded Song dynasty scholar named Su Dong Po left a pot of pork belly braising on his stove during a game of Chinese chess. Upon tasting the pork, he found it to be even more unctuously delicious and melt-in-your-mouth tender than expected. His recipe eventually made its way to Kyushu in southern Japan, where it evolved into Buta no Kakuni. This is my paleofied take on this flavor bomb of a pork belly dish.

LEMONGRASS PORK CHOPS

MAKES 6 SERVINGS
◐ 1½ HOURS
(30 MINUTES HANDS-ON)

NUT-FREE	EGG-FREE

• PORK CHOPS •

2 large lemongrass stalks

1 large shallot, coarsely chopped

6 garlic cloves, peeled

1 tablespoon lime zest

1 teaspoon Diamond Crystal kosher salt

1 teaspoon ground ginger

¼ teaspoon freshly ground black pepper

¼ cup avocado oil

2 tablespoons paleo-friendly fish sauce or No-Fish Sauce (page 28)

1 tablespoon honey

6 (1-inch-thick) bone-in pork chops

• NUOC CHAM SAUCE •

3 tablespoons paleo-friendly fish sauce or No-Fish Sauce (page 28)

3 tablespoons maple syrup

Juice from 1 medium lime

¼ cup water

¼ teaspoon crushed red pepper flakes

1 small garlic clove, minced

• GARNISHES •

1 butter lettuce head, separated into leaves

1 English cucumber, thinly sliced

2 limes, cut into wedges

1 bunch fresh spearmint

1 bunch fresh Thai or Italian basil

1 FIRST, MARINATE THE PORK. GRAB THE LEMONGRASS STALKS AND CUT OFF ABOUT AN INCH FROM THE ROOT ENDS.

2 PEEL OFF THE TOUGH OUTER LAYERS OF THE STALKS UNTIL YOU'RE LEFT WITH THE TENDER CORE.

3 CUT THE STALKS ABOUT 4 TO 5 INCHES FROM THE ROOT END AND DISCARD THE DRY TOPS.

4 ROUGHLY CHOP UP THE LEMONGRASS INTO SMALL PIECES.

5 IN A FOOD PROCESSOR OR BLENDER, ADD THE LEMONGRASS, SHALLOT, GARLIC, LIME ZEST, SALT...

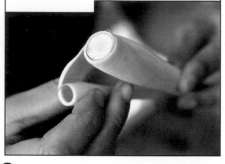

6 ...GINGER, BLACK PEPPER, AVOCADO OIL, FISH SAUCE, AND HONEY.

7 BLITZ UNTIL THE MARINADE IS MOSTLY SMOOTH.

8 PLACE THE PORK CHOPS IN A SHALLOW CONTAINER AND POUR IN THE MARINADE.

Per serving: 604 calories • 18 g carbohydrates • 47 g protein • 38 g fat • 1 g fiber

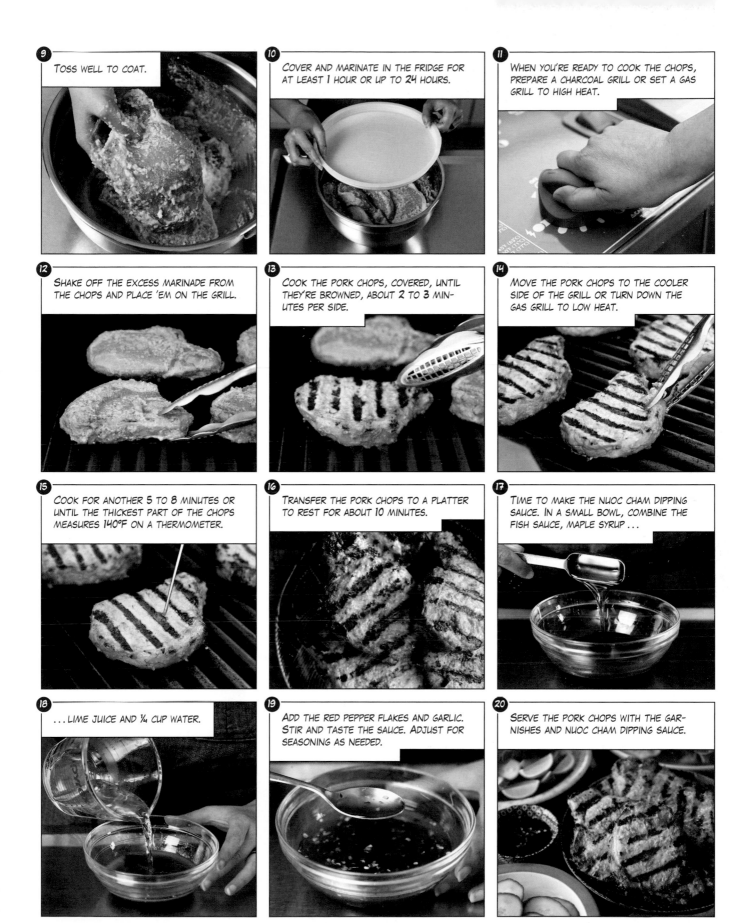

9 TOSS WELL TO COAT.

10 COVER AND MARINATE IN THE FRIDGE FOR AT LEAST 1 HOUR OR UP TO 24 HOURS.

11 WHEN YOU'RE READY TO COOK THE CHOPS, PREPARE A CHARCOAL GRILL OR SET A GAS GRILL TO HIGH HEAT.

12 SHAKE OFF THE EXCESS MARINADE FROM THE CHOPS AND PLACE 'EM ON THE GRILL.

13 COOK THE PORK CHOPS, COVERED, UNTIL THEY'RE BROWNED, ABOUT 2 TO 3 MINUTES PER SIDE.

14 MOVE THE PORK CHOPS TO THE COOLER SIDE OF THE GRILL OR TURN DOWN THE GAS GRILL TO LOW HEAT.

15 COOK FOR ANOTHER 5 TO 8 MINUTES OR UNTIL THE THICKEST PART OF THE CHOPS MEASURES 140°F ON A THERMOMETER.

16 TRANSFER THE PORK CHOPS TO A PLATTER TO REST FOR ABOUT 10 MINUTES.

17 TIME TO MAKE THE NUOC CHAM DIPPING SAUCE. IN A SMALL BOWL, COMBINE THE FISH SAUCE, MAPLE SYRUP . . .

18 . . . LIME JUICE AND ¼ CUP WATER.

19 ADD THE RED PEPPER FLAKES AND GARLIC. STIR AND TASTE THE SAUCE. ADJUST FOR SEASONING AS NEEDED.

20 SERVE THE PORK CHOPS WITH THE GARNISHES AND NUOC CHAM DIPPING SAUCE.

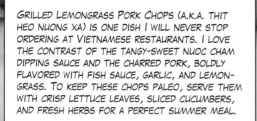

GRILLED LEMONGRASS PORK CHOPS (A.K.A. THIT HEO NUONG XA) IS ONE DISH I WILL NEVER STOP ORDERING AT VIETNAMESE RESTAURANTS. I LOVE THE CONTRAST OF THE TANGY-SWEET NUOC CHAM DIPPING SAUCE AND THE CHARRED PORK, BOLDLY FLAVORED WITH FISH SAUCE, GARLIC, AND LEMONGRASS. TO KEEP THESE CHOPS PALEO, SERVE THEM WITH CRISP LETTUCE LEAVES, SLICED CUCUMBERS, AND FRESH HERBS FOR A PERFECT SUMMER MEAL.

CHAR SIU (CHINESE BARBECUE PORK)

MAKES 8 SERVINGS

●●●● **4 HOURS**
(1½ HOURS HANDS-ON)

WHOLE30® (IF MODIFIED)	
KETO-FRIENDLY	EGG-FREE

½ cup plum, peach, or apricot jam, sweetened only with fruit juice

¼ cup coconut aminos

3 tablespoons tomato paste

1 tablespoon almond butter

1 tablespoon honey (optional, not Whole30)

1 teaspoon paleo-friendly fish sauce or No-Fish Sauce (page 28)

½ teaspoon Chinese five-spice powder

½ teaspoon ground ginger

3 pounds boneless pork shoulder roast

2 teaspoons Diamond Crystal kosher salt

2 scallions, thinly sliced (optional)

USE THIS FOR:

- Scallion Pancake Tacos (page 84)

- Singapore Noodles (page 128)

- Shoyu Ramen (page 134)

1 POUR THE JAM INTO A SMALL SAUCEPAN. (TO STAY PALEO-FRIENDLY, BE SURE TO USE A HIGH-QUALITY, 100% FRUIT JAM.)

2 NEXT, TOSS IN THE COCONUT AMINOS, TOMATO PASTE, ALMOND BUTTER, HONEY (IF DESIRED), FISH SAUCE, CHINESE FIVE-SPICE POWDER, AND GROUND GINGER.

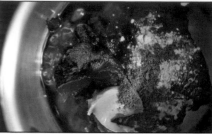

3 WHISK THE MARINADE AS YOU HEAT IT TO A SIMMER OVER MEDIUM HEAT.

4 ONCE THE MARINADE IS BUBBLING AND SMOOTH, TRANSFER IT TO A MEASURING CUP AND LET IT COOL TO ROOM TEMPERATURE. (NOT READY TO ROAST THE PORK? YOU CAN STORE THE SAUCE IN THE FRIDGE FOR UP TO 4 DAYS.)

5 NEXT, PREPARE THE PORK. BLOT THE PORK SHOULDER DRY WITH A PAPER TOWEL.

6 THEN, SLICE THE PORK SHOULDER INTO 2-INCH STRIPS OF EVEN THICKNESS.

7 THE PORK STRIPS SHOULD BE ROUGHLY UNIFORM IN SIZE. IT'S FINE TO HAVE FATTY PIECES OF PORK BECAUSE: (1) IT'S TASTY, AND (2) YOU DON'T WANT TO END UP WITH DRY CHAR SIU.

8 SPRINKLE 2 TEASPOONS KOSHER SALT ALL OVER THE PORK PIECES.

Per serving: 531 calories • 11 g carbohydrates • 41 g protein • 33 g fat • 1 g fiber

9 PLACE THE PORK IN A LARGE BOWL OR A ZIPPERED FOOD STORAGE BAG.

10 POUR ALL EXCEPT ⅓ CUP OF THE COOLED MARINADE ONTO THE PORK. COVER AND REFRIGERATE THE RESERVED MARINADE.

11 USE YOUR HANDS (A.K.A. NATURE'S TONGS) TO COAT THE MARINADE ALL OVER THE PORK STRIPS.

12 COVER THE BOWL AND REFRIGERATE IT FOR 2 TO 24 HOURS.

13 WHEN YOU'RE READY TO ROAST THE PORK, HEAT THE OVEN TO 350°F WITH THE RACK IN THE MIDDLE POSITION.

14 ARRANGE THE PORK ON AN OVEN-SAFE WIRE RACK IN A RIMMED BAKING SHEET.

15 ROAST FOR 30 MINUTES, FLIPPING THE PORK PIECES AT THE HALFWAY POINT.

16 TAKE THE PORK OUT OF THE OVEN AND INCREASE THE TEMPERATURE TO 400°F.

17 BRUSH HALF OF THE RESERVED MARINADE ON THE TOPS OF THE PORK PIECES.

18 POUR ENOUGH WATER INTO THE BOTTOM OF THE PAN SO THAT YOU HAVE A THIN LAYER COATING THE BOTTOM. THIS WILL KEEP THE DRIPPINGS FROM BURNING WHILE THE PORK COOKS.

19 ROAST FOR 25 MINUTES. THEN, FLIP THE PORK PIECES OVER . . .

20 . . . AND BRUSH ON THE REMAINING MARINADE.

(RECIPE CONTINUED ON THE NEXT PAGE!)

21 COOK FOR ANOTHER 20 TO 30 MINUTES OR UNTIL THE PORK IS SLIGHTLY CHARRED ON THE EDGES.

22 REST THE PORK FOR 10 MINUTES, AND THEN SLICE AGAINST THE GRAIN INTO BITE-SIZE PIECES.

23 ARRANGE THE PORK ON A SERVING DISH . . .

24 . . . AND GARNISH WITH 2 SLICED SCALLIONS.

I ADORE CHAR SIU, CANTONESE ROASTED PORK LACQUERED WITH A STICKY-SWEET MARINADE. YOU KNOW WHAT I'M TALKING ABOUT: THE BRIGHT RED HUNKS OF MEAT THAT HANG IN THE FOGGED-UP WINDOWS OF CHINATOWN BARBECUE RESTAURANTS.

As a kid, I would linger at my mom's elbow every time she sliced up her char siu, panting like a puppy desperate for a scrap of leftovers. Never one to be subtle, I'd refuse to budge until my mom slipped me a juicy piece of pork right from the cutting board. Fueled by these happy food memories, I made it my mission to invent a paleo version of this porky delight. It took a dozen tries, but I finally nailed it!

TREATS

CHOCOLATE GANACHE

MAKES 1 CUP
⏲ 10 MINUTES

NUT-FREE	EGG-FREE
NIGHTSHADE-FREE	VEGAN

⅔ cup full-fat coconut milk

4 ounces dark chocolate, finely chopped

USE THIS FOR:

- Profiteroles (page 329)
- Coffee Ice Cream (page 332)
- Coconut Vanilla Ice Cream (page 334)

THIS DAIRY-FREE CHOCOLATE GANACHE IS THE GLOSSY, DECADENT TOPPING THAT ALL OF YOUR DESSERTS DESERVE!

1 IN A SMALL SAUCEPAN SET OVER MEDIUM HEAT, WARM THE COCONUT MILK UNTIL IT BEGINS TO SIMMER.

2 PLACE THE CHOCOLATE IN A BOWL, POUR THE HOT COCONUT MILK OVER IT, AND LET IT SIT FOR 1 TO 2 MINUTES.

3 STIR, ALLOWING THE HEAT OF THE HOT COCONUT MILK TO MELT THE CHOCOLATE.

4 DRIZZLE IT OVER YOUR FAVORITE TREATS, LIKE COFFEE ICE CREAM (PAGE **332**)!

Per 2 tablespoons: 122 calories • 7 g carbohydrates • 2 g protein • 10 g fat • 2 g fiber

WHIPPED COCONUT CREAM

MAKES 1 CUP
⚠ 5 TO 8 HOURS
(10 MINUTES HANDS-ON)

NUT-FREE	EGG-FREE
NIGHTSHADE-FREE	VEGAN

1 (13.5-ounce) can full-fat coconut cream, chilled overnight in the refrigerator

1 tablespoon maple sugar (optional)

1 teaspoon vanilla extract

USE THIS FOR:

- Blueberry Galette (page 304)
- Fruit Galette (page 307)
- Cherry Clafoutis (page 310)
- Chocolate Mug Cake (page 318)
- Vanilla Mug Cake (page 319)
- Matcha Mug Cake (page 319)
- Pumpkin Mug Cake (page 321)
- Chocolate Pudding (page 331)

CAN'T WAIT OVERNIGHT TO CHILL THE COCONUT CREAM? STICK THE CAN IN THE FREEZER FOR ABOUT 5 HOURS BEFORE WHIPPING!

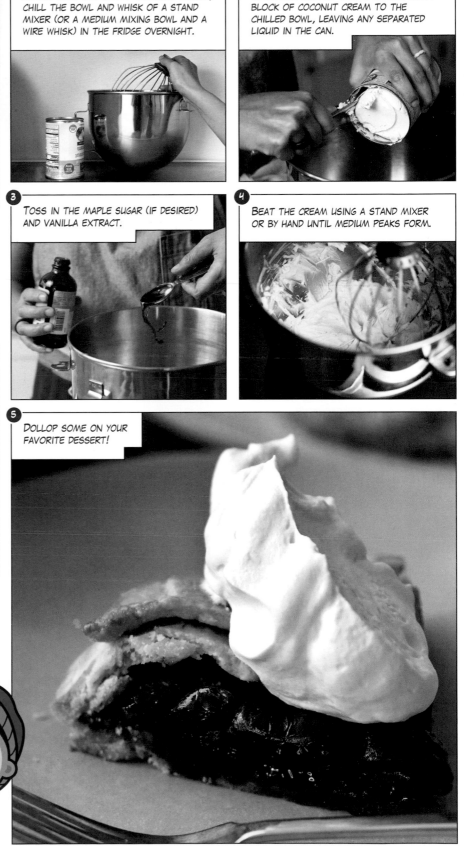

1 ALONG WITH THE CAN OF COCONUT CREAM, CHILL THE BOWL AND WHISK OF A STAND MIXER (OR A MEDIUM MIXING BOWL AND A WIRE WHISK) IN THE FRIDGE OVERNIGHT.

2 OPEN THE CAN AND TRANSFER THE THICK BLOCK OF COCONUT CREAM TO THE CHILLED BOWL, LEAVING ANY SEPARATED LIQUID IN THE CAN.

3 TOSS IN THE MAPLE SUGAR (IF DESIRED) AND VANILLA EXTRACT.

4 BEAT THE CREAM USING A STAND MIXER OR BY HAND UNTIL MEDIUM PEAKS FORM.

5 DOLLOP SOME ON YOUR FAVORITE DESSERT!

Per 2 tablespoons: 101 calories • 3 g carbohydrates • 1 g protein • 10 g fat • 0 g fiber

CHOCOLATE CHERRY GRANOLA

MAKES 18 SERVINGS
● **1 HOUR**
(15 MINUTES HANDS-ON)

EGG-FREE	NIGHTSHADE-FREE
VEGAN	

½ cup maple syrup

¼ cup melted refined coconut oil

1½ teaspoons vanilla extract

½ teaspoon ground cardamom

½ teaspoon Diamond Crystal kosher salt

2 cups raw unsweetened coconut flakes

2 cups raw almonds, roughly chopped

1 cup raw walnuts, roughly chopped

1 cup raw cashews, roughly chopped

½ cup raw pepitas

½ cup dried cherries

1 (3.5-ounce) dark chocolate bar, chopped into small chunks

THIS GRANOLA IS GRAIN-FREE, SO IT'S MADE WITH NUTS AND SEEDS INSTEAD OF OATS. I USED ALMONDS, CASHEWS, WALNUTS, AND PEPITAS HERE, BUT FEEL FREE TO CHANGE UP THE NUTS AND SEEDS IN THIS GRANOLA TO YOUR LIKING!

1 HEAT THE OVEN TO 300°F WITH THE RACK IN THE MIDDLE POSITION. LINE A RIMMED BAKING SHEET WITH PARCHMENT PAPER.

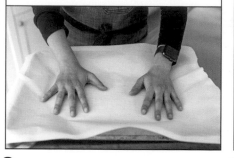

2 IN A LARGE BOWL, WHISK TOGETHER THE MAPLE SYRUP, MELTED COCONUT OIL, VANILLA EXTRACT, CARDAMOM, AND SALT.

3 STIR IN THE COCONUT FLAKES, NUTS, AND SEEDS, AND COAT EVERYTHING EVENLY WITH THE WET INGREDIENTS.

4 DON'T MIX TOO VIGOROUSLY OR THE CO-CONUT FLAKES WILL CRUMBLE AND BREAK!

5 TRANSFER THE GRANOLA ONTO THE PARCH-MENT-LINED BAKING SHEET, AND USE A SPATULA TO EVENLY SPREAD IT OUT.

6 POP THE TRAY IN THE OVEN AND BAKE FOR 30 TO 35 MINUTES OR UNTIL GOLDEN BROWN. TO ENSURE EVEN COOKING, STIR THE GRANOLA AND ROTATE THE TRAY AT THE HALFWAY POINT.

7 TAKE THE TRAY OUT OF THE OVEN. COOL THE GRANOLA COMPLETELY, ABOUT AN HOUR. THEN, BREAK IT UP INTO CHUNKS.

8 MIX IN THE DRIED CHERRIES AND DARK CHOCOLATE CHUNKS. PACK THE GRANOLA IN COVERED CONTAINERS, AND IT'LL KEEP AT ROOM TEMPERATURE FOR UP TO 2 WEEKS.

Per serving: 337 calories • 20 g carbohydrates • 7 g protein • 27 g fat • 5 g fiber

IT'S HARD TO STOP MUNCHING ON THIS CRUNCHY AND NUTTY TREAT, SO SHARE SOME WITH YOUR FRIENDS BEFORE YOU GOBBLE IT UP ALL BY YOURSELF!

COCONUT ALMOND JELLY

MAKES 4 SERVINGS
●●○ **2½ HOURS**
(15 MINUTES HANDS-ON)

EGG-FREE	NIGHTSHADE-FREE

1 (13.5-ounce) can full-fat coconut milk, divided

1 tablespoon gelatin powder

3 tablespoons honey

2 teaspoons almond extract

1 cup canned mandarin orange segments (in fruit juice)

1 cup canned peach slices (in fruit juice)

1 cup mixed berries

> As a kid, whenever my parents took me out for Chinese dim sum, I ordered these jiggly cubes of almond-flavored jelly, topped with a syrup-soaked fruit cocktail. To this day, I still have a soft spot for canned peaches and tangerines.

> But have no fear: my take on this sweet treat uses fresh berries and fruit canned with nothing but juice. After all, this is a Paleo cookbook!

1. Pour ¼ cup of the coconut milk into a measuring cup. Add the gelatin and whisk until well incorporated. Set the mixture aside.

2. In a small saucepan, heat the remaining coconut milk and honey over medium heat, stirring frequently, until well mixed.

3. Cook the sweetened coconut milk mixture until bubbles appear on the edges of the pan. Turn off the heat.

4. Add the reserved hydrated gelatin mixture and almond extract to the pan. Whisk well, making sure there are no lumps.

5. Pour the mixture into a rectangular container.

6. Chill the mixture for 30 minutes uncovered. Then, cover and chill for an additional 1½ hours or until solid. (You can keep the jelly in the fridge for up to 4 days before serving.)

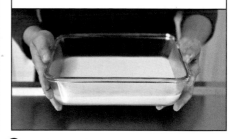

7. When ready to serve, cut the jelly into ½-inch squares.

8. Divide the cubes into bowls and top with the fruit and its juice. Eat it up!

Per serving: 294 calories • 26 g carbohydrates • 4 g protein • 21 g fat • 2 g fiber

BLUEBERRY GALETTE

MAKES 6 SERVINGS
◐◐ 1½ HOURS
(30 MINUTES HANDS-ON)

NUT-FREE	NIGHTSHADE-FREE
VEGETARIAN	

• CRUST •

1 cup (128 grams) cassava flour

¼ cup (36 grams) tapioca flour

1½ teaspoons maple sugar

¼ teaspoon Diamond Crystal kosher salt

2 eggs, divided

½ cup (120 grams) ghee, chilled and coarsely chopped

¼ cup ice water

• FILLING •

1¾ cup (227 grams) blueberries

¼ cup (39 grams) maple sugar or coconut sugar

1 tablespoon (9 grams) tapioca flour

1½ teaspoons lemon juice

⅛ teaspoon Diamond Crystal kosher salt

• OPTIONAL TOPPING •

½ cup Whipped Coconut Cream (page 299)

1 Let's start by making a galette crust. In a food processor, add the cassava flour, tapioca flour...

2 ...sugar, salt, 1 egg, and chilled ghee.

3 Pulse until the ingredients are the texture of coarse cornmeal. Transfer the contents to a large bowl.

4 Knead in just enough ice water so that the dough holds and is no longer sticky when pressed together.

5 Form the dough into a flat puck. Cover and stick it in the fridge for at least 30 minutes. Heat the oven to 400°F with the rack in the middle.

6 Sprinkle a piece of parchment paper with cassava flour. Place the chilled dough on top, and dust it with some more cassava flour.

7 Use a rolling pin to flatten the puck of dough into a circle about ¼ inch thick and 12 inches in diameter.

8 Transfer the flattened dough with the parchment onto a baking sheet, and stick it in the fridge.

Per serving: 313 calories • 40 g carbohydrates • 3 g protein • 17 g fat • 1 g fiber

9 NOW IT'S TIME TO MAKE THE FILLING. IN A LARGE BOWL, TOSS TOGETHER THE BLUEBERRIES, SUGAR, TAPIOCA FLOUR, LEMON JUICE, AND SALT.

10 MIX UNTIL WELL COMBINED.

11 PLOP THE BLUEBERRIES IN THE CENTER OF THE CHILLED DOUGH, LEAVING A 2-INCH BORDER AROUND THE EDGE.

12 USING A PARING KNIFE, CUT 8 EVENLY SPACED SLITS FROM THE EDGE OF THE DOUGH TO THE BERRIES TO FORM FLAPS.

13 FOLD THE SEGMENTED DOUGH FLAPS UP AND OVER THE FILLING . . .

14 . . . OVERLAPPING THE DOUGH AS YOU GO AROUND THE GALETTE. IF THE DOUGH SPLITS, JUST WET YOUR FINGERS AND SEAL UP THE CRACKS. THIS IS SUPPOSED TO BE RUSTIC, PEOPLE!

15 WHISK THE REMAINING EGG IN A SMALL BOWL OR MEASURING CUP.

16 BRUSH THE EGG WASH OVER THE CRUST (BUT NOT THE BERRIES).

17 POP THE GALETTE IN THE OVEN AND BAKE FOR 20 MINUTES.

18 THEN, ROTATE THE TRAY 180° AND BAKE FOR ANOTHER 10 TO 15 MINUTES OR UNTIL THE GALETTE CRUST IS GOLDEN BROWN AND THE FILLING IS THICK AND BUBBLY.

19 TRANSFER THE GALETTE ONTO A WIRE RACK TO COOL TO ROOM TEMPERATURE.

20 SLICE AND SERVE. IF DESIRED, TOP WITH WHIPPED COCONUT CREAM AND DIG IN.

A ROUND PASTRY SHELL WRAPPED AROUND A FRUIT FILLING AND COOKED DIRECTLY ON A BAKING SHEET, A GALETTE IS BASICALLY A SIMPLIFIED PIE. A WELL-MADE GALETTE OFFERS A CRISP, BUTTERY CRUST AND THE PERFECT BALANCE OF SWEET AND TART IN THE FILLING. MY GRAIN-FREE VERSION FEATURES A DOUGH THAT'S SUPER FORGIVING, SO DON'T BE AFRAID TO PLAY AROUND WITH DIFFERENT FRUIT FILLINGS!

SWITCH IT UP:
FRUIT GALETTE

Seriously: you can make galettes with just about any kind of fruit. I've made 'em with blackberries, strawberries, peaches, and apples, but two of my favorite fillings are cherries and nectarines. To make a Cherry Galette, use ½ pound of pitted fresh cherries, and to make a Nectarine Galette, use 2 medium pitted nectarines, sliced.

SWITCH IT UP:
RUSTIC APPLE PIE

JUST FOLLOW MY BLUEBERRY GALETTE RECIPE (PAGE 304), BUT IN PLACE OF THE BERRIES, USE 2 MEDIUM APPLES (I'VE FOUND THAT GRANNY SMITH, JONAGOLD, MUTSU, BRAEBURN, AND PINK LADY APPLES WORK BEST), PEELED, CORED, AND THINLY SLICED. I ALSO WRAP LESS OF THE DOUGH UP-AND-OVER, WHICH RESULTS IN A WIDER, FLATTER PIE WITH MORE EXPOSED FILLING!

CHERRY CLAFOUTIS

MAKES 8 SERVINGS
● 1 HOUR
(15 MINUTES HANDS-ON)

NUT-FREE (IF MODIFIED)	
NIGHTSHADE-FREE	VEGETARIAN

- **1** tablespoon ghee or coconut oil
- **1** (13.5-ounce) can full-fat coconut milk
- **3** large eggs
- **½** cup (72 grams) maple sugar
- **½** cup (64 grams) cassava flour
- **2** teaspoons vanilla extract
- **½** teaspoon almond extract (optional)
- **¼** teaspoon Diamond Crystal kosher salt
- **1½** pounds fresh or frozen sweet cherries, pitted

> A CROSS BETWEEN A PANCAKE AND A FLAN, CLAFOUTIS ARE ONE OF THE SIMPLEST AND MOST ELEGANT WAYS TO INCORPORATE SEASONAL FRUIT. THIS DELICATE FRENCH CLASSIC IS MILDLY SWEET AND PERFECT FOR BOTH DESSERT AND BREAKFAST!

1 HEAT THE OVEN TO 375°F WITH THE RACK IN THE MIDDLE POSITION.

2 GREASE A 9 OR 10-INCH OVEN-SAFE SKILLET WITH GHEE. SET IT ASIDE.

3 TOSS ALL THE INGREDIENTS EXCEPT THE CHERRIES INTO A BLENDER.

4 BLITZ ON HIGH SPEED UNTIL SMOOTH, ABOUT 1 MINUTE.

5 ARRANGE ABOUT ¾ OF THE CHERRIES IN A SINGLE LAYER IN THE GREASED SKILLET.

6 POUR THE BATTER ON TOP OF THE CHERRIES.

7 DOT THE REMAINING CHERRIES ON TOP.

8 BAKE FOR 30 TO 45 MINUTES OR UNTIL THE TOP TURNS GOLDEN BROWN AND THE CENTER SETS. AN INSTANT-READ THERMOMETER SHOULD READ 195°F WHEN INSERTED INTO THE MIDDLE.

Per serving: 269 calories • 35 g carbohydrates • 4 g protein • 14 g fat • 2 g fiber

9   LET THE CLAFOUTIS COOL SLIGHTLY BEFORE SERVING.

RASPBERRY FINANCIERS

MAKES 24 MINI-CAKES
● **1 HOUR**
(30 MINUTES HANDS-ON)

NIGHTSHADE-FREE	VEGETARIAN

5 tablespoons (70 grams) ghee, plus more to coat the muffin tin if not using liners

1 cup (112 grams) finely ground blanched almond flour

½ cup (72 grams) maple sugar

2 tablespoons (16 grams) cassava flour

¼ teaspoon Diamond Crystal kosher salt

3 large egg whites, whisked

½ teaspoon vanilla or almond extract

24 small raspberries

THESE BITE-SIZE FRENCH CAKES ARE CALLED "FINANCIERS" 'CAUSE THEY'RE NORMALLY BAKED IN LITTLE RECTANGULAR MOLDS TO RESEMBLE GOLD BARS. BUT THEY TASTE GREAT NO MATTER WHAT SHAPE THEY TAKE!

THESE ONE-BITE ALMOND FLOUR MINI-CAKES ARE CRUSTY ON THE OUTSIDE AND TENDER ON THE INSIDE. THEY LOOK AND TASTE MIGHTY FANCY, BUT THEY'RE A BREEZE TO MAKE!

① MELT THE GHEE IN THE MICROWAVE OR IN A SMALL SAUCEPAN OVER LOW HEAT. TRANSFER THE GHEE TO A LIQUID MEASURING CUP OR SMALL BOWL AND COOL IT TO ROOM TEMPERATURE.

② HEAT THE OVEN TO 375°F DEGREES WITH THE RACK IN THE MIDDLE POSITION. PLACE MUFFIN LINERS IN A 24-CUP MINI-MUFFIN TIN OR LIGHTLY GREASE THE MUFFIN PAN.

Per mini-cake: 72 calories • 5 g carbohydrates • 1 g protein • 5 g fat • 1 g fiber

3 In a large bowl, combine the almond flour, maple sugar, cassava flour, and salt.

4 Stir it all together.

5 Pour in the egg whites . . .

6 . . . and mix well with a spatula until well combined.

7 Add the melted ghee and vanilla.

8 Then, mix until the batter is uniform.

9 Use a small scooper to divide the batter into the muffin cups, about a tablespoon each.

10 Flatten the tops a bit. Then, gently press a raspberry, butt-end up, into the center of each blob of batter.

11 Pop the muffin tin into the hot oven.

12 Bake for 13 to 15 minutes or until the edges of the financiers are browned and the sides come away from the edges, rotating the muffin tin half-way through baking.

13 Take the raspberry financiers out of the oven and immediately transfer them to a wire rack.

14 Cool the cakes on the wire rack for at least 30 minutes. Gobble them up!

313

PISTACHIO CARDAMOM COOKIES

MAKES 24 COOKIES
●● **2 HOURS**
(40 MINUTES HANDS-ON)

NIGHTSHADE-FREE	VEGETARIAN

¾ cup (108 grams) maple sugar

⅓ cup (72 grams) refined coconut oil, softened at room temperature

1 large egg

2 teaspoons lime zest

2 cups (224 grams) almond flour

⅓ cup (40 grams) tapioca flour

1½ teaspoons ground cardamom

¼ teaspoon Diamond Crystal kosher salt

½ cup (60 grams) roasted, salted, and shelled pistachios, finely chopped

THESE ARE SMALL BUT AMAZING, KINDA LIKE ME!

1 PLOP THE MAPLE SUGAR AND COCONUT OIL INTO A LARGE BOWL.

2 BEAT WITH AN ELECTRIC HAND MIXER 'TIL THE OIL IS INCORPORATED.

3 ADD THE EGG AND LIME ZEST.

4 BEAT UNTIL WELL COMBINED. SET IT ASIDE.

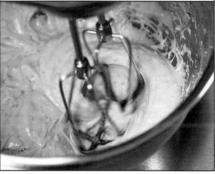

5 IN A SEPARATE MEDIUM BOWL, WHISK THE ALMOND FLOUR, TAPIOCA FLOUR, CARDAMOM, AND SALT TOGETHER.

6 POUR THE DRY INGREDIENTS INTO THE BOWL WITH THE WET INGREDIENTS.

7 USING A SPATULA OR WOODEN SPOON, MIX UNTIL A DOUGH IS FORMED.

8 DUMP IN THE PISTACHIOS.

Per cookie: 128 calories • 11 g carbohydrates • 3 g protein • 9 g fat • 1 g fiber

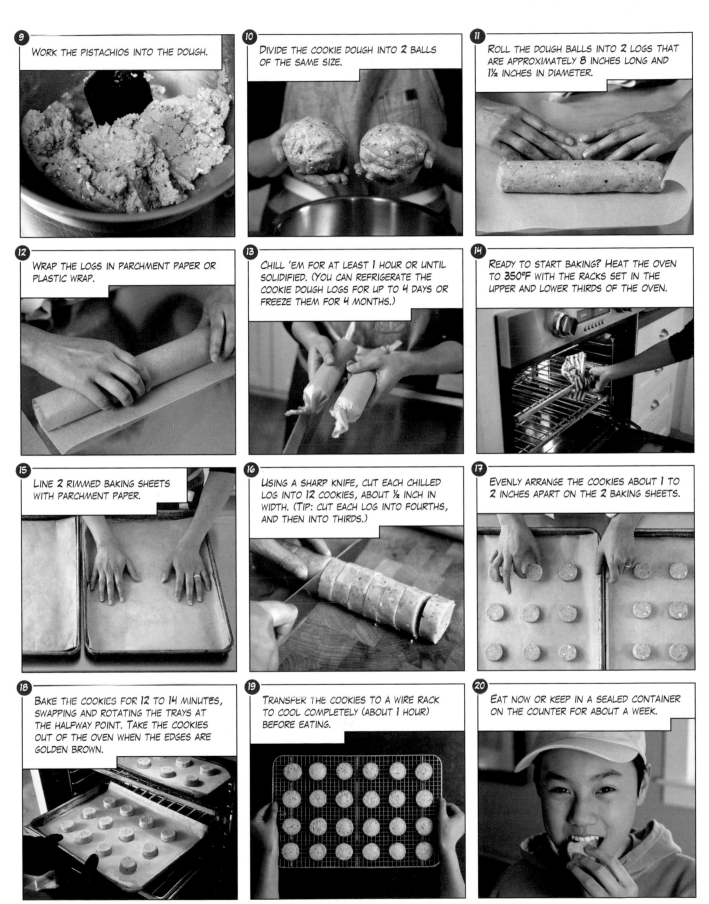

9 WORK THE PISTACHIOS INTO THE DOUGH.

10 DIVIDE THE COOKIE DOUGH INTO 2 BALLS OF THE SAME SIZE.

11 ROLL THE DOUGH BALLS INTO 2 LOGS THAT ARE APPROXIMATELY 8 INCHES LONG AND 1½ INCHES IN DIAMETER.

12 WRAP THE LOGS IN PARCHMENT PAPER OR PLASTIC WRAP.

13 CHILL 'EM FOR AT LEAST 1 HOUR OR UNTIL SOLIDIFIED. (YOU CAN REFRIGERATE THE COOKIE DOUGH LOGS FOR UP TO 4 DAYS OR FREEZE THEM FOR 4 MONTHS.)

14 READY TO START BAKING? HEAT THE OVEN TO 350°F WITH THE RACKS SET IN THE UPPER AND LOWER THIRDS OF THE OVEN.

15 LINE 2 RIMMED BAKING SHEETS WITH PARCHMENT PAPER.

16 USING A SHARP KNIFE, CUT EACH CHILLED LOG INTO 12 COOKIES, ABOUT ½ INCH IN WIDTH. (TIP: CUT EACH LOG INTO FOURTHS, AND THEN INTO THIRDS.)

17 EVENLY ARRANGE THE COOKIES ABOUT 1 TO 2 INCHES APART ON THE 2 BAKING SHEETS.

18 BAKE THE COOKIES FOR 12 TO 14 MINUTES, SWAPPING AND ROTATING THE TRAYS AT THE HALFWAY POINT. TAKE THE COOKIES OUT OF THE OVEN WHEN THE EDGES ARE GOLDEN BROWN.

19 TRANSFER THE COOKIES TO A WIRE RACK TO COOL COMPLETELY (ABOUT 1 HOUR) BEFORE EATING.

20 EAT NOW OR KEEP IN A SEALED CONTAINER ON THE COUNTER FOR ABOUT A WEEK.

THESE PERSIAN-INSPIRED TEA COOKIES COMBINE SALTY PISTACHIOS, AROMATIC CARDAMOM, AND LIME ZEST INTO AN IRRESISTIBLE BITE!

PISTACHIO CARDAMOM COOKIES ARE A CROWD FAVORITE AND PERFECT FOR D.I.Y. HOLIDAY GIFTING. THEY'RE STURDY ENOUGH THAT YOU CAN EVEN PACK AND SHIP THEM.

CHOCOLATE MUG CAKE

MAKES 1 SERVING
⏱ **5 MINUTES**

NIGHTSHADE-FREE	VEGETARIAN

3 tablespoons (21 grams) finely ground blanched almond flour

1 tablespoon unsweetened cocoa

⅛ teaspoon baking soda

⅛ teaspoon Diamond Crystal kosher salt

1½ tablespoons maple syrup

1 tablespoon avocado oil

¼ teaspoon vanilla extract

1 large egg

• OPTIONAL TOPPING •

Whipped Coconut Cream (page 299)

YOU MAY NEED TO ADJUST THE COOKING TIME DEPENDING ON THE STRENGTH OF YOUR MICROWAVE. IN MY 900-WATT MICROWAVE OVEN, THIS MIRACLE TREAT IS READY IN 90 SECONDS!

1 TOSS THE DRY INGREDIENTS INTO A MEASURING CUP.

2 STIR TOGETHER UNTIL UNIFORM.

3 ADD THE WET INGREDIENTS.

4 WHISK TOGETHER UNTIL SMOOTH.

5 POUR THE BATTER INTO A MICROWAVE-SAFE 6 TO 8-OUNCE MUG.

6 PLACE THE MUG AT THE CENTER OF THE MICROWAVE AND COOK ON HIGH POWER FOR 1 TO 2 MINUTES OR UNTIL A TOOTHPICK INSERTED IN THE CAKE COMES OUT CLEAN.

7 LET THE CAKE COOL FOR A FEW MINUTES ...

8 ... AND TOP WITH WHIPPED COCONUT CREAM IF DESIRED.

Per cake: 401 calories • 25 g carbohydrates • 12 g protein • 29 g fat • 2 g fiber

CHOCOLATE'S AMAZING, BUT THAT DOESN'T MEAN YOU CAN'T MIX THINGS UP. WHIP UP THESE VANILLA AND MATCHA VARIATIONS ON THIS PALEO MUG CAKE RECIPE, OR TRY EXPERIMENTING WITH OTHER FLAVORS!

SWITCH IT UP: VANILLA MUG CAKE

IN STEP 1, LEAVE OUT THE COCOA, AND IN STEP 3, USE 1 TEASPOON OF VANILLA EXTRACT (INSTEAD OF ¼ TEASPOON).

SWITCH IT UP: MATCHA MUG CAKE

LEAVE OUT THE UNSWEETENED COCOA IN STEP 1, AND ADD 1 TEASPOON OF HIGH-QUALITY MATCHA POWDER IN ITS PLACE.

FOLLOW MY RECIPE FOR CHOCOLATE MUG CAKE (PAGE 318), BUT IN STEP 1, LEAVE OUT THE COCOA, AND ADD ¾ TEASPOON OF PUMPKIN SPICE BLEND INSTEAD. THEN, IN STEP 3, ADD 1 TABLESPOON (15 GRAMS) OF CANNED PUMPKIN PURÉE. THIS MUG CAKE IS THE PERFECT 90-SECOND AUTUMN TREAT!

DAN TAT (HONG KONG EGG TARTS)

MAKES 16 TARTS
●● 1¾ HOURS
(1 HOUR HANDS-ON)

NUT-FREE	NIGHTSHADE-FREE
VEGETARIAN	

• CRUST •

1 cup (128 grams) cassava flour, plus more for rolling out the dough

¼ cup (36 grams) tapioca flour

1½ teaspoons maple sugar

¼ teaspoon Diamond Crystal kosher salt

1 large egg

½ cup (120 grams) ghee, chilled and coarsely chopped

¼ cup ice water, plus more if needed

• FILLING •

½ cup (170 grams) light-colored honey

¾ cup hot water

½ cup full-fat coconut milk

3 large eggs

1 teaspoon vanilla extract

> EVEN MY PICKY PARENTS GAVE THESE DIM SUM FAVORITES A BIG THUMBS-UP!

1 START BY MAKING THE CRUST. IN THE WORK BOWL OF A FOOD PROCESSOR, ADD THE CASSAVA FLOUR, TAPIOCA FLOUR, SUGAR, SALT, 1 EGG, AND CHILLED GHEE.

2 PULSE UNTIL THE INGREDIENTS ARE THE TEXTURE OF COARSE CRUMBS. TRANSFER THE CONTENTS TO A LARGE BOWL.

3 MIX IN SOME ICE WATER A LITTLE AT A TIME UNTIL THE DOUGH HOLDS AND IS NO LONGER STICKY WHEN PRESSED TOGETHER.

4 SMUSH THE DOUGH INTO A FLAT PUCK AND WRAP IT IN PARCHMENT OR PLASTIC WRAP. REFRIGERATE FOR AT LEAST 30 MINUTES.

5 WHILE THE DOUGH IS CHILLING, HEAT THE OVEN TO 400°F WITH THE RACK SET IN THE LOWER-THIRD POSITION.

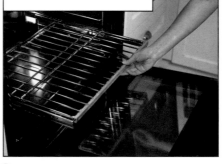

6 IN A MEASURING CUP OR BOWL, STIR THE HONEY INTO THE HOT WATER UNTIL IT HAS DISSOLVED. SET THE SYRUP ASIDE TO COOL UNTIL LUKEWARM.

7 IN A SEPARATE, LARGER MEASURING CUP OR BOWL, WHISK TOGETHER THE COCONUT MILK, 3 EGGS, AND VANILLA EXTRACT.

8 ADD THE COOLED HONEY SYRUP TO THE COCONUT MILK MIXTURE AND STIR UNTIL UNIFORM. SET IT ASIDE.

Per tart: 145 calories • 17 g carbohydrates • 2 g protein • 8 g fat • 1 g fiber

9 PLACE 16 SMALL (2¾-INCH-DIAMETER) EGG TART MOLDS ON A RIMMED BAKING SHEET.

10 TAKE THE DOUGH OUT OF THE REFRIGERATOR. SPRINKLE SOME CASSAVA FLOUR ON THE COUNTER, AND ROLL THE DOUGH OUT UNTIL IT'S ⅛ INCH THICK. (OR ROLL IT IN BETWEEN 2 PIECES OF PARCHMENT PAPER.)

11 USE A 3½-INCH CIRCULAR PASTRY MOLD TO CUT OUT AT LEAST 8 DOUGH ROUNDS.

12 PRESS EACH ROUND INTO A TART MOLD, REMOVING ANY EXCESS DOUGH. GATHER AND REFRIGERATE THE DOUGH SCRAPS FOR 15 MINUTES IF TOO SOFT.

13 ROLL OUT EXCESS DOUGH AND PUNCH OUT 8 MORE ROUNDS TO FILL THE REMAINING EGG TART MOLDS.

14 BACK TO THE FILLING! POUR THE COCONUT MILK AND EGG MIXTURE THROUGH A FINE-MESH SIEVE INTO A LARGE LIQUID MEASURING CUP (OR A PITCHER WITH A SPOUT).

15 FILL EACH TART SHELL TO THE TOP WITH THE MIXTURE. USE A TOOTHPICK TO POP ANY BUBBLES THAT SURFACE.

16 CAREFULLY TRANSFER THE TRAY TO THE OVEN AND BAKE FOR 15 MINUTES.

17 ROTATE THE TRAY AROUND AND DECREASE THE HEAT TO 325°F.

18 BAKE FOR ANOTHER 8 TO 10 MINUTES OR UNTIL THE PASTRY SHELL IS GOLDEN BROWN AND A TOOTHPICK STANDS UP IN THE EGG CUSTARD.

19 TRANSFER THE EGG CUSTARD TARTS TO A WIRE RACK TO COOL.

20 CAREFULLY REMOVE THE TARTS FROM THE MOLDS AND SERVE.

HONG KONG EGG TARTS ARE A MASH-UP OF ENGLISH CUSTARD TARTS AND PORTUGUESE PASTÉIS DE NATA. THEY WERE FIRST POPULARIZED IN THE 1940S, WHEN DIM SUM RESTAURANTS IN THE THEN-BRITISH COLONY BEGAN SERVING THESE SWEET TREATS AS A COMPLEMENT TO SAVORY DUMPLINGS AND HOT TEA. WITH A BRIGHT, EGGY CUSTARD FILLING IN GOLDEN SHELLS MADE OF SHORT PASTRY (OR SOMETIMES PUFF PASTRY), DAN TAT HAVE BECOME THE MOST POPULAR CANTONESE DESSERT IN THE WORLD. SO NATURALLY, I HAD TO CREATE A PALEO-FRIENDLY VERSION!

CREAM PUFFS

MAKES 12 CREAM PUFFS
◐ 1½ HOURS
(1 HOUR HANDS-ON)

NUT-FREE	NIGHTSHADE-FREE
VEGETARIAN (IF MODIFIED)	

2 cups Vanilla Pudding (page 330), Chocolate Pudding (page 331), or Whipped Coconut Cream (page 299)

¼ cup (60 grams) ghee

½ cup full-fat coconut milk

1 teaspoon maple sugar

¼ teaspoon Diamond Crystal kosher salt

½ cup (64 grams) cassava flour

3 large eggs

1 teaspoon Swerve Confectioners' Sweetener (optional)

CREAM PUFFS? MORE LIKE DREAM PUFFS!

1 Got some Vanilla Pudding (page 330), Chocolate Pudding (page 331), or Whipped Coconut Cream (page 299)? You'll need some for this recipe.

2 Heat the oven to 375°F with the rack in the middle. Line a baking sheet with parchment paper and set it aside.

3 In a small saucepan over medium heat, combine the ghee, coconut milk, maple sugar, and salt.

4 Bring it all to a boil, stirring occasionally.

5 Once the mixture reaches a full boil, remove the saucepan from the heat and quickly stir in the cassava flour until a grainy paste develops.

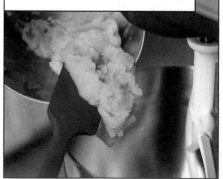

6 Return the pot to low heat and cook for 2 to 3 minutes, stirring with a smearing motion, until the paste is slightly shiny and sticky and leaves a film on the bottom of the saucepan.

7 Transfer the paste to a stand mixer fitted with a paddle blade.

8 Mix on low speed for 30 seconds to cool down the mixture a bit.

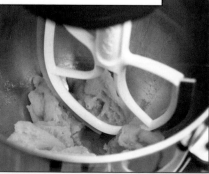

Per cream puff: 168 calories • 10 g carbohydrates • 3 g protein • 13 g fat • 1 g fiber

9 CRANK UP THE MIXER TO MEDIUM SPEED. ADD 1 EGG AT A TIME UNTIL THE LAST EGG IS INCORPORATED.

10 BEAT THE DOUGH AT MEDIUM SPEED, SCRAPING DOWN THE SIDES, FOR 1 MINUTE OR UNTIL SHINY AND ELASTIC.

11 FILL A 14-INCH PASTRY BAG FITTED WITH A ½-INCH PLAIN ROUND TIP WITH THE DOUGH.

12 CAREFULLY PIPE THE DOUGH INTO 2-INCH MOUNDS ON THE PARCHMENT-LINED BAKING SHEET, MAKING SURE THEY'RE AT LEAST 1½ INCHES APART.

13 YOU SHOULD BE ABLE TO FIT ABOUT 12 MOUNDS ON THE BAKING SHEET.

14 DIP A FINGER IN COLD WATER AND USE IT TO SMOOTH OUT THE TOP OF EACH OF THE MOUNDS.

15 BAKE 'EM FOR 30 TO 40 MINUTES OR UNTIL THE CREAM PUFFS ARE GOLDEN BROWN AND SOUND HOLLOW WHEN TAPPED.

16 TRANSFER THE PUFFS ONTO A WIRE RACK.

17 WITH A PARING KNIFE, CUT A SMALL SLIT IN THE SIDE OF EACH PUFF AND ALLOW THEM TO COOL COMPLETELY ON THE RACK.

18 PLACE THE PUDDING OR WHIPPED CREAM IN A PASTRY BAG FITTED WITH A SMALL TIP. POKE THE TIP INTO THE SLIT ON EACH CREAM PUFF AND INJECT IT WITH FILLING.

19 IF DESIRED, DUST THE CREAM PUFFS WITH SWERVE CONFECTIONERS' SWEETENER.

20 SERVE!

PALEO AND GRAIN-FREE CREAM PUFFS MAY SEEM LIKE AN IMPOSSIBLE DREAM, BUT GUESS WHAT? I MADE THEM A REALITY! THIS SHOWSTOPPER OF A DESSERT MIGHT TAKE A BIT OF PRACTICE, BUT TRUST ME: EVEN YOUR LOPSIDED TEST BATCH OF CREAM PUFFS WILL BE EAGERLY DEVOURED.

SWITCH IT UP: PROFITEROLES

SURE, YOU CAN FILL CREAM PUFF SHELLS WITH WHIPPED CREAM, PUDDING, CUSTARD, OR EVEN JAM. BUT IS THERE ANYTHING MORE DECADENT THAN A BIG PLATE OF PROFITEROLES? (ANSWER: HECK NO.)

SO GO STUFF YOUR PUFFS WITH ICE CREAM AND TOP 'EM WITH CHOCOLATE GANACHE (PAGE 298). NO NEED TO WAIT FOR A FANCY SOIRÉE TO PROFITEROLE IT UP!

1 MAKE SOME CREAM PUFFS (PAGE 326), BUT AFTER STEP 16, USE A SHARP KNIFE TO CUT EACH PUFF IN HALF HORIZONTALLY. COOL THE PUFFS TO ROOM TEMPERATURE.

2 SCOOP YOUR FAVORITE ICE CREAM ONTO EACH BOTTOM HALF. I USED COFFEE ICE CREAM (PAGE 332).

3 ASSEMBLE A PLATE OF BITE-SIZE ICE CREAM SANDWICHES, AND TOP THEM WITH CHOCOLATE GANACHE AND A GENEROUS SHOWER OF TOASTED SLICED ALMONDS.

COFFEE ICE CREAM

MAKES 6 SERVINGS
●●●●◑ 4½ HOURS
(30 MINUTES HANDS-ON)

NUT-FREE	EGG-FREE
NIGHTSHADE-FREE	VEGAN

1 (13.5-ounce) can full-fat coconut milk, divided

1 (13.5-ounce) can coconut cream

¾ cup (108 grams) maple sugar

3 tablespoons (15 grams) medium-ground coffee

½ teaspoon Diamond Crystal kosher salt

1½ tablespoons (13.5 grams) tapioca flour

2 teaspoons vanilla extract

USE THIS FOR:

- Profiteroles (page 329)

There's nothing better than homemade churned ice cream. And coffee happens to be my favorite ice cream flavor of all time!

Creamy and bracingly bold, this dairy-free Coffee Ice Cream is one silky-smooth treat that's sure to perk you up!

1 POUR ¼ CUP OF COCONUT MILK IN A SMALL MEASURING CUP AND SET IT ASIDE.

2 IN A MEDIUM SAUCEPAN, POUR IN THE REMAINING COCONUT MILK, COCONUT CREAM, MAPLE SUGAR, COFFEE, AND SALT.

Per serving: 451 calories • 35 g carbohydrates • 4 g protein • 36 g fat • 1 g fiber

3 Bring the contents to a simmer over medium heat, stirring frequently.

4 Carefully pour the liquid through a fine-mesh sieve or coffee filter into a large measuring cup or bowl.

5 Wipe out the saucepan, and transfer the strained liquid back into the pan.

6 In a small bowl or cup, whisk the reserved coconut milk and tapioca flour together . . .

7 . . . and add it to the filtered ice cream base in the saucepan.

8 Cook over medium heat, stirring frequently. Turn off the heat once the mixture has thickened slightly.

9 Add the vanilla extract.

10 Blitz the ice cream base with an immersion blender for 30 seconds.

11 Pour the liquid ice cream base into a container. Cover and refrigerate until chilled, about 4 hours. (To speed up the process, you can put the container in an ice bath or freezer.)

12 Churn the chilled base in an ice cream maker according to manufacturer's instructions.

13 Immediately transfer the ice cream to an airtight container and freeze until solid. You can keep the ice cream in the freezer for up to 1 month.

14 Scoop into bowls and eat it all up.

SWITCH IT UP:
COCONUT VANILLA
ICE CREAM

NOT A COFFEE FANATIC? TRY WHIPPING UP
SOME COCONUT VANILLA ICE CREAM USING
THE SAME RECIPE AS THE ONE ON THE
PREVIOUS PAGE. IT'S A CINCH: JUST LEAVE
OUT THE GROUND COFFEE IN STEP 2, AND
SKIP STEPS 4 AND 5 ENTIRELY.

AND DON'T FORGET: THIS FROZEN TREAT
GOES GREAT WITH A GENEROUS DRIZZLE OF
CHOCOLATE GANACHE (PAGE 298).

339

TEMPERATURE

200°F	95°C
225°F	110°C
250°F	120°C
275°F	135°C
300°F	150°C
325°F	165°C
350°F	175°C
375°F	190°C
400°F	200°C
425°F	220°C
450°F	230°C
475°F	245°C
500°F	260°C
525°F	275°C

WEIGHT

¼ oz	7 g
½ oz	14 g
¾ oz	21 g
1 oz	28 g
1¼ oz	35 g
1½ oz	42 g
1¾ oz	50 g
2 oz	57 g
3 oz	85 g
4 oz	113 g
5 oz	142 g
6 oz	170 g
7 oz	198 g
8 oz	227 g
16 oz	454 g

LENGTH

¼ in	6 mm
½ in	1¼ cm
1 in	2½ cm
2 in	5 cm
2½ in	6 cm
4 in	10 cm
5 in	13 cm
6 in	15¼ cm
12 in	30 cm

VOLUME

⅛ tsp	0.5 ml	
¼ tsp	1 ml	
½ tsp	2.5 ml	
¾ tsp	4 ml	
1 tsp	5 ml	
1¼ tsp	6 ml	
1½ tsp	7.5 ml	
1¾ tsp	8.5 ml	
2 tsp	10 ml	⅓ fl oz
1 T	15 ml	½ fl oz
2 T	30 ml	1 fl oz
¼ C	60 ml	2 fl oz
⅓ C	80 ml	3 fl oz
½ C	120 ml	4 fl oz
¾ C	180 ml	6 fl oz
1 C	240 ml	8 fl oz

CONVERSIONS

Information compiled from a variety of sources, including *Recipes into Type* by Joan Whitman and Dolores Simon (Newton, MA: Biscuit Books, 2000); *The New Food Lover's Companion* by Sharon Tyler Herbst (Hauppauge, NY: Barron's, 1995); and *Rosemary Brown's Big Kitchen Instruction Book* (Kansas City, MO: Andrews McMeel, 1998).

THANK YOU!

I'm pretty sure no one ever reads the acknowledgments at the end of a cookbook. It's secretly thrilling to know that the contents of this page are hidden in plain sight; I can write anything I want here—even if it has nothing to do with thanking anyone.

This means I can fill this page with life hacks, like our trick for reminding the boys to run the dishwasher before bedtime (Henry stuck a sign on the ceiling above their beds). Or I can use this space to apologize for my tactlessness; I'm sorry for freezing up when I meet people, and for habitually saying the quiet parts out loud (like blurting "wow, that dog has a really ugly butt!" when its owner is well within earshot).

I can air my grievances, from measuring spoons too wide to fit into spice bottles to Internet trolls who tell me to "shut up and cook" when I post about anything other than food. I can even use this page to settle scores against my childhood tormentors (YOU KNOW WHO YOU ARE). I'm not all positivity and light, folks; my high school English teacher, Mrs. Griscom, didn't call me "Michelle from Hell" for nothing.

Then again, I'm told that gratitude leads to improved health and positivity, so maybe I should use this space as it's intended: to thank those who made this book possible.

First up: family. As always, my sister, **Fiona Kennedy**, served as my second brain and sounding board. Many of the recipes here were inspired by those made by our food-obsessed parents, **Rebecca** and **Gene Tam** and **Wendy** and **Kenny Fong**. And our teenagers(!), **Owen** and **Ollie**, taste-tested every dish we cooked for this book.

We're blessed with an incredible team, including our editor, **Jean Lucas**, our publisher, **Kirsty Melville**, the entire **Andrews McMeel** family, and our PR wizards, **Carrie Bachman** and **Dee Dee DeBartlo**. Once again, my friend and favorite professional recipe tester **Sheri Codiana** meticulously cooked, tasted, and graded our dishes along with **Larry Klein**. (They managed this on top of their royal duties as the First Couple of Sunnyvale, California.) **Angelina Hong**, our amazing behind-the-scenes conductor at Nom Nom Paleo, deserves special mention—she project-managed this book and even photographed a handful of the recipes!

Sidney Majalya, **Jory Steele**, and **Matthew Majalya** are like family to us and fed us whenever we were too bleary-eyed to cook. Jory shared her easy and delicious salad dressing recipe for this book, too. (It's been Owen's favorite since he was little!) When I was suffering from (recipe) writer's block, my buddy **Shiraaz Bhabha** came to the rescue with ideas for a pair of tasty dishes. Along with our pals **Maria Zajac** and **Susan Papp**, we made the most of our socially distanced gossip sessions.

During the pandemic, many of our friends kept us smiling even when we couldn't see them in person, including **Amanda Haas**, **Diana Rodgers**, **Gregory Gourdet**, **Kaja Taft**, **Rebecca Katz**, **Evelyn Nadeau**, and **Lauren Trinh**. We're grateful for the support of Henry's friends and colleagues at **LinkedIn**, as well as to **Sanjan Joshi** for teaching Ollie how to curse without actually cursing. Thank you also to **Cora**, **Fleur**, **Laurie**, and **Matt Suran** for helping to keep our home fires lit in Portland.

Lots of love to our food world friends, too—especially **Teri Turner**, **Diane Sanfilippo**, **Melissa Urban**, **Danielle Walker**, **Melissa King**, **Andrea Nguyen**, **Cassy Joy Garcia**, **Juli Bauer Roth**, **Mina Makram**, **Tu David Phu**, **Kyle** and **Lisa Hildebrant**, **Bill** and **Hayley Staley**, **Emma Christensen**, **Tori Ritchie**, **Suzanne Ryan**, and **Norma Quon**.

Special thanks to **Mindy Kaling** for convincing our kids that we're (somewhat) cool.

Last but not least, we're grateful for you, our loyal Nomsters, for cooking with us, sticking with us, and inspiring us. You're the reason we do what we do!